The Catholic Philanthropic Tradition in America

THE CATHOLIC PHILANTHROPIC TRADITION IN AMERICA

Mary J. Oates

Indiana University Press

Bloomington and Indianapolis

The paper used in this publication meets the minimum requirements of American
National Standard for Information Sciences—Permanence of Paper for Printed
Library Materials, ANSI Z39.48-1984.

Manufactured in the United States of America

Library of Congress Cataloging-in-Publication Data

Oates, Mary J.
The Catholic philanthropic tradition in America / Mary J. Oates.
p.   cm.—(Philanthropic studies)
Includes bibliographical references and index.
ISBN 0-253-34159-0 (alk. paper)
1. Catholic Church—United States—Charities—History.   I. Title.
II. Series.
BX2347.019   1995
361.7′5′08822—dc20   94-13027

1 2 3 4 5 00 99 98 97 96 95

In memory of my mother

Mary Folan Oates

1906–1981

Contents

Acknowledgments

IT IS A great pleasure to thank the Lilly Endowment for funding the research and writing of this book. Its generosity enabled me to undertake research in archives across the country, freed me from teaching responsibilities for two years, and provided essential research and clerical assistance. I am very grateful, also, for the warm interest and encouragement proffered by Lilly officers, especially Robert Wood Lynn, Fred Hofheinz, and Jeanne Knoerle, throughout the course of the project. The Association of American Colleges and the Cushwa Center for the Study of American Catholicism at Notre Dame University have my gratitude for earlier grants supporting initial research on two aspects of Catholic benevolence.

I thank collectively the numerous archivists and librarians who accorded me expert professional assistance and cordial hospitality on my visits to their depositories. In particular, I would like to recognize the contributions of Armine Bagdasarian, Jeffrey Burns, Joseph Casino, Mary Joan Faller, Peter Hogan, Mary Kraft, Joanne O'Keefe, Margaret O'Rourke, Charles Nolan, Ronald Patkus, Margaret Quinn, Celeste Rabaut, Philip Runkel, Timothy Slavin, Blaithin Sullivan, Paul Thomas, Elaine Wheeler, and Anthony Zito.

In writing this book, I have incurred debts to many individuals who have aided me in diverse ways. I appreciate especially the assistance of Francis Butler, Joan Challinor, Conrad Cherry, Magdalen Coughlin, Dorothy Cunningham, Jay Dolan, Rosenda Gill, James Hennesey, William Hutchison, Thom Jeavons, Christopher Kauffman, Karen Kennelly, Catherine McShane, Margaret W. Rossiter, and Susan Williamson. For perceptive criticisms that helped me refine my arguments significantly, I am very grateful to two anonymous reviewers. I thank also the many colleagues who commented on my presentations at research seminars and scholarly conferences over the past several years.

Robert Sloan, my editor at Indiana University Press, provided valuable insights as well as patient support, and he has my warm gratitude. So does Joseph Perry, my research assistant, whose care in collecting and organizing materials greatly advanced my work. I am also indebted to fifteen foundation officers who responded graciously and in thoughtful detail to my questions about the structure, priorities, and activities of their organizations.

Finally, I want to acknowledge the critical contributions made by my family and by my associates in the Congregation of the Sisters of St. Joseph of Boston. Their interest and moral support sustained me throughout the writing of this book. Very special thanks are due to my father, Thomas F. Oates, whose wise counsel and never-failing enthusiasm for my work have always meant more to me than I can say.

Introduction

RELIGION HAS ALWAYS played a critical role in shaping the American social conscience and in defining the nation's independent sector. While the obligation to charity is a tenet of all religious faiths in the Judeo-Christian tradition, important differences in benevolent priorities and styles have marked its traditional expression. These differences exist not only among religious groups but also within groups at different points in their history.

Dedication to democracy, individualism, and progress already distinguished the American character by 1790. Members of the small Catholic community stood on the periphery of society not simply because they adhered to religious doctrines objectionable to mainstream citizens, but also because in its structure their church appeared to challenge these honored civic virtues. Since hierarchy, uniformity, and tradition governed its discipline in matters of faith and moral law, most Americans assumed that these attributes marked every area of its religious life.

In its philanthropic sphere, however, the church offered diverse opportunities for members to express their individuality and to join in implementing socially progressive ideas. Democracy, personal initiative, and adaptability to civic needs already animated church benevolence in the half century following John Carroll's appointment as the first American bishop in 1790 and continued, despite severe challenges, to affect its distinctive course over the next 150 years. While bishops held foremost authority in the areas of dogma, sacrament, and discipline, in the domain of charity they had to weigh their personal agendas against those of the laity who provided financial support. At the same time, benevolent laity and members of religious orders freely inaugurated good works, but for these activities to have official status, they needed episcopal endorsement. A rapidly growing church community, although marked by widening class and ethnic differences, gradually developed the extensive network of orphanages, hospitals, schools, and social agencies that came to represent so visibly the Catholic way of giving.

Religious philanthropy, or charity, is defined in this study as the giving of financial resources and voluntary service, under the aegis of the church, to benefit others. Not all contributions to the church are philanthropic. For example, contributions to support the local pastor, church, and parish programs which chiefly benefit the congregation itself, do not qualify as charitable giving.

Nor do gifts by individual Catholics to extra-ecclesial philanthropic causes, substantial though these may be, qualify as charitable giving. This book, then, is a study of "organized philanthropy" and as such focuses on secular changes over time in the philanthropic tradition of the church as a community rather than on individual benevolence, even toward Catholic causes, or on short-lived collective responses to immediate civic crises.

Although the altruistic experience of the nation's largest religious denomination represents a critical part of American social history, it has received meager attention from historians. There is general agreement that its patterns differed substantially from those which developed among American Protestants. Yet there is no clear understanding of how these differences influenced the course of Catholic giving over time, or why Catholics, eager for mainstream acceptance, did not simply imitate the giving style and spirit of the majority. Similarly unexamined have been the mechanisms by which a population that remained heavily working class until the mid-twentieth century developed and financed its benevolent institutions and agencies.

From their earliest days in America, Catholics organized to initiate and support charitable activities. Their collective voluntarism reveals not only their understanding of the gospel mandate to charity but also their interpretation of the critical problems facing American society. Changing economic, political, and social conditions and a rapidly growing membership provoked sharp debate within the church about the obligation to give, priorities in giving, appropriate organization of religious charity, and the locus of authority over philanthropic resources. The struggle of Catholics to adapt their philanthropic strategies to changing social needs continued as they advanced economically and socially in the two hundred years following 1790. That collective effort has contributed distinctively to American understanding of the role of private giving in furthering the common good.

American Catholics have traditionally been very generous. In recent decades, however, their reputation for benevolence has begun to erode. Individual contributions to the church, relative to income, have fallen steadily since the mid-1960s. For all its past accomplishments, Catholic philanthropy today is in a precarious state, even as church membership becomes richer and better educated. This development has serious implications not only for religious giving but also for private giving more generally.

This book argues that the uncertain state of Catholic philanthropy today reflects not so much a weakening will to give as a secular narrowing of opportunities to give more than money. While the poor still hold priority of place in the benevolence of the nation's 59 million Catholics, local, decentralized infrastructures that encourage contributions of direct personal service to those in need have been diminishing since the 1920s. The challenge facing Catholics today is to restore and integrate their time-honored benevolent values with the best features of modern charity organization. An exploration of the historic roots, progress, and present state of Catholic philanthropy since 1790 provides important lessons not only for Catholics but also for all who seek to build a more compassionate society.

The Catholic Philanthropic Tradition in America

1

American Society and Benevolent Enterprise

The poor need your help today, not next week.
—Catherine McAuley, c. 1835

FORMAL ORGANIZATION OF the American church did not commence until after the Revolutionary War. Until then, Jesuit missionaries traveled among scattered communities of Catholics, most of them in the East. Substantial gifts of property and money received for this work during the eighteenth century allowed the clergy to be fairly self-supporting. In addition, Maryland Jesuits had acquired land from Indian chiefs and benefited from the "Conditions of Plantation" which gave substantial land grants to sponsors of early settlers. The early church relied on the modest income from these estates to fund its activities.[1]

By the time John Carroll of Baltimore became the first American bishop in 1790, church membership totaled twenty-five priests and about thirty thousand congregants, with 60 percent of the laity and most of the priests living in Maryland. At that time, lay Catholics were contributing virtually nothing to support the church. Because their numbers were few and concentrated in only two states, clergy could live, according to Carroll, "independent of any contributions from the justice or the charity of the respective congregations."[2]

Lack of organization was a critical problem for a geographically dispersed community. Following the Protestant model, laity who built churches sought also to incorporate them and choose their pastors. Faced with a serious shortage of priests, Carroll at first tolerated lay incorporation, provided that the local pastor had a seat on the board. But as disputes between lay trustees and clergy over parish resources became common and increasingly acrimonious, Carroll moved to assume control of the churches, a step interrupted by his death in 1815.[3] After Rome decreed in 1829 that property of new churches must be incorporated in the name of the bishop, public dissension declined.

As membership expanded and new settlements appeared, Carroll begged his people to begin to support their churches and pastors properly and also to consider the needs of the poor. Offertory collections at Sunday masses were introduced in the parishes at this time. Contributions barely covered basic parish expenses, and if a church had to be constructed, the situation could quickly become desperate. In 1824, for example, New York parishioners found that payments due on the debt they had incurred in constructing their church, although absorbing the entire Sunday offering, could not be made. They saw no alternative but to withhold the pastor's salary. Such an injustice mobilized them to undertake an aggressive campaign to pay off the church debt immediately, hoping that thereafter pew rents and regular collections would cover both the pastor's salary and ordinary parish operating expenses. The relieved and grateful pastor pronounced the planning meeting "the brightest of my existence—this moment as the happiest of my life."[4]

The New York initiative represents one of the first collections organized by Catholics to incorporate a commitment to future contributions. Its lay organizers publicized the campaign well in advance and assigned collectors to every street in the parish. The pastor helped by preaching on the sacred duty to give. Armed with collection books, volunteers solicited from everyone, Protestant and Catholic alike. The expectation was that Catholics would not only give as much as their means allowed on the collection day itself, but would promise future contributions on a weekly or monthly schedule. The subscription approach soon marked most fundraising appeals.[5]

Because voluntary offerings in Sunday collections were unpredictable, pastors introduced pew rents to stabilize parish finances. Originating in Germany, the pew rent system was commonplace in America by the 1840s, appearing first in New York and Philadelphia, sites of heavy German settlement. In the 1820s, John England, bishop of Charleston, South Carolina, had spoken out strongly against pew rents as contrary to the principle of democracy that should prevail in the religious sphere. Although he conceded that more homogeneous Protestant congregations might be able to tolerate them, he questioned how a church with many poor members could. Pew rents, after all, seemed to honor the rich and humiliate the poor.[6] Financial exigencies soon overrode such objections, and pew rents became an indispensable source of parish revenue. Pews were rented annually at auction, with front seats commanding higher prices. By the 1830s, fewer than one in four Catholics could afford them, a situation that did not improve as the number of poor congregants increased in succeeding decades. Even so, they provided at least half of annual parish incomes in this decade. Typical were several New York City parishes. In St. James's Church, pew rents accounted for 61 percent of yearly parish receipts and in St. Paul's, they provided 70 percent. Income in Transfiguration Parish came in equal proportions from pew rents and the regular Sunday collections.[7]

Pew rents gradually declined in importance relative to other revenue sources. Regular Sunday collections by the 1870s were providing nearly three-fourths of parish funds, pew rents 13 percent, and various fundraising projects the rest. There was, of course, considerable diversity among parishes, occasioned by the types and extent of fundraising activities, but pew rents generally were less important than they had been in the past. On the other hand, the practice of charging non-pewholders "seat money," a ten-cent admission fee, to attend Sunday services had grown more popular.[8] Despite its condemnation by Rome and by the American hierarchy in two Baltimore Councils, the scheme spread quickly throughout the country after its introduction in Cleveland in the late 1850s.[9] In 1886, Archbishop Michael Corrigan of New York forbade charging admission to mass on Sundays and other days of obligation. "It is not more unlawful, other things being equal, to pay for a seat Sunday after Sunday than to pay pew-rent by the quarter or by the year," he agreed. "But it is incongruity, to say the least, to require attendance at Mass and the payment of money to fulfill that necessary duty."[10]

Fundraising, even for local parish needs, was still sluggish at best when John Carroll made his first national appeal in 1803 for funds to construct a cathedral in Baltimore. He took a two-pronged approach. First, he asked every wage-earning Catholic in the country to subscribe one dollar for four successive years to the cause. Second, in order to attract those who could afford to give more, he inaugurated the first Catholic lottery, naming local merchant and former Presbyterian David Williamson to direct it. Lotteries had long been popular fundraising devices in mainstream churches and in civic and educational institutions as well. In the city of Baltimore, for example, both St. Paul's church and the Presbyterian church had held three lotteries between 1762 and 1805, and the Baltimore Market House benefited from another in 1763. Harvard College increased its income in three such fundraisers between 1772 and 1806. The net goal of the Baltimore cathedral lottery was $31,500, as 85 percent of the proceeds from an anticipated sale of 21,000 tickets, at ten dollars each, was reserved for prizes.[11]

Response to the subscription campaign was most disappointing. "Small as this demand was," Carroll complained to his priests, "it has not been complied with, except in a very partial manner."[12] The lottery did not generate much enthusiasm either. The first prize in the 1805 drawing was an attractive $20,000, but $10 tickets were beyond the means of most Catholics. And although he donated the money to the building fund, the fact that Carroll himself was the winner of the first lottery considerably lessened interest in the second, held by his successor in 1819. Legislative approval for a third lottery in 1826 was in hand, but it was never held. Catholics, for the most part, whether in urban or rural settings, simply ignored church lotteries. A western priest, unable to sell tickets for the 1805 lottery, assured Carroll that his views on "the parsimony of Catholics towards the support of the Church are generally applicable in Kentucky."[13]

A dearth of wealthy parishioners sympathetic to the needs of their growing dioceses led early bishops to appeal to European Catholics for assistance. The Society for the Propagation of the Faith, founded in France in 1822, and the Austrian Leopoldine Society, formed seven years later, were the earliest of several large mission societies that aided the young American church. The approach of the French society resembled "penny-a-week" programs popular among Anglicans of the era, whereby groups of ten, one hundred, or one thousand persons saved pennies for the missions. Parish priests collected the small weekly membership fees, and the societies, buoyed by the immense fascination of Europeans with the New World, saw their enrollments soar. In the distribution of the funds, frontier dioceses and Indian missions benefited disproportionately.[14] Beyond these predilections, European societies made no effort to control how the money was spent. They dealt directly with bishops and superiors of religious orders and were confident that the "pennies for the poor" were reaching those in need with a minimum of administrative cost.

Benevolent associations like the Leopoldine Society characteristically preferred to make substantial grants that would permit bishops to make significant strides, rather than "to deal out the money in small bits and give relief, practically, to nobody."[15] For example, in 1830, Cincinnati's bishop, Edward Fenwick, received a munificent gift of more than $22,000. The arrival of such large sums of foreign money aroused ethnic and religious rancor in some quarters. Samuel F. B. Morse, for example, furiously denounced the Leopoldine Society's work as a scheme by Austria and the Catholic Church to take over the United States.[16]

Foreign benevolence remained important throughout the nineteenth century, expressed not only in monetary gifts, but also in the large numbers of clergy and religious who emigrated to work in American dioceses. Greater success attended bishops who traveled to Europe to make appeals for help in person. They combined visits to mission aid society headquarters with extended preaching tours intended to inspire clergy and religious sisters to volunteer to work in their dioceses. These tours had the added effect of persuading donors that their modest contributions were indeed making a significant difference in the life of the church in America. Among the more indefatigable episcopal preachers was Benedict Flaget of Bardstown, Kentucky, who in 1838 visited forty-six French dioceses, speaking in six to fifteen parishes in each place. By praising not only large donations, but also the small gifts of children, the elderly, and the poor, he attracted immense support for his cause.[17]

Simon Bruté, pioneer bishop of Vincennes, wrote movingly to the Leopoldine Society in 1838 of the struggle of French settlers to provide for the Indiana church. They had circulated a subscription list to cover his salary, but were able to raise less than $200, most of it to be paid in grain. Bruté pointed out that while the pastor of a small parish might get along on that sum, a bishop had greater and more diverse expenses to meet. Of special concern to him were the education of seminarians and the care of the poor. Yet, he went on to say, "the revenue from Pews in my Cathedral is so small as barely to supply what is necessary for the Altar and current Expenses of the Church itself."[18]

Although immigration from Germany, France, and Ireland had swelled Catholic ranks in the 1830s, French and German Catholics, unused to paying pastors and supporting parish churches, were relatively apathetic to episcopal reminders of their obligations in these matters. The Irish, more accustomed to appeals for church support, responded somewhat better. At the Third Provincial Council of Baltimore in 1837, the hierarchy particularly stressed the obligation of Catholics to pay their pastors a satisfactory salary. Because elderly and sick priests were being left without resources and without help, the bishops saw no alternative but to institute a Clerical Fund in every diocese.[19]

Although constructing churches and providing seminaries preoccupied most early bishops, they worked hard to stir Catholics to philanthropy. In 1830, Francis Kenrick chose charity as the theme of his first message to the Philadelphia congregation: "Let not, the spiritual works of mercy so engross your attention as to cause a neglect of the exercises of charity towards the suffering members of Jesus Christ. The poor must be the objects of your predilection."[20] Several years later, Bishop John Dubois of New York ordered that all church collections on Christmas Day go to the care of orphans, and, in 1838, he allocated all collections on Easter Sunday to that purpose as well.[21]

Organized benevolent work, while not common in the early nineteenth century, was certainly not unknown. In 1797, for example, Philadelphia parishioners met to consider how to provide for children orphaned in the recurring yellow fever outbreaks that plagued the city. By 1806, they had organized the Roman Catholic Society of St. Joseph for the Maintenance and Education of Orphans to support St. Joseph's Orphan Asylum and had hired a matron to manage it. Pastors and laity initiating such projects, however, faced one very serious obstacle. The institutional approach to charity was extremely labor intensive, and while it was difficult enough to raise funds to provide a house, it was almost impossible to raise enough money to pay competent managers on an ongoing basis.

The first step to a solution emerged in 1809 in Emmitsburg, Maryland, where a New York widow, and convert to Catholicism, Elizabeth Seton, had established the pioneer American sisterhood, the Sisters of Charity, to assist the

poor, especially children. Officers of the Philadelphia benevolent society immediately requested that the sisters manage their orphanage. By 1814, the religious
community was in a position to respond, and three sisters arrived to take charge
of the institution. They found thirteen unsupervised children, both sexes sharing facilities, and an institution in serious debt. The women of the parish
formed a Society of Lady Managers to raise funds to cover the sisters' annual
salaries of thirty-six dollars, their transportation, and the annual cost of their
shoes.[22]

Parishioners supported the sisters and children as generously as their
means allowed, although early donations came more often in kind than in cash.
"Sometimes when we would return from early Mass on a week day," wrote one
sister, "we would find a barrell [sic] of flour at our kitchen door; sometimes find
the kitchen table strewn with produce of the market, and our kind friends
would leave us to guess the name of the donor."[23] Although the officers of the
orphan society could provide the sisters only $600 yearly to cover all operating
expenses, the institution flourished under their direction. Within three years the
$5,000 debt was paid, although the number of children being cared for had dou-
bled. The single major factor in these accomplishments was the contributed services of the sisters.[24]

Word of the success of the Philadelphia orphanage spread quickly, and bishops, speaking for laity as well as for themselves, appealed to the Sisters of Charity to manage their foundering institutions. Bishop John Connolly of New York,
for example, informed Elizabeth Seton in 1817 that "many pious and zealous
Catholics of this City are most anxious that we should have here for the relief
and education of destitute Catholic children, such an Orphan Asylum as exists
at Philadelphia, under the care of the Sisters of your Religious Society whom
you were so kind as to grant for that purpose."[25] Three sisters were soon caring
for twenty-eight children in the New York orphanage.

The Roman Catholic Orphan Society in New York took shape in 1826, when
thirty-five men, including some Protestants, held an organizational meeting in
Brooklyn. Four years later, the society elected a president and formally commenced its work. Although contributions in the first year totaled a disappointing $161.05, spirits improved considerably when one member, Cornelius
Heeney, made substantial gifts of property and funds. Catholics like Heeney,
who had become rich before 1840, for the most part made their money in real
estate and commercial activities. Thus it was not surprising that they expressed
their charity as often in gifts of property as cash.[26] Heeney was typical in this
regard. He arrived in New York from Ireland in 1784 at the age of thirty, made
a fortune in merchandising as a partner of John Jacob Astor, and also invested
heavily and profitably in Brooklyn real estate. With his help, the Roman Catho-

lic Orphan Society was able to support the New York orphanage more adequately after 1835. His beneficence toward it continued after his death through the Brooklyn Benevolent Society which he endowed in 1845 to continue his charitable work. Local men's social clubs, like the Emerald Society, earmarked a share of the proceeds from their social functions for the orphanage as well. Orphanage directors were always laymen until 1853, when the bishop of Brooklyn assumed the office of president of the board.[27]

As long as the Catholic population remained small, benevolent societies organized city-wide, segregated by sex. Organizers were usually wealthy parishioners, but memberships were more likely to be working class than well-to-do. William Quarter, a New York pastor, later bishop of Chicago, observed that "the poor especially experience much consolation in attaching themselves to any pious sodality or confraternity; while the rich seldom attach themselves to these associations."[28] Representative of women's societies was the Catholic Female Benevolent Society of Detroit, formed by fifty women in 1834 to assist orphans and worthy poor. Members adopted a distinctive uniform to wear while visiting the poor and the almshouse. Within two years they were also supporting a small orphanage and school. Faced with large numbers of poor Catholics and a shortage of clergy, bishops actively encouraged the formation of such lay societies. In 1829, for example, Ambrose Maréchal enlisted women to join the Maria-Marthian Society in Baltimore to help white poor and sick of all religious faiths. A year earlier, the city's African Americans had formed the Tobias Society to address the same needs within their community.[29]

Tensions between Catholics and Protestants influenced both the choice of good works to be supported and organizational strategies. By the 1820s, Catholics saw Protestant benevolent agencies as mainly proselytizing forums, and public institutions, since they were managed by Protestants, as equally dangerous. Though municipalities and states relied heavily on private charities to care for the destitute, support of Catholic charities from public funds remained uncommon. A notable exception was New Orleans, where a small annual subsidy, the "city alimony," was allotted to charity institutions of all denominations.[30] Catholics concurred that children of their own faith should take first priority in their collective philanthropy, since they, more than adults, were vulnerable to Protestant evangelists. As long as Catholic families could not absorb them, separate Catholic institutions were essential.

Fear of proselytization was not the only reason for the proclivity for an institutional approach to charity. Well-managed social agencies would give incontrovertible witness to mainstream citizens that Catholics were patriotic and socially concerned Americans. Ethnic values also contributed to the popularity of the charitable institution. Religious discrimination in Ireland had engendered in Catholics of every social class an attachment to highly visible projects that would demonstrate the philanthropy of the church. In the 1820s, for example, Catherine McAuley, a wealthy Dublin woman, debated how best to use her fortune to aid the sick and destitute. A clerical friend counseled her to open an institution in a prosperous part of the city, because, he insisted, the only way Catholics could hold their own with Protestants was to "bring their charitable institutions more prominently before the world."[31] Finally, the proclivity for institutional charity over the "outdoor relief," or cash assistance, so prevalent among mainstream groups, was partially a result of the way the church itself was organized. With the local parish already the center of Catholic life by the 1830s, there was general agreement that the best way to foster lay support was through vigorous parish institutions, societies, and devotions.[32]

As a result, most lay benevolent societies, male as well as female, were parish-based at this time. Women of Cincinnati's St. Peter's parish, for example, organized the Martha and Mary Society in 1836, stirred by the generosity of local Protestant women who had recently raised six hundred dollars in a fair to benefit the Catholic orphanage. Its members paid $1.50 in annual dues, and each month elected a committee of eight to identify the destitute, give them spiritual as well as temporal relief, and report their situation to the membership the following month.[33] Typical of male societies was the Young Catholic's Friend Society formed in 1835 by eight young men in Boston's cathedral parish to teach and give material help to poor neighborhood children. They raised funds for these purposes by sponsoring an annual lecture series open to the general public. Eminent Protestants like Rufus Choate, Wendell Phillips, and Josiah Quincy participated, and the series became so popular that it remained the society's only fundraiser for more than a decade. The Young Catholic's Friend Society continued as the city's leading Catholic charitable organization until 1860 when Bishop John Fitzpatrick, unable to quell intense internal rivalry and embarrassed by the sensational publicity accompanying it, signaled its demise by withdrawing his episcopal approval.[34]

Because the benevolent society before 1840 was usually formed to support a parish charitable institution, usually a small orphanage, its fundraising efforts, conducted mainly within parish boundaries, rarely generated enough funds to cover institutional costs, especially when parishioners were themselves poor. Without endowment or reserves, the parish institution, relying entirely on voluntary gifts, saw its operating income fluctuate erratically from year to year. As public memory of the disaster which had precipitated its founding faded in the face of new social crises, contributions to the institution waned, and its financial situation became increasingly tenuous.

The charitable institution favored or founded by a bishop attracted broader support and publicity and, hence, was relatively more secure financially. Among the first projects of John Purcell on his arrival in Cincinnati in 1833, for example, was to set the local orphanage on a stable financial basis. For its first five years, it had been supported almost entirely by its managers, the Sisters of Charity, and Purcell intended to lift this burden. He preached a charity sermon for the institution in 1834 as a preliminary to the establishment of St. Peter's Benevolent Association, a lay organization that thereafter assumed responsibility for the material well-being of the orphanage.[35]

Lay leadership in philanthropy developed slowly, since the number of prosperous and educated Catholics remained small. In addition, trustee controversies had discouraged initiative, even in matters of obvious lay concern. Irish and German mutual-benefit societies and social clubs, however, served as early forums in which working-class men learned to pool their resources and to organize collectively. In the 1830s, the Erin Fraternal Association in Brooklyn, for example, was charging a five dollar entrance fee and dues of twenty-five cents per month and offering benefits of three dollars weekly for illness and twenty-five dollars for burial. The Shamrock Benevolent Society appeared in the same city in 1841, with an entrance fee of only $3, but similar dues and benefits. Encouraged by John England, Irish laborers in Charleston, South Carolina, established a mutual-aid society, the Brotherhood of San Marino, in 1838, to pay for a hospital to care for victims in perennial epidemics of "Stranger's Fever" which struck so heavily in poor neighborhoods. Benevolent societies frequently emerged from such roots.[36]

As thousands of German and Irish immigrants arrived to work on road and canal construction at this time, the size, geographic concentration, and economic status of the church changed swiftly. Most of the newcomers settled in New York and Philadelphia and, to a lesser extent, in Baltimore, Charleston, and New Orleans. By 1840, 663,000 Catholics comprised nearly 4 percent of the American population. The advent of so many poor immigrants presented a small Catholic community with an unprecedented challenge. Its extent is revealed in a debate in the 1830s over the most appropriate work for Sisters of Charity to undertake. An 1828 invitation to staff the Mullanphy Hospital in St. Louis kindled the discussion. Rev. Simon Bruté argued that eight sisters conducting a school of 200 pupils would be more socially useful than if the eight devoted themselves to nursing about twenty sick persons "silently moldering under the roof of *one* infirmary."[37] Within a very few years, however, swelling numbers of sick poor in major cities seemed to vindicate the sisters' decision to accept the Mullanphy Hospital. Commenting in 1837, its first director wrote that she and her companions were "wad[ing] in human misery."[38]

At this time, Catholics were supporting about thirty-nine charitable institutions nationally. Clergy and lay leaders strenuously recruited parishioners to join benevolent societies so that more could be opened. But monetary contributions remained inadequate in the face of widespread social distress. Occasionally, unable to find sisters or brothers for a charitable institution, members of a lay society would attempt to staff as well as finance it themselves. In New Orleans, for example, a local priest and several laymen, in the aftermath of a cholera epidemic, formed in 1835 the Catholic Association for Orphan Relief. They intended to develop a financially stable orphanage by establishing an endowment fund and by selling agricultural products raised on the orphanage grounds. But they were unable to resolve a critical problem, how to find and pay competent personnel. The institution soon floundered, contributions shriveled, and seventy-five children were left in "most frightful misery." Only after religious communities assumed care of the children did popular support resume and the orphanage enjoy a modicum of prosperity.[39]

In fact, institutions managed by laity either quickly failed or were transferred to the jurisdiction of religious orders. The reason was almost entirely financial. Benevolent laity, both individually and in societies, appreciated the fact that alliance with religious orders would allow their limited funds to be used more effectively. Conversely, the occasional sisterhood that attempted to conduct an unendowed institution without the support of a lay auxiliary quickly failed. In 1834, for example, John and Nicholas Devereux of Utica, New York, gave ten thousand dollars to a sisterhood to open an orphanage and school. With no benevolent society to support the establishment, contributions were random and small, and the sisters and children were soon in severe straits. When the sisters threatened to leave, the Devereux brothers saved the project by promising "a liberal yearly contribution."[40] Since very few charities had such individual patrons, the lay benevolent society soon became essential in Catholic charitable organization.

The very wealthy preferred to give personally to their favorite charities, a propensity that brought them opportunities for close and frequent contact with bishops and prominent clergy. In addition to their financial support, these patrons also offered friendship and professional advice to bishops struggling with mainstream challenges and burgeoning dioceses. Although they gave money to initiate a variety of charitable works, the very wealthy did not often provide regular income to maintain them. Among the few who did was St. Louis cotton merchant and realtor John Mullanphy who in 1828 not only contributed land for a hospital for "indigent & sick persons without regard to color, country or religion," but also assigned rents of $600 annually from other properties to cover its operating expenses.[41] Rich donors occasionally placed peculiar conditions on their gifts. Mullanphy, for instance, gave a house to Sacred Heart Sisters for the first girls' school in St. Louis on condition that the institution always enroll twenty orphans. But since he was of the opinion that such children were destined for a lowly place in life, he forbade the sisters to serve them tea or coffee, allowed them corn, but not wheat bread, and insisted that "at least the smaller ones" go without shoes in summer.[42]

Middle-class professional men also liked to give personally, usually allying themselves directly with one or more of their favorite charitable institutions. Physicians and dentists would care for orphans free of charge, and business leaders and lawyers would contribute their expert advice to institutional directors. A dentist spoke for many in 1834 when he described what motivated him to volunteer his services to children from the parish orphanage whom he had seen at Sunday mass: "It struck me they would be in need of the skillful operation of a Dentist, so that their permanent teeth should be brought regularly forward, in order in after life that they might possess the great blessing of a good sett [*sic*]."[43]

The inclination of the rich toward an independent giving style guaranteed that the typical benevolent society of the 1830s would remain heavily working and middle class in membership. Nonetheless, its officers struggled to find ways to make the organization attractive to the rich. One device was the life subscription. Thirty-three prominent Philadelphians, including Clement C. Biddle and Matthew Carey, signed on in the 1830s as life subscribers for St. John's Orphanage. Life subscriptions cost twenty-five dollars, annual subscriptions two dollars, and income differences between men and women were very apparent in lists of subscribers. While nearly half the 328 annual subscribers in the mid-1830s were female, women accounted for only 15 percent of the life subscribers.[44]

On the whole, wealthy women were more likely than wealthy men to join voluntary societies. The distress of children, occasioned mainly by frequent epidemics, mobilized many to unite for benevolent purposes. An 1832 cholera epidemic in Boston, for example, gave rise to the Roman Catholic Female Charitable Society in Baltimore, that set as its first goal to raise money for a Boston orphanage. Mobile, Alabama, women took similar action a few years later, organizing the Catholic Female Charitable Society to house and educate children left destitute there in the wake of an epidemic.[45] Early female societies shared the goals spelled out by the Ladies' Benevolent Society of St. Patrick's Parish in Philadelphia, whose members by the 1840s were largely Irish "working-out girls." "Whereas . . . many are permitted to feel the pressure of want and distress, that others more favored with worldly store may exercise the heaven-born virtue, Charity—which, while it blesses the receiver, draws down a blessing on the giver: We, therefore, the subscribers, have resolved to form a Society to aid the distressed."[46]

Few disputed that poor and working-class parishioners were not only vastly more numerous, but also more generous, relative to their means, than their upper-class co-religionists. Thus how to involve grassroots parishioners in benevolent works on a continuing basis was a paramount concern of lay and clerical charity workers. At first, benevolent societies favored the traditional subscription method. Because annual dues were low, most parishioners could participate, thereby ensuring a substantial and stable yearly income for an institution. One society's appeal in the 1830s observed that its $1.50 annual subscription was only "a small sum from each contributor, but if the society should become numerous, the aggregate, applied under the prudent management of the Sisters of Charity, will enable them to wipe the tears from many an eye."[47]

Given the public's lukewarm response to direct requests for money, and general indifference to lotteries, benevolent societies turned increasingly to crowd-pleasing social events to raise more money and to lessen the relentless pressure to get and keep subscribers. Benevolent fairs, popular in Protestant churches in the 1820s, found instant appeal among Catholics as well. Games, entertainments, auctions, food, and handicrafts attracted citizens of all social classes. Urban fairs frequently became major festivals, drawing immense crowds and continuing for days.

The large assemblies of Catholics that these fairs generated aroused mainstream wrath, particularly at times of heightened nativist activity. Announcement of an 1834 fair for a Philadelphia parish orphanage, for example, produced heated editorials in the local press. The pastor, John Hughes, later archbishop of New York, responded in kind, reminding his readers that Protestants had been running fairs for years without public outcry and that surely Catholics ought to be able to conduct their fairs "without license from the editor of *The Presbyterian* and his associates."[48] Denominational sensibilities stirred by this debate proved advantageous to the cause, since it occasioned an extraordinary turnout of Catholics, and, as a result, the Ladies' Fair raised a huge $4,715.32. Hughes bragged to his Cincinnati counterpart that he had surmounted those difficulties which inevitably accompany "the combination of female effort on so large a scale."[49] More impartial observers, however, gave the women full credit for the fair's success. While the average fair was not nearly so lucrative, its proceeds usually covered a substantial fraction of an institution's annual operating expenses. Typical was a two-week ladies' fair held in 1843 to benefit fifty-five children in Baltimore's St. Mary's Female Orphan Asylum. The $1,600 raised represented nearly two-thirds of the asylum's annual income.[50]

Sisters conducting orphanages also raised money for their support by opening small day schools for local children and contributing tuitions earned to the cause of the orphans. Because the tuition payments were, at first, left to the discretion of parents, these revenues were relatively small. Nonetheless, they provided about 10 percent of orphanage income in the 1830s. In times of financial crisis, sisters would also diversify the services they offered in order to cover operating costs. For example, when a Louisville orphanage was about to close for lack of funds, they simply converted a building into an infirmary for paying patients in order that "the sick would receive the benefit of the Sisters' nursing, and the proceeds would help support the Asylum."[51]

By the 1830s, benevolent laywomen were more often found in "ladies' auxiliaries" attached to specific institutions than in independent societies or parish associations. There were several reasons for this shift. Middle-class graduates of convent day and boarding schools, already moderately numerous, were eager to work hand-in-hand with sisters in all types of charitable activities. When, for example, in the aftermath of a cholera epidemic in the 1830s, sisters in a small Kentucky orphanage were inundated with children, they reported that "several pious ladies, mostly old pupils from Nazareth . . . organized into a regular body to obtain funds for the orphans."[52] Laywomen were vocal champions of sisters, valuing them as trusted advisers on matters spiritual and secular. An Indiana priest, endeavoring in 1832 to secure sisters to work among his Davies County parishioners, informed the superior of one community that the sisters' presence "is very much desired by many, *particularly the ladies* as they expect it would be an advantage for them."[53]

Laywomen quickly earned respect for their ability to organize successful fundraising events. Fairs held in 1832 and 1833 by a Louisville female auxiliary were typically popular and profitable, raising $1,150 and $1,000 respectively, for the local orphanage. However, their very success could provoke occasional conflicts between laywomen and sisters. Several years later, the members of the Louisville auxiliary, with the approval of the pastor, argued that because they had raised funds for the orphanage, they should be able to review accounts and supervise the work of the sisters. The convent analyst recorded the sisters' less than enthusiastic reaction: "This was found to be productive of little or no benefit and it was often exceedingly annoying."[54]

The religious principle that the gift of personal service was an essential component of the definition of charity came alive with the development of religious sisterhoods dedicated to philanthropic service. Most of these groups witnessed to the egalitarian spirit of American charity. Founded to help the poor, they welcomed applicants from every social class. In the years before 1840, the number of women joining sisterhoods slowly increased, while men of the era exhibited little interest in becoming either priests or religious brothers. When John Connolly found only four priests in the New York diocese when he arrived there as its bishop in 1814, he concluded that "the American youth have an almost invincible repugnance to the ecclesiastical state."[55] Less appealing than the priesthood was the brotherhood, whose members took religious vows but were not ordained clergy. Brothers remained few in number, according to Rev. Edward Sorin of Notre Dame, Indiana, writing in 1841, simply because "the spirit of liberty as it is understood in the United States is too directly opposed to the spirit of obedience and submission of a community to leave any hopes for a long time to come of any addition of subjects."[56] Appeals to men, especially tradesmen, to join brotherhoods to care for homeless boys increased in the 1840s, with little result. Rev. George Haskins searched internationally, traveling extensively throughout the United States, Canada, and Europe, from 1854 until his death in 1872, in search of brothers to manage a boys' industrial school in Boston, to no avail.[57]

Although their numbers rose in time, priests were perennially in short supply, given the rapidly growing church membership. They constructed churches and schools, served as spiritual and community leaders, and urged their congregants to support local charities. But they could rarely be spared from pastoral duties to direct benevolent institutions. This situation opened the entire field of philanthropy to women. Those who joined sisterhoods actively dedicated to the poor were not so constrained by church law and local custom as semi-cloistered groups like the Ursuline nuns who since 1727 had conducted a convent school in New Orleans. Given New World conditions, eighteenth-century church authorities, as well as the French government, had allowed them to attend the sick of the city. After 1763, however, the Spanish government forced them to return to their cloister where they remained until the Louisiana Purchase of 1803.[58] In contrast, nineteenth-century sisterhoods like the Sisters of Charity could freely undertake whatever social works they chose collectively to do. These active sisterhoods flourished in America.

Before 1840, most new sisterhoods were of American origin. Thereafter, heavy immigration from Ireland and Germany motivated many European orders to send members to work among ethnic groups in American cities and rural settlements. Bishops became more aggressive in seeking workers for schools and charitable institutions in their dioceses. In 1839, for example, John Purcell of Cincinnati paid a successful visit to the motherhouse of Sisters of Notre Dame in Namur, Belgium, to request sisters for Ohio. A second trip to Europe, six years later, was similarly productive.[59] The exciting prospect of working in America appealed to European sisters. When Michael O'Connor of Pittsburgh in 1843 asked Sisters of Mercy in Carlow, Ireland, to consider working in his diocese, the entire convent volunteered to go.[60] However, clerics like Louis Gillet of Raisin River, Michigan, located far from populous urban centers, had less success in their search for sisters. He concluded that European women shied away from frontier settlements like his that "had nothing to offer them but privations."[61] Therefore, he and his colleagues continued to establish local sisterhoods and to recruit American-born women for them.

Relative to their working-class contemporaries, wealthy women did not find the active sisterhoods appealing. With notable exceptions, they gravitated to semi-cloistered groups like the Ursulines, the Visitation Nuns, and the Religious of the Sacred Heart that specialized in conducting boarding schools for upper-class girls. Despite their willingness to contribute financially to the work of the active sisterhoods, the benevolent rich were unenthusiastic at the prospect of their own daughters joining groups that worked directly with the indigent. Their attitude did not soften much over time, although it remained a real puzzle to the sisters themselves. One Sister of Mercy commented to another in 1913 about a wealthy acquaintance: "How few, of that kind come to the Convent though many, having larger inheritances do not hesitate to confide themselves and their fortunes to gentlemen some of whom are honorable and some are not."[62]

Paradoxically, wealthy laywomen more than others tended to romanticize convent life, with the result that they often made their financial contributions contingent on assurance that they might spend their retirement years within convent walls, exempt, of course, from the sisters' strict regimen. In 1822, for instance, Mrs. Charles Smith of Opelousas, Louisiana, offered extensive property to the Sacred Heart Sisters for a school and later an orphanage "upon the sole condition that she might spend her remaining days in the Convent there."[63] Such requests, by no means uncommon, persisted throughout the nineteenth century. In the 1870s, Anna Hunt, a wealthy St. Louis woman, placed conditions on her gift to a women's reformatory in order to benefit women of her own social class. She offered to construct a convalescent home and school for the Good Shepherd Sisters if they would agree to reserve rooms in the convent for "ladies of the higher class who might wish to avail themselves of an opportunity of leading a peaceful, retired life far removed from the commotion of the world."[64]

Middle-class laity also presented the occasional unconventional request in return for their donations. In 1830, for example, a Frederick, Maryland, couple proposed that Sisters of Charity conducting St. John's Orphanage there, and their charges, move into the couple's home. If the sisters would care for them until their deaths, the Atwoods promised to bequeath the property to them. The sisters agreed, and the move was made. However, as Mr. Atwood died soon and his wife "repented the bargain," the sisters and orphans had to return to their original quarters. A half-century later, sisters conducting St. Joseph Orphan Asylum in Green Bay, Wisconsin, reported a variation on this plan. They had "received two *Orphans*—the brother was 65 years of age and his sister was 63 years of age. . . . The old orphans gave their farm and cash money which helped to pay the last of the *debts* of the house."[65]

Although rich applicants to sisterhoods were relatively few in number, they were nonetheless very important to their communities, since their fortunes could mean the difference between a modest living standard for the entire membership and considerable hardship. The experience of Ann O'Connor, a young Baltimore widow, bears this out. She arrived in Kentucky to join pioneer Sisters of Charity in 1821, replete with furniture, several slaves, and ample funds. The community used her money to purchase a 273-acre plantation for its motherhouse. And Eliza Jane Tiernan, daughter of a rich Pittsburgh family, became in 1843 one of the first Americans to join the Irish Sisters of Mercy in that city. Her large estate considerably improved the circumstances of her community. Life in sisterhoods serving the poor, especially before 1870, was especially arduous for women from comfortable circumstances. Ann O'Connor's untimely death, within three years of her arrival in Kentucky, was directly attributed by the community chronicler to the unaccustomed adversity she encountered there.[66]

Although members of sisterhoods happily contributed their labor at minimal wages to a range of charitable activities, they endeavored from the start to preserve some decision-making autonomy as congregations. However, patriarchal attitudes in early-nineteenth-century America and the greater authority bishops wielded over female versus male religious communities left them vulnerable to external pressures. The idea of collective female authority distressed many bishops who considered it their prerogative to allocate the sisters' valuable labor to works they, not the sisters, determined to be priorities within their dioceses. Distant motherhouses, slow travel, and poor communications frustrated negotiations between bishops and superiors of sisterhoods. Especially galling to many bishops was the need to deal with superiors of European-based sisterhoods who were unwilling to adapt their community regulations to accommodate a bishop's particular plans.

In the 1830s, John England of Charleston, a progressive prelate in terms of lay participation in church affairs, absolutely refused to negotiate with sisters. Recognizing that the rules of established sisterhoods already protected their independence somewhat, he simply founded a "diocesan sisterhood," wrote its rules himself, and recruited women to join it. His example was followed by his colleagues in dioceses across the country. His rationale became theirs as well: "I do not wish to make my institutions depend upon Superiors over whom I have neither control or influence."[67] Although bishops differed considerably in style and priorities, by 1840 they were in full agreement that in order to control the progress and policies of diocesan charities, it was essential that they control the caregivers. The bishops recognized that monetary gifts from poor and working-class laity could not possibly address even a fraction of expanding social needs. Only when these financial resources were joined with labor contributions of sisterhoods and brotherhoods could the philanthropy of a poor and working-class church community significantly ameliorate social ills.

Early-nineteenth-century congregants, despite their sparse resources, compared themselves favorably with their Protestant neighbors in their concern for those in need. They saw the democratic values they admired in American society clearly reflected in their own developing charity organization which honored donations from every social class and ethnic group. Rich and poor alike gave priority in their philanthropy to building institutions for children in need, and they valued the popular, inclusory character of these establishments. While rich laity played leadership roles in benevolent societies, no one doubted that most of the money and labor supporting Catholic charities was coming from grassroots laity and members of religious communities.

By 1840, members of a hierarchical church were learning to accommodate lay initiative, democratic decision making, and diversity in their pioneer philanthropic efforts. Although ethnic and class differences were becoming more noticeable, the common enterprise of charity continued to provide a bond of unity for members of an outsider church. Until 1840, the scattered character of Catholic settlement and the relative paucity of religious sisters and brothers promoted a fairly independent, small scale, and parish-based approach to philanthropy. Heavily pressed to finance the construction of churches and to educate clergy, American Catholics nonetheless mobilized to attend to wider social needs. Poor and working-class parishioners, who themselves had few financial reserves in case of illness, injury, or unemployment, readily identified with those in economic distress. Tensions within the church in this early period were less about the obligation to give or the limits of ecclesiastical authority than about priorities among good works and strategies for addressing them.

As early as 1820, a few clerics were recommending that Catholics unite in their philanthropy. Philadelphian John Dubois, later bishop of New York, was one. He contended that the limited benevolent assets of the Catholic community would go much farther if sisters teaching in local parish schools would reside at the orphanage and commute to the schools. This idea had several merits, Dubois insisted. It would spare parishes the expense of providing separate housing for their sister-teachers. And the orphanage would benefit greatly, in seeking public support, from the added visibility a single large convent would provide. Most important, by cooperating rather than competing in their philanthropy, Catholics of every ethnic background would strengthen their church community. "The Catholics of your city will form but one family of Brethren under one

Mother."[68] Such ideas found few supporters before 1840, however. Religious orders and lay societies alike enjoyed the autonomy they held over benevolent activities. Since their good works did not intrude directly upon the sacramental and doctrinal domains, bishops recognized that to impose priorities running counter to those of their congregations could stifle the developing spirit of religious voluntarism. After 1840, growing ethnic differences and a remarkable growth in church membership were to introduce even more variety in philanthropic objects and strategies.

2

Resource Mobilization in a
Working-Class Church

Charity, practiced by the many, is an essential element of true
and abiding democracy.
—Patrick Hayes, 1925

B Y MID-NINETEENTH century, the Catholic community had established rough
areas of specialization in philanthropy. The construction and support of
seminaries for the education of clergy were the particular responsibility of the
wealthy, while average laity were more often reminded of their obligations toward the poor. The bishops formalized this division of beneficence in an 1843
pastoral letter, taking care, however, to praise all types of charity: "Those to
whom the wealth of this world has been given, cannot better employ a portion
of it than in providing for the education of ministers of the altar. We are far,
however, from meaning to undervalue the offerings which faith may inspire for
the erection of temples to the glory of God, or charity may present for the clothing and maintenance of the orphan."[1] The pastoral of the 1884 Plenary Council
of Baltimore was to repeat this message.

Social exclusion, widespread poverty, and growing ethnic heterogeneity in
the 1840–1890 period shaped the ways American Catholics expressed their charity. Sustained immigration introduced new social needs and presented particular challenges to the development of philanthropic perspectives that honored
American civic virtues. After 1850, the church did not develop gradually like
most denominations, but rather in abrupt and very large increments. The small,
parish-based charities of earlier decades were increasingly ineffective in addressing the needs of growing numbers of poor crowded into urban slums. A
working-class community set about reviewing its giving style and mobilizing
its charitable forces more resourcefully. Casual practices of the past, such as sup-
plementing donations for orphans by tuitions from day schools, worked only
as long as orphanages remained small. By the 1850s, these charitable projects
had to rely almost entirely on less predictable voluntary philanthropy.

The rapid increase in the number of Catholics ensured that clergy would continue to be preoccupied with the construction of churches and with the exercise of pastoral and sacramental responsibilities. This was true not only in congested urban parishes, but also in sparsely populated, but geographically vast western dioceses and vicariates. While officially bishops were leaders of all the charitable enterprises in their dioceses, responsibility for their financial support and day-to-day operations rested primarily on the initiative and voluntary service of members of benevolent societies and religious communities, and on the charitable donations of individual parishioners.

As social needs exhausted financial resources, bishops and clergy underscored more forcefully than ever the religious merits of voluntary service. Church teaching had always emphasized that religious philanthropy entailed more than gifts of money. Full observance of the charitable mandate required personal involvement as well. While economic circumstances might limit the money one could give, everyone, poor and rich, could offer some kind of voluntary service to those in need.

As young women heeded this message, the charitable sisterhoods expanded quickly after 1850. Still a novelty in many parts of the country, they soon became a universally recognized symbol of Catholic charity. When Michael O'Connor of Pittsburgh introduced Irish Sisters of Mercy into his diocese in the 1840s, for example, he met criticism from Catholics as well as Protestants. "People did not understand for what object I had brought them," he remarked. "They were looked upon with suspicion by Protestants, with coldness by Catholics and with fear that they would add to their burdens, without any advantage which they could understand."[2] Whereas in 1850 priests and sisters were fairly equal in number, by 1900, the nation's more than 40,000 sisters outnumbered priests by a margin of 3.5 to 1.[3] While many mid-nineteenth-century sisters were foreign-born, Americans soon outnumbered them. Typical were Irish Sisters of Mercy who in 1857 established themselves in Manchester, New Hampshire. Until 1880, 55 percent of the community membership was Irish-born, while that was true of only 29 percent of women joining between 1880 and 1907.[4] The trend was the same in other parts of the country and in small as well as larger congregations. In the 1880s, for example, of sixteen North Carolina Sisters of Mercy, eleven were southerners, four Irish-born, and one a native of Belgium. Before that decade, Irish sisters had dominated the membership by three to one.[5]

Communities directly engaged in social work, nursing, and teaching in small parish schools grew rapidly. So popular had they become in major cities by the 1860s that concern was occasionally voiced about a "surplus" of sisters. As one New Orleans resident remarked in 1865: "Becoming nuns and sisters is the existing epidemic in the city."[6] For most Catholics, however, the social distress so evident in every crowded city testified to the premature character of such judgments. They definitely shared Edward Sorin's conclusion that the sisters' work was not one of "supererogation, but quite to the contrary, a work raised up precisely to meet some of the most pressing wants of existing society."[7]

Sisterhoods soon were the most commented upon feature of Catholic charity organization, and indeed they represented an original development in American philanthropy more generally. Given the rhetoric of the day concerning women's proper sphere and their exclusion from clerical offices in the church, their prominence in its voluntary sector was a phenomenon remarked upon by Protestant and Catholic alike. Although mainstream suspicion of them lingered, sisters were soon interacting easily with the Catholic laity. Their public vows, distinctive dress, ecclesiastical approbation, and essential social mission brought them considerable status within the church and, to a lesser extent, in the wider society as well.

At first, most sisterhoods excluded the care of boys from among their chosen works. However, a permanent shortage of brothers, the pitiful condition of male orphans, and considerable episcopal pressure prompted many to modify their stand. As a result, women quickly dominated in the care of needy children, the major philanthropic work of nineteenth-century Catholics. By 1879, for example, sisters at the New York Roman Catholic Orphan Asylum were caring for 91 percent of the 1,360 children enrolled there, brothers for 9 percent, a representative proportion.[8]

The dearth of brothers explains only part of the female monopoly of charitable institutions, however. Sisters became key actors in all types of charity work because of a significant differential in the salaries paid male and female religious. Brothers both expected and received much higher compensation than sisters for the same work. In 1856, for example, sisters conducting a Washington, D.C., orphanage received sixty dollars per year in addition to their board and room, a figure that varied little over time and place. In the 1880s, Sisters of Charity in Cincinnati were being paid an annual salary of fifty dollars for the same work. In contrast, Christian Brothers conducting a boys' home in Eddington, Pennsylvania, in that decade received a $204 annual salary. The last obligation honored by institutional boards of directors faced with debt was the sisters' compensation. Some simply omitted this cost item from their books. A diocesan-owned orphanage in Fort Wayne, Indiana, for instance, paid no salaries at all to the Holy Cross sisters during its first twenty years. In 1887, the bishop finally offered them a twenty-five dollar annual salary.[9]

As a result of the sisterhoods' extraordinary popularity, a division of responsibility for benevolent institutions was incorporated in formal instructions on the obligation to give by the 1850s. "The great organized works of general charity must be carried on by the clergy or religious societies," and the laity must support them "liberally and abundantly,"[10] contended leading clerics and writers. An 1856 fundraising circular for a San Francisco hospital reminded laity that "the religious must look to a benevolent public for funds to carry out these various objects of humanity, as all they have to give is their time, labor, and every energy of mind & body."[11] Rich and poor alike agreed with this perspective. For wealthy donors, the dichotomy of roles tended to be very sharply defined. Sarah Worthington King Peter, a wealthy Cincinnati convert who subsidized many local charities there, was one who saw her role as strictly limited to the provision of essential funds. She did not offer her voluntary service in the charitable institutions; that was the sisters' responsibility. "I shall work hard this summer . . . to get my charities in motion," she explained in 1857, "and then I think I shall feel at liberty to retire, while they do my work, as a capitalist retires on his revenues."[12]

In pragmatic terms, this division of labor was the most efficient way to use the sisters' valuable contributed labor. The number of benevolent associations and auxiliaries multiplied dramatically as new charity institutions appeared, giving grassroots parishioners as well as the rich considerable choice in expressing their personal philanthropy. Nonetheless, the typical charity establishment of the 1850s was overcrowded and financially strained. John Timon, bishop of Buffalo, reported that an orphanage housing 120 boys was "not only without revenue, but also in debt for the very house that shelters the orphans."[13] Like most bishops of the era, however, he disliked asking poor and working-class parishioners for more money to support it. Parishes were beginning to open parochial schools, establishments he described bleakly as filled with ragged, hungry children. The Civil War, however, provoked even more calls for asylums for homeless children. Originally intended as temporary expedients, they soon were permanent and oversubscribed. Yearly state stipends of $100 for children of veterans killed in the war allowed the Catholic Home for Destitute Children in Philadelphia to shelter twelve orphans in 1863. By 1900, with subsidies long expired, the institution was caring for 230 children.[14]

Benevolent women, especially sensitive to the effects of the double standard of morality that prevailed at mid-century, focused on benevolent works that would give women in distress extra help. Mrs. J. V. Bouvier, a leading supporter of the New York Foundling Hospital, explained their outlook: "In this pharisaical world where the woman and the man are judged by different standards, and the lapse of one is the crime of the other, too sympathetic an aid cannot be extended to the erring mother."[15] The upsurge of orphans in the 1860s only strengthened the long-held conviction that children were women's special responsibility: "More than twenty thousand Catholic children in New York, homeless, uncared for, ignorant, and abandoned! Can we Catholic mothers think of this and sit quietly in our homes with our little ones around us? . . . The Sisters of Charity or Mercy are ready and longing to care for these little desolate ones. We have only to put the means in their hands."[16]

That its lay benevolent auxiliary had become the financial mainstay of the charitable institution is best appreciated by considering its plight without it. In the early 1870s, for example, with some assistance from their motherhouse, but no steady income and no lay auxiliary, Dominican sisters opened St. Catherine's Hospital for charity patients on Long Island. "Questing sisters" were soon begging for support. While they collected the minimum needed to keep the institution afloat, such an activity was time-consuming and definitely not the work they had joined a community to do.[17]

Laity had assumed responsibility for organized fundraising by the 1850s, and sisters did not usually join in organized public appeals. When in 1854 a priest asked Archbishop Anthony Blanc to allow a Holy Cross sister to join a "very respectable lady" in a formal collection for a New Orleans girls' orphanage, he acknowledged that his request was "very unusual" and assured the bishop that the collection would be undertaken "in a very proper way."[18] After the Civil War, laity more often took the initiative in identifying social needs as well as in developing strategies to respond to them. In 1869, under the leadership of Mrs. Paul Thébaud, a group of local women organized the New York Foundling Society to finance a hospital of the same name, enlisting Sisters of Charity to conduct it. Mrs. Thébaud represents well the auxiliary woman of her day. A convent school graduate and wife of a prominent New York physician, she had known the Sisters of Charity since childhood and remained their loyal supporter all her life. While Sister Irene Fitzgibbons, the hospital's first director, was eulogized as "the most remarkable woman of her age in her sphere of philanthropy," Mrs. Thébaud was recalled as "ever at her side, aiding and cheering. . . . It was her happiness to share in the Sisters' labors."[19]

Women at this time, however, were strongly discouraged from any activity that would draw them into the public arena. Their influence was to be exerted indirectly and privately. Thus charitable laywomen did not serve on the boards of directors of the charities they financed. Instead, the institutions developed "advisory boards," composed of business and professional men, including at least one member of the clergy. These boards dealt with the legal and financial concerns of the institutions and headed public campaigns for their support. Female benevolent organizations, even those not allied to a specific institution, had to have their male advisory committees. For example, the Association for Befriending Children and Young Girls, formed in 1870 by New York women, not only had twenty-seven "lady managers," elected from the membership, but also "an advisory committee of fourteen gentlemen,"[20] chaired by a priest.

Sisterhoods had always tried to preserve their authority in institutions they founded. In 1857, for example, the eight sisters who incorporated a Baltimore infant asylum made their intent clear in the institution's charter: "The Sister Superior of St. Vincent's Asylum shall be ex-officio member and President of the Board. . . . The members of this Association shall always be chosen from among the Sisters . . . it being intended that this Corporation shall at all times be composed of females devoted to works of Benevolence."[21] As time went on, however, such charters became unusual, as sisterhoods were far less likely to own the land and buildings of institutions they staffed. The erosion of their authority by the 1880s is illustrated in a description of the governing board of St. Joseph's Orphan Asylum in Philadelphia as "controlled by a Board of twelve Managers, all Catholics, and gentlemen but not necessarily of our parish. . . . The affairs of the institution are not at all controlled by the Sisters' Board."[22]

Given the public character of their duties, it is hardly surprising that the general public, Catholic as well as Protestant, considered the prominent men who served as board members to be the main financial actors in Catholic philanthropy. This obscured the critical contribution of women as formidable fundraisers. If a cause especially appealed to them, results were notable. One such female venture was the General Fair, held in 1867 to benefit the New York Catholic Protectory and especially "to make up an ample *building fund* to be sacredly appropriated to the benefit of poor friendless little *girls*, left either destitute or dangerously exposed." Net of expenses, $100,000 was raised, an achievement that astonished the male society managers, who gave due credit to "the enthusiastic and successful perseverance of the lady-directors and promoters of the fair."[23]

Church leaders and members alike generally understood by mid-century that collaboration in charity was more expressive of "the church in her collective capacity" than individual giving. They concurred that while lay benevolent societies admirably reflected this, the religious communities were in fact "the most perfect organs of this Christian work."[24] "Religious communities," however, meant sisterhoods. Priests in religious orders certainly did not see direct personal charity work as part of their responsibilities, a stand that aroused some criticism in poor city parishes of the 1850s. One Jesuit superior suggested that members of his community serving as pastors in Cincinnati churches open soup kitchens and collect clothing and housewares for the local poor. The pastors refused, maintaining that such a course of action would "give offense" and that women's groups ought properly to do such work.[25] The church press agreed with the priests that such voluntary service was more appropriate for women than for ordained clergy. "The wisdom of Christian charity has adapted to these extreme wants vocations equally extreme, in the devotion of religious orders; and this duty has devolved especially upon the female sex, because it is better gifted than the male for the ministry of compassion."[26] As such distinctions became entrenched, the democratic spirit of benevolent initiative of earlier decades began to fade.

Mainstream dismay at rising public relief rolls aggravated religious tensions. Of 40,000 destitute foreigners in New York in 1850, Irish Catholics alone comprised between one-third and two-thirds, and immigrants, a majority of them Irish, filled public almshouses by the end of the decade. These figures only weakly indicate prevailing distress, since most poor Irish did not apply for public relief, relying instead on relatives and private charity. Their needs strained church resources, human and financial, in every major city. "We are so overrun at this time with immigrants and other poor," observed a New York City priest, "that I do not know what is to become of us."[27]

Irish fraternal societies first appeared in the late eighteenth century. Because they welcomed upper-class men without religious distinction, their Catholic membership grew steadily. In the 1840s, these groups mobilized laymen to meet unprecedented local distress, occasioned by the extended agricultural crisis in Ireland, by forming either new benevolent societies or special committees for immediate action. In 1847, for example, a Philadelphia fraternal society, the Friendly Sons of St. Patrick, formed the Hibernian Society for the Relief of Emigrants from Ireland. They also canceled their annual gala social event, a St. Patrick's Day dinner, applying the funds instead to establish a building fund for a hospital for poor Irish. The hospital was functioning within two years.[28]

Baltimore men responded more directly to the same crisis in their city. As ships bearing hundreds of starving and sick Irish landed, the city's Hibernian Society appointed a committee of members to collect funds for their relief. At the same time, society members personally assisted the immigrants, carrying the ill from the landing dock to a city infirmary where Sisters of Charity cared for them, and provided a large building to house the rest. When many of its residents soon died, society men made their coffins, as "the carpenters had fled, terror-stricken, from the building."[29] Finally, in a step they saw as a civic and religious duty, they opened an orphanage for the forty children left parentless. The home would be a "means of preventing vice . . . in which the children, by honorable labor, should support themselves, without calling continually on the public for aid."[30]

Lay associations favored patriotic and ethnic themes in fundraising projects. In the 1850s, ethnic religious holidays were also fundraising days. On St.

Patrick's Day in 1855, for example, a concert by the orphans in a Boston industrial school drew an audience of about three thousand and raised over one thousand dollars for the cause. Organizers of a San Francisco fair in the next decade explained that they settled on St. Patrick's Day because it would "supply a *safe amusement* for the Irish who look for extra pleasures on that day."[31] By the 1880s, American holidays were the more popular fair dates. Managers of one charity festival typically announced a two-fold objective in 1889: to raise money for St. Mary's Infant Asylum and to honor the centennial of Washington's inauguration.[32]

To be termed "Catholic," the benevolent society, of course, had to obtain episcopal approval for its activities. As a lingering consequence of the trustee controversy, however, bishops tended to be suspicious of lay organizations they did not direct. Even laity serving at their personal request on institutional boards of directors did not necessarily win the bishops' wholehearted trust. All the lay directors of St. Mary's Asylum in Boston resigned in 1848, maintaining that neither clergy nor bishop would cooperate with them.[33] Because it organized its conferences within local parishes, the St. Vincent de Paul Society, a laymen's benevolent association that appeared in America in 1845, aroused less episcopal concern than more independent lay societies and institutional boards, like the one in Boston. Within a few years, it had become the largest lay benevolent organization in the church. Parish conferences were separate units, their activities coordinated by a particular council composed of elected presidents and vice presidents of parish units. Although particular councils were later to sponsor activities crossing parish lines, such as clothing distribution and prison visiting, the heart of the society's work remained firmly based in the parishes.[34]

St. Vincent de Paul Society men learned quickly that unless they worked closely with the clergy, their benevolent projects were doomed to failure. Members of the first conference in St. Louis began their work by assigning two men to each of the city's four parishes. They were to seek out those in need, provide modest emergency funds, and report any problems they discovered to the respective pastors. The pastors, however, viewed these initiatives as unwarranted incursions by laity into their domain and a usurpation of clerical authority. They warned male parishioners against joining the new society, and its membership plummeted accordingly. Society officers resolved the impasse by inviting each of the pastors to serve as custodian of charity funds raised by the society for the poor of his parish. Society membership soon soared.[35]

With the exception of this benevolent society which, despite its large national membership, was parish-based, bishops disliked consolidated lay societies, especially federations with large working-class constituencies. They discouraged proposals from these groups for nationally organized benevolent projects and patronized their officers. When leaders of the Irish Catholic Benevolent Union, a national federation of Irish societies established in 1869, proposed to develop a network of protectories for destitute children, the bishops told them bluntly that member societies should instead focus their energies on the charities of their own dioceses. Richmond's James Gibbons dismissed the laymen with the peremptory order: "Co-operate with your local Ordinaries." Other bishops made light of the union's proposal by commenting on the working-class background of most of its membership. William McCloskey of Louisville, for example, pointedly referring to the union's limited financial resources, asked it to give him fifty thousand dollars for an industrial school in his diocese, knowing such a sum was far beyond its means. Patrick Ryan, coadjutor bishop of St. Louis, briskly dismissed the union's proposal by simply assessing member societies located in St. Louis for the support of St. Louis charities.[36] Such reactions from the hierarchy dampened lay overtures to undertake national benevolent programs.

Although heavily Irish in membership, the St. Vincent de Paul Society gradually attracted men from every ethnic group. By 1860 it had the numbers and resources to undertake, in addition to its regular work among the parish poor, special works in child and family welfare at diocesan and national levels. Between 1865 and 1886, this society held four national assemblies, and by the 1880s it was the leading forum for laymen in church philanthropy.

In addition to the lack of encouragement from the hierarchy, several other factors also hindered the development of national benevolent organizations in the late nineteenth century. First, ethnic communities did not want to collaborate. Irish and German fraternal and mutual-aid societies clung to their independence even when consolidation clearly promised better membership benefits and more effective benevolence. The 1878 refusal by the Catholic Aid Association, a Minnesota German mutual life insurance society, to consider the proposal of local Irish insurance societies that the groups merge to form the Catholic Insurance Society of Minnesota was more the rule than the exception. Second, sustained, heavy immigration of Catholics from Europe led bishops and clergy to fear nativist reactions. They therefore cautioned benevolent laity to work quietly at the parish level and to avoid large public assemblies. Only a few bishops, like Richard Gilmour of Cleveland, opposed this advice as inimical to Catholic progress. In the 1870s, he urged the Irish Catholic Benevolent Union to join forces with a German society to demonstrate effectively the benevolence and civic consciousness of the Catholic community. "We ought in our numbers and in our strength present a calm manly front," he argued. "We are not here in America by toleration, we are here by right."[37]

A third important factor discouraging the development of national benevolent organizations was the poor and working-class composition of the church membership. Efforts by Germans to organize nationally got underway in St. Louis as early as 1855 when the German Roman Catholic Central-Verein proposed to unite the numerous German mutual-aid societies. Although these had developed primarily to provide insurance benefits for working-class men and their families in case of accident, sickness, death, or unemployment, they also undertook benevolent work. However, the fact that most society members were working class severely limited the scope of the Verein's philanthropy. President Henry Spaunhorst explained in the mid 1870s: "With us it is lamentably true that the so-called better classes do but seldom take much interest in societies designated as Benevolent Societies and hence we have to move very cautiously and not undertake too much."[38]

Finally, strict gender segregation rendered the development of national societies difficult. Women's benevolent societies, even those functioning independently, continued to be heavily local in their memberships and priorities. Bishops did not look favorably upon even limited autonomy in female activities, whether lay or religious, and the women's benevolent societies did not have even the modest legal protections enjoyed by sisterhoods. Early attempts, like that of Brooklyn women in the 1840s to develop St. Paul's Catholic Guild into a national organization for "the practice of Christian charity," came to nothing.[39] Most benevolent women belonged to institutional auxiliaries, and these retained the decentralized pattern of the early parish female societies. The strong attachment of women's auxiliaries to specific institutions engendered competition rather than collaboration among them in charity fundraising. The idea of a joint fundraising campaign even for two local institutions was stoutly resisted. Margaret Gaffney Haughery, a prominent supporter of New Orleans charities, crushed an 1850 suggestion that two charity fairs, scheduled to benefit the girls' and the boys' orphanage respectively, be combined by threatening to withhold her substantial financial support from the girls' institution. Sisters of Charity, who managed both institutions, reassured her by agreeing that it was indeed one thing to ask members of a women's auxiliary to work for their own institution, but to ask them do the same for "another not connected" was simply preposterous.[40]

In the antebellum period, the preference for expressing charity through institutions had reflected a concern to protect the poor, especially children, from evangelization by Protestant charity workers. But its persistence suggests other explanatory factors as well. The mainstream outdoor relief approach demanded relatively more money than labor. But since the relatively abundant benevolent resource of the Catholic community was the voluntary corps of religious, the large institution seemed to be the organizational structure that would allow it to be most efficiently employed. Religious sisters and brothers could care for large numbers in a single facility, minimizing costs of land, buildings, and maintenance. While church officials celebrated the growing network of charity institutions as evidence of religious devotion and social responsibility, in fact, economic constraints, buttressed by occasional denominational friction, played a major role in explaining the enduring commitment to the institutional approach.

By mid-century their preference for very large institutions was placing Catholics increasingly at odds with "scientific philanthropists." This did not worry directors of charitable institutions very much, however. The significant cost reductions promised by sisters obscured the merits of alternative approaches to benevolent work. In the 1860s, for example, St. Vincent de Paul Society men in Boston decided that destitute infants ought to be one of their special works. While initially they placed the infants in foster homes, paying a ten-dollar monthly board for each, they soon asked Sisters of Charity at the Carney Hospital to open a special ward for these children. They preferred the institutional setting to the foster home, not simply because of the real difficulties they confronted in finding suitable Catholic foster homes, but even more because the sisters could care for the children at a 40 percent lower cost, a savings that permitted the society to "increase the work."[41]

Projections in 1870 for a New York City shelter for homeless women spelled out the Catholic position plainly: "The cost of such hospitality here would not exceed fifteen cents per night, and not as much if these houses were under the care of a religious community, saving by this the salaries of matrons and other employees."[42] Officers of Brooklyn orphan asylums expressed unfeigned relief upon completing staffing negotiations with a sisterhood in the 1880s: "Now, with the Sisters in charge of the various institutions, our work is light. Formerly, with a comparatively small Catholic population, and more limited means, the work must have tested even the brave hearts who laid the foundation of this charity."[43]

Interest in utilizing contributed labor efficiently did not entirely explain the bias toward institutions over outdoor relief. By mid-century the importance of preparing orphans, especially boys, for gainful employment had triggered investment in residential industrial schools. At this time, boys left orphanages at the age of twelve. If Catholics continued to concentrate most of their benevolent resources in institutions for younger children, concerned philanthropists argued, they would be leaving a major social need unaddressed. To bind over twelve-year-olds with no skills to a master, or to expect them to find jobs on their own, was, in effect, to abandon them in a harsh world.

The tendency to locate charity institutions in urban centers reflected the mid-century urban character of Catholic settlement and the vagaries of fund-raising. Charity officers recognized that city institutions would garner more financial support than those situated in the country or even at the edge of town. The manager of a Cincinnati orphanage pointed out the chief advantage of a city location: "Our children such as are able go to the Cathedral twice every Sunday. This keeps them before the public who love to see them and encourages them to contribute to their support."[44] St. John's Orphan Asylum directors discussed, but rejected, an 1851 proposal to move the Philadelphia institution to a healthier rural environment because "the interest which the Catholics of this community manifest for the Institution, would thus be more or less weakened, by its being withdrawn, as it were, from their view."[45] In the 1860s, an overcrowded boys' home in Washington, D.C., declined a gift of land in a more physically attractive location. The land, its directors explained, was "too remote for charitable visitors, too remote for the lively interest created by the neighborhood, presenting no chance for the favors of the passerby."[46]

A related factor in selecting a site for a charitable establishment was the need to find prominent citizens to sit on its board of directors. These men generated essential public attention and attracted new subscribers. After Philadelphia banker Francis A. Drexel joined the board of a city orphanage in 1852, the number of its subscribers increased nearly five-fold in one year. Economics dictated that establishments locate where benevolent societies could readily forge personal links between benefactors and institutions and where unused land could be leased at good rents to provide a steady income.[47]

Financial considerations also explain why many Catholic charitable institutions provided unrelated social services under one roof. Using funds bequeathed by John Mullanphy, Sisters of Charity erected a building in the 1850s for the care of elderly St. Louis women. However, since other sisters in their community were already caring for foundlings in a rented house in the city, they economized by moving both groups into the new building. By the end of the next decade, the institution bore the imposing name of St. Ann's Widows' Home, Lying-in Hospital, and Foundling Asylum.[48] Institutional names did not always reveal the breadth of services provided. In the same era, one hundred children in St. Patrick's Orphan Asylum in Manchester, New Hampshire, already shared quarters with aged women, and plans were underway for "a new school building which would also be a combination of school, orphanage and old folks' home."[49] The City Orphan Asylum in Salem, Massachusetts, likewise, in addition to its proclaimed work, was functioning in the 1880s as a hospital, a residence for unemployed women, and a home for elderly women.[50] By this time, such mingling of disparate services in a single institution was drawing stiff criticism from mainstream social reformers and from a few progressive Catholics as well.

Growing ethnic diversity continued to shape perceptions of the role of collective charity in the life of the church. While national groups, attached to their own languages, cultures, and customs, shared a common faith, they definitely wanted to express their benevolence independently. The rapid development of the parish as the basic unit of the American church was the most important influence in this area. Since place of residence determined one's parish, and since members of ethnic groups clustered together geographically, parish ties were strong, and parishes functioned autonomously. As a consequence, ethnic charity initiatives were constrained by parish boundaries, and Catholic charity organization became increasingly decentralized after 1850. While this development fostered considerable flexibility and local initiative, it also presented serious problems in fundraising and cultivated an already strong separatist mentality, relative to mainstream philanthropy.[51]

Benevolent-society fundraisers had discovered by the 1840s that heavy reliance on subscriptions was risky, since the enthusiasm of subscribers often withered quickly. Volunteers seeking subscribers for St. John's Orphanage in Philadelphia attributed waning interest in their institution to "competing appeals" from other Catholic charitable institutions opening in the city. The society's annual subscription payments peaked at approximately $1,175 in 1843, but fell precipitously in just eight years to one-third of that sum. Its annual fair supplied 34 percent of 1853 revenue, subscriptions only 8 percent.[52] The charity fair, in fact, was by now far more popular than membership in a subscription society. After all, it offered benevolent Catholics social enjoyment, whereas subscriptions only obliged them to future payments.

From the perspective of the institution as well, the charity fair was becoming the fundraising strategy of choice since its returns were cash in hand. Subscription pledges, on the other hand, were not always paid. The difference could be significant. In 1856, for example, benevolent men set out to raise money to pay the $13,000 debt of a San Francisco charity hospital by printing a circular and soliciting subscriptions. Their female counterparts organized a "ladies' fair" for the same cause. While the men raised $6,670 in three months, the women produced $8,500 in a week. Although fairs were becoming essential for most charities, they were by no means always successful. According to its organizers, bad weather contributed to the failure of a Boston orphan's fair in 1845. The next, not held for another five years, "was fully up to expectation," however, netting $3,500, about five times more than its predecessor.[53] Given these fluctuations, orphanage boards of directors at this time began to admit more children whose relatives could pay something toward their care. Understandable though it was, this step compromised somewhat the traditional priority of these institutions for society's most destitute children.

Already common in the 1830s, the charity sermon emerged in the 1850s as a major fundraising device. The more persuasive the preacher and the larger the parish, the bigger the collection. Institutions vied with one another to attract the most compelling speakers and to get permission from pastors to collect in the wealthier parishes. The charity sermon typically stressed the spiritual rewards that accompanied charity to the poor, especially to helpless orphans. Often with the children present, the preacher would assure donors that the orphans represented the child Jesus. "Deal with them as you would deal with Him if He came to you personally."[54] Charity sermons could mean the difference between a financially distressed institution closing or remaining open. A New Orleans sister, clearly seeing it as a last resort, beseeched the local archbishop to enlist some "eloquent divines" to preach on behalf of her orphanage.[55] Charity sermons soon became so popular and competition among institutions for them so great that bishops were forced to regulate them. In Philadelphia in the 1850s, for example, no more than three were allowed in one parish annually. In addition, proceeds from charity sermons were to be pooled and then divided among all charitable institutions of the city. Although this solution relieved Sunday congregations of a seemingly endless series of fundraising sermons, it displeased larger, well established institutions that had benefited more than the rest from the old approach.[56]

The charity sermon did not disappear, however, since it allowed bishops to appeal personally for a variety of diocesan charities, thereby reinforcing their pastoral letters on the subject. Episcopal charity sermons were often extremely dramatic. Thomas Hendricken, bishop of Providence, Rhode Island, distressed by lagging contributions for the support of orphans, gave such a sermon in the 1870s. He described, for a packed cathedral assembled for Christmas services, the serious consequences of the failure of a recent orphans' fair. At that point, he stopped to allow 176 children from the local asylum to march from the vestry into the sanctuary of the church. A journalist depicted the scene: "Placing themselves kneeling in a line before the altar, there at once arose from their little hearts, in voice of song, the touching verses of the beautiful Christmas hymn, Adeste Fidelis." The orphans then filed out. Then followed the bishop's charity sermon, based on the gospel text: "Taking a child, He placed him in the midst of them, and embracing the child, He turned to them and said: Whosoever shall receive one such child in My name, shall receive Me."[57] That his message reached the shamed congregation was evident in the large collection that followed.

The search for dependable income sources to augment fairs, subscriptions, and charity sermons continued throughout the nineteenth century. In the 1870s, John Drumgoole, a New York City priest, formed St. Joseph's Union, a subscription society, to fund the St. Vincent de Paul Newsboys' Lodging House.[58] Unlike many other such associations, this one flourished because he kept his subscribers interested through a small magazine. For an annual subscription of 25 cents, subscribers received *The Homeless Child and Messenger of St. Joseph's Union*. It publicized activities and conditions at the home, emphasized the spiritual benefits donors could expect, and discussed topics of general Catholic interest. In addition, extra spiritual benefits were promised to solicitors who recruited four new members for the Union. This special group of benefactors would participate in the masses and personal prayers of Father Drumgoole himself. His goal was to maximize the number of subscribers, since the likelihood of finding major donors was slim. The magazine kept interest high, and circulation reached 500,000 within three years, with over half the membership from New York City. The merits of this approach were quickly confirmed: "The united 'mites' of the grand army of St. Joseph's Union" soon permitted purchase of land worth nearly $70,000, "paid down in cash . . . not one cent of debt remaining on it."[59]

By the 1860s, as parishes in major cities became predominantly Irish or German, those of the same ethnic composition were actively discussing the advantages of joining together to fund their charities on a city-wide basis. Germans, who had been particularly successful in developing large benevolent societies, were the pioneers in this movement. Within a year of its establishment in 1850, for example, the German St. Vincent's Orphan Society of St. Louis recruited 350 members to support a German orphanage and soon opened a branch in every German parish in the city. In general, Germans dismissed outright any proposal, even when made by their bishop, that children of all ethnic backgrounds might be well cared for in one institution.[60]

Gaining city-wide support was not always easy. The Angel Guardian German Catholic Orphan Society, founded in Chicago in 1865, canvassed the city's five German parishes on behalf of an asylum for German children orphaned in the Civil War. However, although pastors of these parishes had agreed to collect for the project, results were indifferent in the first year. The society then revamped its structure to include on its board of directors the five German pastors as well as two laymen from each of their parishes. Society officers also asked the bishop to approve a special annual collection for the orphans in the five German parishes only. This, supplemented by income from a city-wide bazaar, yielded quite satisfactory operating income for the institution. For unusual projects, such as the construction of buildings, however, society officers continued to depend heavily on in-kind and service contributions. As an example, in 1876 most materials and labor for a new building were donated, with the result that a single benefit picnic permitted all construction bills to be met.[61] Germans in other cities followed similar organizational strategies.

Requests that bishops reserve ethnic parish charity collections for institutions serving persons of the same nationality were, in fact, becoming common by the 1880s. Charity collections in "English-speaking" parishes in Milwaukee routinely went to Irish institutions, while returns from the German parishes went to German institutions. Less commonly, ethnic benevolent societies extended their support to institutions beyond city limits.[62]

A few overtures toward making church benevolence a diocesan rather than a parish responsibility had occurred as early as the 1840s, all of them linked to the need to finance children's institutions more effectively. Peter Kenrick of St. Louis, for example, formed a Board of Managers in his archdiocese to oversee orphanages there. He also assigned surplus revenues of the archdiocesan cemetery association to the two Irish orphanages and ordered biannual collections in the German parishes to support the German orphanage.[63] Since public interest in established institutions tended to wane as new needs appeared, their support soon devolved almost entirely on the parishes where they happened to be located. Donations from other city parishes for their support remained sparse. Directors of St. Paul's parish orphanage in Brooklyn proposed to Bishop John Hughes in 1840 that every parish in the city schedule a charity sermon once a year to benefit that orphanage. In this way, they argued, responsibility for supporting the children would be shared more equitably by all New York Catholics. As Hughes refused to challenge pastoral autonomy in this area, the people of St. Paul's parish continued to hear most of the charity sermons and to provide most of the funds to maintain the orphanage.[64]

With little episcopal support, pastors and orphanage directors found it difficult to develop a sense of city-wide responsibility for the parish institution. Some tried to give it a less local identity. In 1845, for example, the pastor of St. Joseph's parish in Albany, New York, named his new parish orphanage in honor of St. Vincent rather than St. Joseph, hoping "that it might have less of a parochial character, and so share in the general contributions of the faithful."[65] And directors of St. John's Orphanage in Philadelphia requested the bishop to join the board of managers as president. "There is nothing local or partial, but everything general, or universal, in the character of this charity," they emphasized. However, even though collection books were sent to every pastor in the city, extra-parish contributions remained minimal. The directors complained that a neighboring parish, St. Paul's, sent more children to St. John's orphanage than any other city parish, yet did not contribute a cent toward the children's support. The directors blamed the situation squarely on the various pastors who refused to collect for the cause. Finally, they offered to quit and let the clergy take responsibility for an orphanage of 144 children, which, they declared, had become "an incubus upon a few, when there are so many who might with ease, and ought even at a little pain, rescue it from the necessity of these constant appeals."[66] The Catholic press, preferring to chastise laity rather than clergy, reminded readers that "words and wishes will not feed the hungry, clothe the naked, or assist in meeting the expense of the establishment."[67]

The financial condition of so many child-caring institutions struggling independently to support themselves, with only modest success in most cases, led more bishops to call forcefully in the 1860s for a warmer spirit of corporate responsibility among Catholics of their diocese. Martin Spalding of Baltimore was one. "Our asylums like our other charities [a hospital and a home for the aged] are not local but Catholic,"[68] he insisted. He took tentative steps to act on this conviction by requiring all charitable institutions to obtain his permission for their fundraising events, and he personally determined their dates and times. This, he hoped, would foster "brotherly harmony, and concert of action in carrying on their works of mercy."

By this decade, bishops were becoming much more wary about granting permission for the establishment of new charitable institutions in their dioceses, unless proposers guaranteed that they had the means, or at least feasible plans, for their support. Diocesan resources were already strained to support existing charities and to construct churches and seminaries, and they concurred that these commitments should take priority over new benevolent projects. Groups proposing to open new charity institutions knew from the start that they might receive occasional allocations from diocesan funds, but they could not count on any regular income from this source. The Little Sisters of the Poor, for example, were able to open their home for the elderly poor in Indianapolis in 1873 only after they had convinced Bishop Maurice de Saint-Palais that they would not expect financial support from the diocese.[69]

In fact, by the 1870s dioceses were being called on more often to save venerable, but now financially bereft, parish charity institutions. St. Joseph's Orphan Society in St. Paul, Minnesota, had supported a German parish orphanage since the 1850s from annual subscriptions of $1.20 for men and $1 for women. As society founders grew old, however, new subscribers were hard to find, and many of these neglected to pay their monthly dues. By 1877, society membership had dwindled to the point that a legal election could not be held. Finally, in 1881 the society turned the institution over to the bishop, its funding to be provided thereafter by the diocese, supplemented by whatever the society could raise.[70] Charities that depended heavily on fairs faced similar financial problems. For example, although the annual three-day orphans' fair for the Minneapolis Catholic Orphan Asylum was one of the city's major social events, after 1878 the funds it raised no longer covered institutional needs. A decade later, in an effort to remedy the situation, the bishop proposed to replace the fair with parish assessments. Without mechanisms to ensure the cooperation of pastors, these did not prove much more remunerative than the fair. In 1894, the benevolent society reluctantly transferred ownership of its orphanage to the archdiocese, a move which seemed the only way to secure for it some degree of financial security.[71]

The Civil War years had not only kindled demand for more homes for children, but had also highlighted the inadequacy of traditional fundraising methods. Bishops seeking financial support for their diocesan projects found that the constant fundraising activities of numerous charitable institutions worked against them. An orphan collection in every parish seemed to many to be a good way to address the problem. This idea had strong precedent, since for decades some important dioceses had traditionally reserved for the orphans the parish collections on one or both days of highest church attendance, Christmas and Easter. For example, the archdiocese of New York had been allocating both of these lucrative collections to the orphans for several decades. By the 1880s, more bishops preferred to designate another day for the orphan collection, so that they could use the Christmas and Easter collections for other diocesan needs.[72]

The early diocesan-wide collections for orphans faced a perennial problem. Some parishes gave in accord with their means, but many others did not. Since the enthusiasm of pastors seemed to be a critical factor in explaining interparish variations, bishops set out to reduce pastoral influence by levying annual assessments for the orphan collection on every parish, with dollar amounts established according to the economic status of the parish. By the mid-1880s, the Providence, Rhode Island, diocese had eliminated all charity fairs for the Providence R. C. Orphan Asylum. The institution thereafter was to be supported by "an annual tax on all the churches of the city of Providence."[73]

The quota scheme, while apparently simple, was by no means always successful. The experience in Cleveland in the 1890s was not unusual. The diocese had been divided into districts, each responsible for the support of one of the charitable institutions of the diocese. City parishes were assigned quotas that they usually met by holding an orphans' fair. That quotas did not elicit the warm cooperation of the laity was evident in persisting institutional deficits and the need for sisters to beg to meet operating expenses. Smaller dioceses generally continued to follow traditional ways of fundraising. The Natchez, Mississippi, diocese, for instance, still supported its two orphanages in the 1880s by an annual Orphans' Fair and a Christmas Day collection in all parishes of the diocese.[74]

As dioceses gradually assumed more financial responsibility for troubled institutions, the authority of lay directors declined. Particular arrangements varied, but the sequence was a familiar one. In 1885, for example, a diocesan synod in Detroit established an orphan board composed of three priests and announced that henceforth only children admitted to the orphanage by this board would be supported "at a specified rate" from an "annual tax on the ordinary revenues of the various churches of the diocese."[75] While this ostensibly left the institution's directors free to continue to admit other children, they had to raise funds for the support of these children independently, a requirement that severely constrained their autonomy in this important area.

Given the fundraising problems that faced independent parish orphanages, by the late nineteenth century an increasing number of pastors wanted to close them. In Lowell, Massachusetts, for example, St. Peter's Orphan Asylum had opened with the strong support of pastor and parishioners in 1870. When the pastor died, his successor simply announced unilaterally that he was going to close the orphanage and that parishioners should withhold contributions for its support. When they ignored his message, he complained to the archbishop that the orphanage had become a "source of dissension and discord," an accusation that prompted the Sisters of Charity to withdraw their services.[76]

Most independent parish orphanages, by this time, were eager to qualify for a share of the annual orphans' collection mandated for the parishes. But acceptance of diocesan regulations and a willingness to appoint the bishop, or his clerical representative, as president of their boards of directors were conditions for participation. The reconstitution of a Milwaukee orphanage society board in 1882 was fairly typical. While a lay vice president presided over society meetings, "counting the archbishop always as director, the full board thereafter numbered sixteen. There were to be ten priests on the board."[77] In addition, the treasurer of the society was to be the orphanage chaplain.

Despite their authority as spiritual and temporal leaders, nineteenth-century bishops discovered that the hierarchical approach did not work well in the voluntary sector of the church. Those who tried to impose their personal benevolent priorities on the laity found themselves without sufficient funds. Lay enthusiasm for the cause was essential. In the 1840s, William Quarter of Chicago learned a painful lesson in this regard. Meeting widespread indifference to his priority project, a diocesan seminary, he finally acknowledged that "without the charitable cooperation of the faithful throughout the Diocese, little, comparatively, can be done by the Bishop; with it, much can be effected."[78] But rather than attributing the poor result to his autocratic style, he blamed it on the poor economic circumstances of his scattered parishioners and left on a collecting tour in the more populated and prosperous East. There his colleagues had little choice but to let him collect, but they did not welcome him with open arms, as he noted in his diary: "When the Bishop arrived in New York he applied to Bishop Hughes for permission to collect funds in the different Catholic churches of the city and Diocese to enable him to build a Catholic college and seminary in Chicago. The permission was granted, although not very cheerfully."[79]

Bishops, not all of them from poor or sparsely populated frontier dioceses, continued to rely on collecting tours, despite the cool receptions they occasionally received. Many found the annuities from European mission societies increasingly inadequate in the face of mounting needs in the 1860s and 1870s. Results of these tours varied with episcopal eloquence. James Gibbons of Richmond, Virginia, for example, reported on a trek throughout New York State: "Should my success keep pace with the past two Sundays," he wrote in 1871, "I will easily succeed before leaving Albany, in realizing the next installment ($3,000 with interest) on the Sisters' property."[80]

Lay response to episcopal appeals was far stronger when they were made for specific institutions that promised to address a social problem of pressing lay concern. Martin Spalding's proposal at the close of the Civil War to build a diocesan protectory in Baltimore for homeless teenage boys, where they would be "reformed and competent to earn their daily bread," met overwhelming approval from rich and poor alike. Of the $50,000 he needed for the project, more than one-third came from wealthy persons attending an initial planning meeting, and 100 acres of land were donated at that time as well. Contributions poured in from all parts of the archdiocese, and the school opened in 1866, under the management of Xaverian Brothers.[81] In contrast, bishops taking an autocratic approach in fundraising, even when the cause was popular, faced strong lay resistance. One such bishop was John Luers, of Fort Wayne, Indiana, who planned, in 1865, to open a diocesan home for Civil War orphans. Convinced that unmarried wage earners gave little or nothing to charity, he decided to shame them into giving by publishing the names of donors and the amounts they pledged for the cause. The plan collapsed as parishioners throughout the diocese, offended by such pressure, simply made large pledges and then refused to honor them. Two years later, a disappointed Luers reported the results of his campaign: "It stands as yet on paper, like wheat in the field, not yet come to maturity."[82]

Perhaps the best example of disharmony in benevolence between bishops and people was an episcopal effort to relocate Irish immigrants from urban slums to western farm lands. The Minnesota Irish Emigration Society, established for this purpose in 1864 by Bishop Thomas Grace of St. Paul, Minnesota, took on new life in 1875 under his energetic coadjutor, John Ireland. Ireland set out to raise money for the society, now known as the Catholic Colonization Bureau of Minnesota, by organizing "charitable saving banks," such as the Catholic Colonization Land Stock Company, and then selling stock in them throughout the country at $10 a share. Although this scheme failed, the project was revived later in the Irish Catholic Colonization Association of the United States. From 1879 until 1891, under the leadership of William Onahan, a prominent Chicago layman, the association sold stock certificates. Again results were poor, and, in fact, few settlers ever reached association lands in Nebraska and Minnesota.[83]

John Lancaster Spalding, bishop of Peoria and staunch backer of colonization plans, deplored the narrow charitable horizons of the Catholic laity. "Stronger evidence could not be desired of the dearth of large and enlightened views among wealthy Catholics on the work and wants of the Church in the United States. Even the better sort seem to have little idea of anything that reaches beyond a parish charity."[84] While Spalding was correct in his assessment of the provincial character of Catholic benevolence, he did not acknowledge that the promotion of colonization projects almost exclusively as business schemes, promising brisk returns to investors, rather than as genuine philanthropic programs, contributed to their failure.

Although child care still dominated Catholic priorities in the latter half of the nineteenth century, other areas were attracting some benevolent concern as well. One was the establishment of hospitals where priests would be welcome to visit and patients would be protected from proselytization. Sisterhoods provided initial funds for many early hospitals, and these limited resources were supplemented by fairs and benefits organized by interested laity. Since few hospitals received large individual gifts, the sisters typically borrowed to fund major expansion projects and sometimes to cover operating costs. One New York sister superior quipped, only half in jest, in 1856: "I shall be put in prison for debt."[85]

Until 1840, poor Catholics had used existing public hospitals when necessary and had met little religious intolerance in them. Expanding numbers of poor immigrants in succeeding decades, however, put heavy pressures on these free facilities, generating, in the process, considerable class and religious conflict. Therefore, Catholics followed the same separatist route in providing health care that they had taken in caring for orphans. Local physicians and prominent citizens occasionally promoted hospitals to care for "deserving journeymen, domestics in families, and operatives of various kinds."[86] These were working-class groups rather than poor, but promoters pointed out that when they became sick they became unemployed and would soon be in need of charity. Since subscription funds and donations invariably fell short of financial requirements, hospitals began to charge fees to patients who could pay. The fees were used to meet operating costs and to support destitute patients.

Among the first groups attended in Catholic hospitals were the mentally ill. Sisters of Charity, who for seven years had staffed the Maryland Hospital for the Insane, a public institution, left in 1840 to open a Catholic hospital, the Mount Hope Institution. They received patients from all parts of the country, charging those with financial resources, and treating the poor without charge. The latter comprised approximately 15 to 20 percent of patients in the institution's early decades. By 1855, now known as Mount Hope Retreat, it was caring for an average of 122 patients, two-thirds of them women. At this time, its directors established a fund to endow free beds for the indigent, an uncommon step for a Catholic charitable institution of this period. "Three thousand dollars would maintain a free bed or apartment perpetually or as long as the Institution exists," they announced, "and this apartment so endowed would always be designated by the name of the donor."[87]

The issue of charging fees for hospital care became a heated one in charity circles. Those in favor of the practice pointed out that many people avoided hospitals because they saw them as places for the destitute. By charging small fees, this stigma was removed. At the same time, working-class patients, unlikely to become involved in endowing free beds for the indigent, would be happy to see part of the small fee they paid used to support the destitute sick.[88] Fees at Boston's Carney Hospital were typical of the 1860s. Men paid a weekly fee of six dollars and women paid five dollars. The poor were admitted free.

Because paying patients were mainly working class, fees collected never covered total costs, and sisterhoods subsidized hospitals, not only by contributing their services as nurses and domestic workers, but also by raising money for the cause. In some instances, their cash gifts were not voluntary. For example, in 1869 the bishop of Louisville, William McCloskey, informed Sisters of Charity that he would provide five thousand dollars annually to cover operating expenses of a diocesan charity hospital then under construction if the sisters would match that sum yearly and, in addition, request no salaries from the diocese for managing the hospital. He explained that while his proposal might appear to be doing them an injustice, in fact, just the opposite was true, since it would "infuse into the Sisters that love of poverty and that devotion to the sick and suffering poor, which your very name implies."[89]

Sisterhoods, who had long and voluntarily underwritten diocesan charities, were deeply offended by such arrogance. Sisters of St. Joseph were typical of many communities when, in the 1890s, they "kindly declined the offer" of the St. Paul archdiocese to begin paying sisters working in archdiocesan orphanages $100 per year.[90] And in New Orleans, at the turn of the century, sisters at

St. John Berchmans' Asylum for Colored Orphan Girls received only a small public subsidy to care for the institution's sixty children. The city's Board of Prisons and Asylums acknowledged that diocesan funding was minimal: "The Sisters in charge support the asylum by the revenues from the convent attached."[91]

Unlike the Louisville hospital, most hospitals were owned by sisterhoods, not by parishes or dioceses, a feature that affected episcopal interest in them. While bishops approved their establishment, they could not control the corporate boards and hence felt little financial obligation toward the hospitals.[92] This made their support a perennial problem. Until the 1880s, religious denominations in some cities occasionally concurred that because hospitals accepted patients without regard to religion, all should receive their support. At this time, Protestant and Catholic churches in Boston were still holding an annual "Hospital-Sunday" collection and dividing the pooled donations among hospitals in the city. These ecumenical collections did not last long, however. Although patient fees were covering only about one-third of annual costs, Catholics believed that these fees covered total costs and that, relative to other charitable institutions, hospitals did not need philanthropic support.[93]

In western territories, early hospitals were genuinely pioneer enterprises. When St. Joseph's Hospital in St. Paul opened in 1854, it was Minnesota Territory's first charitable institution. As work in railroad construction and mines attracted more immigrant laborers, hospitals were needed for care of those injured in industrial accidents and for general medical care as well. In some instances, miners importuned sisters to open hospitals. In Silver Reef, Utah, in 1879, Holy Cross Sisters financed St. John's Hospital from miners' subscriptions of one dollar monthly, a contribution that allowed the miners access to the hospital's services.[94] Financing such institutions in sparsely populated territories was an ongoing challenge. Rather than collecting subscriptions for their hospital, Michigan Sisters of Charity traveled to lumber camps in the same decade to sell five-dollar vouchers, good for a year's hospital care. Similarly, "Hospital Admission" tickets could be purchased for ten dollars annually for care in any of three hospitals conducted by Benedictine Sisters in Dakota Territory in the late 1880s. These tickets were valid for treatment of any ailment except "insanity, contagious, infectious, veneral [sic] diseases, or injury received before the date of the ticket, or arising from the use of intoxicating drink or fighting."[95] Such financial arrangements became very popular throughout the West.

In order to keep hospitals afloat, sisters occasionally adopted unorthodox strategies. In the 1870s, for example, Sister Alexis, the director of the St. Louis Mullanphy Hospital, financed a $150,000 building by borrowing $12,000 at 8 percent. Over the next year, she advertised in the local press that the sisters at the hospital would accept deposits and pay 8 percent for deposits exceeding $100, 7 percent for smaller amounts. These desirable rates attracted large deposits by banks as well as individuals. Sister Alexis used the deposits to meet payments on the mounting hospital debt, keeping on hand only enough to pay interest and to cover likely withdrawals. When the scheme became known to her superiors, she was replaced, leaving her successor, who "feared the sheriff would come,"[96] to pay off the debts.

By this time, charity cases comprised about half the admissions in Catholic hospitals. Yet their fundraising strategies continued to reinforce the perception of church members that hospitals were not religious charities in the strict sense of the word.[97] The practice of charging fees for service seemed to many to violate a basic tenet of Catholic charity, since, given a limited number of beds, the more paying patients an institution admitted, the fewer destitute patients it could accept. Proponents of the fee system countered that just as tuitions from boarding academies had long subsidized orphanages, so fees from paying patients provided the means to allow sisters to nurse the sick poor. But there was one critical difference, and the average parishioner recognized it. Gifts of tuition revenues to orphanages had been made voluntarily by the sisters, whereas hospital fees were not gifts at all, but rather payments for services received. Furthermore, heavy dependence on patient fees to cover operating costs inevitably resulted in paying patients taking precedence when beds were in short supply during epidemics and natural disasters.

Despite this conflict, hospitals continued to charge fees according to their patients' ability to pay, and neither bishops nor charity leaders objected to the practice. Sharp criticism came from another quarter, however. Sister Alphonsa Lathrop, who founded St. Rose's Free Home for Incurable Cancer in New York City in 1897, had strong convictions on the matter. Her pioneer institution charged no fees, relying entirely on private benevolence for its support. A charity institution could not simultaneously be fee dependent, she declared: "Fearing future abuses because of a mingling of paying and non-paying patients, as is known often to be the result in hospitals, 'no pay beds' are allowed."[98] Within two decades, her free hospital was admitting an average of 340 patients annually, one quarter of whom were Protestant, and 4 percent African Americans.[99] Few other Catholic hospitals followed her example.

Catholics had long maintained that their philanthropic works were not primarily denominational, but rather a collective contribution to the common good. Although they differentiated religious charity from the work of public welfare agencies and private secular benevolent organizations, they never claimed that they were entirely separate. Through the virtue of charity, they maintained, Christianity showed its divine foundation, but like secular philanthropy, it aimed to benefit others. Because their charitable institutions helped the state meet its responsibility to its citizens, they felt justified in requesting state funds for their support.[100] Bishops, clergy, and prominent laymen usually took the initiative in applying for public funds for Catholic charities. On occasion, however, sisters took the first step. For example, aware that "words alone would not make [their] visits agreeable to ignorant, hungry creatures," Sisters of Mercy in Wilmington, North Carolina, decided to call on the mayor in 1869 to request financial support: "One sultry evening we fixed up with gloves, parasol etc. and ascended the steps of a respectable looking house, and found ourselves talking to his Honor, the Mayor, who graciously acceding to our request allowed us a weekly sum for our charities. The little success was a great encouragement to us."[101] However, public monies for the support of institutions were less easily obtained at this time. Mainstream opposition remained strong, even though charity leaders like Erastus Brooks warned that this could be a self-defeating stance: "Be careful where you strike," he reminded legislators, "or, like Samson, you may bring the whole temple at your feet, and destroy all in your zeal to prostrate those you dislike."[102] *Harper's Weekly* editor George W. Curtis agreed that "if the State, as we have determined, is to aid charities, it cannot avoid, at least proportionately, helping those institutions which are under the care of the Roman Church."[103]

Public funding for Catholic institutions varied widely in time, place, and amount by late nineteenth century. Some states and municipalities offered, then withdrew assistance, while others never provided any funds. Support was given selectively. Some charitable institutions received it, others did not. In the 1870s, for example, New York and New Jersey were paying charitable institutions for the care of wards of the court, but Massachusetts offered no stipends for the care of such children. The topic of public support remained a sensitive political issue in New England, so funds from this source were unreliable. While Boston's Carney Hospital received $10,000 from the state in 1887 and again in 1891 to care for charity patients, its 1892 application was denied on the grounds that this would be "sectarian aid."[104]

Charity leaders throughout the country nonetheless persisted in their applications for municipal and state appropriations. Public contracts for the care of even a fraction of the children would insulate an institution from the vagaries of private support. Public funding, despite its financial benefits, was to have untoward consequences on grassroots giving, however. In 1869, for example, directors of St. Mary's Industrial School in Baltimore convinced local and government officials that since the school was providing a desperately needed public service, it merited a city subsidy. To compete with the only other private industrial school in the city for public funding, the school's trustees amended its charter so that it could admit boys referred by the courts. Their aim was "to convert the simple, charitable School into a great State and City incorporation, with all the powers and franchises of a sister institution, the House of Refuge."[105] Such aggressive pursuit of public funds had a striking impact on lay attitudes toward the school. As its enrollment grew, benevolent interest tapered off. In 1873, city appropriations represented 25 percent of its annual income, private giving, through a fair, 36 percent, and church collections 23 percent. Within four years, public funds were accounting for nearly three-fourths of institutional receipts, but no church collections were taken up to benefit the school.[106] By this time, with court wards comprising 80 percent of its enrollment, mainstream opponents accused the school's directors of being motivated more by pecuniary than benevolent impulse. At the same time, Catholics were viewing the school as a public establishment toward which they had no special benevolent obligation. Although religious brothers continued to manage the school, the enthusiastic lay support that it had received when Martin Spalding first proposed it virtually disappeared. The effect of public funding on religious giving was to become more pronounced as this revenue source became more available and more substantial in the twentieth century.

Relative to poor and working-class Catholics, the number of wealthy parishioners grew slowly during the nineteenth century, and financial support for the expanding charities depended on small gifts from many individuals of limited means. This was a source of pride in denominational debates of the 1860s. Claims that, collectively, Catholics gave more money in Sunday collections than other denominations and gave larger proportions of their incomes as well were commonly heard.[107] Mainstream response to the first point was to dismiss it by pointing out that the average Protestant congregation was much smaller than the Catholic parish. "For the people of the parish it was easy enough," commented one journalist. "Are there not fifteen thousand of them? If each contributes ten cents a week, does it not come to seventy-eight thousand dollars a year?" The second claim, however, was acknowledged to have more merit: "The poor, besides being more generous than the rich, are hundreds of times more numerous, and their pennies flow in a continuous stream. Nor do they confine their gifts to copper coin."[108] By the turn of the century, the view was about the same. "Whoever studies our Catholic charities will notice two features," remarked a St. Vincent de Paul Society officer, "the relatively large demands which are made upon them, for we have many poor; and the comparative insufficiency of means that can be obtained to support them, for we have few Catholics who are wealthy."[109]

The development of opportunities for voluntary service that increasingly marked Catholic philanthropy in the second half of the nineteenth century was extremely significant, since it allowed the immense working class to participate fully and on equal terms with the wealthy. Those unable to give much money could offer their time or small in-kind gifts to support institutions of their choice. Since direct provision of charitable services was not generally seen as appropriate work for clergy, laity, women as well as men, could assume leadership roles in the church's philanthropic sector. "It is not necessary that a Catholic should be a bishop or a priest to fix upon him this responsibility," Levi Silliman Ives reminded lay colleagues in the 1860s.[110] A distinctive approach to charity, unlike that taken by major Protestant denominations, developed among Catholics as their giving became almost exclusively confined to institutional settings. Because charity work did not yet require much professional training, lay involvement in the institutions was varied, voluntaristic, and somewhat freewheeling.

Changing social needs in the second half of the nineteenth century strengthened grassroots appreciation of philanthropy as the democratic heart of their hierarchical church. In their struggle to contribute as a community to the social good, members of an outsider church became more confident of their place in American society. However, competition among proliferating charitable institutions for limited benevolent funds was generating increasing criticism from charity reformers of the 1880s, and the stage was set for twentieth-century changes in Catholic charity organization.

3

Social Needs and
Mainstream Challenges

One can give to the poor without being charitable, but one cannot be charitable
without giving to the poor.
—Anon.

RELATIONS BETWEEN CATHOLICS and their neighbors in rural communities of the eighteenth century were cordial. Religious differences did not matter very much in small communities struggling to survive. Poor Mennonites helped German Catholics erect a church in 1741 in Goshenhoppen, Pennsylvania, for example, and the priest, in turn, gave them land on which an old Mennonite meeting house stood in appreciation for their charity. A half century later, although Protestants outnumbered them by a margin of sixty-eight to one, Maryland Catholics met little discrimination and cooperated actively in local philanthropies. Bishop John Carroll was among the founders of the Maryland Society for Promoting Useful Knowledge in 1800, and he played a leadership role in the drive to establish Baltimore's first library.[1]

Tensions between mainstream citizens and Catholics intensified in the 1820s, however, and cooperative ventures in benevolence declined. Although fundraising appeals for charitable projects were still addressed to Protestant and Catholic alike, mutual support waned as denominational rhetoric intensified. In 1832, Philadelphia pastor John Hughes invited wealthy Protestant acquaintances to attend the dedication of St. John's Church. Hoping to move them to contribute to the church building fund, he engaged, as guest preacher, John Power, widely acclaimed for his eloquent charity sermons. But instead of focusing on ecumenical topics, Power took the occasion to respond to recent anti-Catholic outbursts in the city. His inflammatory discourse on the marks of the "true church" left the flabbergasted Hughes to groan: "My dear sir, you have ruined me!"[2]

Religious animosities were more virulent in the East than in other sections of the country. Catholic and Protestant women in St. Louis in the 1820s cooperated amicably to establish the Female Charitable Society. Protestants were as eager as Catholics to engage Sisters of Loretto to assume the care of the orphans and sick poor in that city. Mainstream citizens and Catholics were also collaborating on charity projects in New Orleans in the 1830s. Protestant directors of the Poydras Orphan Asylum there hired Sisters of Charity to conduct the institution and to instruct the children. The sisters were sought out for their professional skills, not to save on labor costs, and each sister received an annual salary of $150, a munificent sum relative to what Catholic institutions were able to offer them.[3]

Hostile religious feeling thawed, at least temporarily, in the face of common needs. In the 1830s, local government officials in major cities called on the sisterhoods for help in recurring epidemics. Their positive response evoked the good will of citizens of every denomination. Baltimore Mayor William Steuart, for example, praised the "unostentatious charity" of Sisters of Charity during an 1832 epidemic in his city, and Philadelphia officials asked "these amiable philanthropists" who had nursed victims there to stay on after the crisis to manage the almshouse hospital.[4]

The fact that sisters gave their nursing services gratuitously left citizens "doubly [their] debtors,"[5] and Catholics, for their part, viewed the work of sisters in these crises as a reflection of the public spirit and generosity of the entire church community. Charleston Sisters of Mercy, for example, at the request of city officials, had provided services during the yellow fever epidemic that struck Augusta, Georgia, in 1839. On their departure several months later, the Augusta city council voted to reimburse them for travel and living expenses. However, they refused the money, according to a local pastor, because "the Catholics of Charleston felt that in the affliction of their sister city, they ought not at least make any charge for charitable aid, and the more especially as a great portion of the patients were Roman Catholics."[6]

Although separatism marked Catholic philanthropy in ordinary times, every city reported some cooperative endeavors. In the late 1840s, for example, Sisters of Charity in Natchez, Mississippi, had raised half the funds needed to open an orphanage and free school by subscriptions and had borrowed the rest. A local Protestant endorsed their notes and paid them when due. In the same decade, Brooklyn Catholics took up a special diocesan collection on Thanksgiving Day to benefit the lying-in hospital "where many of our people go."[7]

While mainstream appreciation for the contributions of Catholics in times of community crisis was wholehearted, nativist sentiment remained strong in the 1850s, and charity fundraising had to take it into account. Sisters conducting a Louisville orphanage had to borrow emergency funds from another sisterhood because, they explained, "the present state of public feelings" occasioned by virulently anti-Catholic Know-Nothing agitation had prevented the institution's lady managers from holding their charity fair.[8] During the next decade, although denominational barriers again thawed in the face of war, the Know-Nothing Movement still had enough national support to make the appearance of sisters as volunteers in military hospitals and on battlefields an occasion of considerable consternation. Only an order from the Surgeon General's office in 1861 silenced the opposition of Dorothea Dix, Superintendent of Female Nurses, to the participation of sisters in the nursing corps. Although Dix never really accepted them, the sisters eventually won the friendship of the Protestant nurses and volunteers with whom they worked. Commented one sister-nurse: "Later, a great deal of the prejudice against us was softened, and the ladies were very kind and good to us. Indeed, the prejudice was only in their heads, never in their hearts."[9]

Since many of the six hundred sisters who worked as nurses on battlefields, in ambulance corps, and in military hospitals were immigrants, unflattering press descriptions of Catholics as foreign intruders died down somewhat. The fact that they nursed the troops without pay elicited positive tributes to Catholic patriotism and to charity work in general. When Sister Lucy Dosh, who had cared for military typhoid victims, succumbed to typhoid, men from both armies demanded that she have a full military funeral. An honor guard in blue and gray uniforms accompanied her body back to her Kentucky convent for burial.[10]

Mainstream attitudes toward Catholic philanthropic efforts varied considerably according to geography. Relative to the East, where collaborative efforts in charity were already rare by the 1860s, there was less religious animosity in western regions, where Catholics had been among the first settlers. By the 1860s, western parishioners were testifying that their charitable projects received widespread community support and that "the advances of the Church are regarded without dismay."[11] Soon after several French Sisters of Charity arrived in Galveston, Texas, in 1866 to open a hospital, local Catholics and Baptists joined to sponsor a fair and benefit concert, splitting the proceeds between the Baptist church and the new hospital. The local press, remarking that the singers, members of an Italian opera company, were probably all Catholic, applauded the project. "Such instances go farther in breaking down the partition walls of sectarianism between Catholics and Protestants than all the homilies ever written."[12] Nor was this event unique. A month later a second benefit concert for the hospital featured the Episcopal church choir.

Economic hardships accompanying the Civil War exacerbated the challenges of immigration and kindled controversy within the church over aspects

of its collective benevolence. Acrimonious public disputes with mainstream social reformers over how best to assist the poor led some parishioners to call for
a reassessment of their traditional giving style. Three issues, in particular, occasioned energetic debate: the separatist stance of Catholics in conducting their
charitable enterprises; their strong preference for relief over social reform projects; and their benevolent record, relative to that of other Christian churches,
toward African Americans and Indians. These conflicts, in time, evoked new
appreciation of the social benefits and shortcomings of Catholic giving.

After the Civil War, a small contingent of Catholics, clerical and lay, began
to question publicly the strict isolation that marked the charitable work of their
church. They argued that its original purpose, to protect the poor, especially
children, from proselytization, was no longer compelling and that modern social problems demanded that Catholics collaborate in charity work with other
private benevolent agencies. However, although bishops of the 1870s occasionally approved local cooperative projects, they continued to insist that Catholic
charity differed critically from that of other religious denominations. Conceding that generous Protestants financed many hospitals and benevolent works,
William Byrne, vicar of the Boston archdiocese, nonetheless emphasized that,
while altruistic, these activities were not true religious charity because they
lacked one essential element, namely, voluntary service. He did not claim that
the Catholic laity volunteered service more often than did Protestants. However,
he maintained that in the aggregate Catholic benevolence had a much larger
voluntary-service component than that of other religious groups because of the
contributed labor of thousands of religious sisters and brothers. Such reasoning
led to the uneasy inference that only the religious orders distinguished Catholic
giving from "mere humanitarianism."[13]

Although, by this time, the religious orders were certainly a prominent feature of Catholic philanthropy, the financial distress of so many of the charitable
institutions they managed undercut flattering comparisons with the benevolence of other churches. Inordinate emphasis on the contributed services of the
religious orders delayed critical evaluation of the actual record of lay giving.
Middle-class parishioners did not appear to be any more generous in their financial contributions than members of other faiths; they might indeed be less.
By the 1850s, however, church leaders were worrying that their giving propen-
sities too closely resembled those of mainstream citizens. If Catholic charity is
an intellectual rather than a sentimental act, one writer noted pointedly, then
why were Catholics soliciting charity support by entertaining donors? "The
charity, which follows the new banners, is all mixed up with pleasure and os-
tentation. . . . The ingenious science of economy, in modern times, has enabled

men to feel that they contribute to the support of the poor not only without sub-tracting anything from their own usual amusements, but even in proportion as they multiply them; so that the most dissipated are the most merciful."[14]

Middle- and upper-class Catholics of the 1860s and 1870s were interacting more frequently with Protestants in business and the professions and were eager for full acceptance in mainstream society. They dismissed such criticisms as unreasonable and outmoded. It was neither necessary nor intelligent to reject modern fundraising strategies out-of-hand simply because mainstream groups adopted them. And, they agreed, mainstream criticisms of Catholic charitable methods might have some merit. Disputes continued within the church com-munity, however, about the meaning of religious giving and the degree to which mainstream philanthropic values ought to be accepted as normative.

The sporadic collaboration of sisters with mainstream groups in times of epidemic had opened the door to ongoing collaboration, albeit modest, in times of prosperity. An exemplary case is provided by parochial school teachers in Vicksburg, Mississippi, who stepped in to manage the city hospital when yellow fever struck in 1878. The move took considerable courage and was not soon for-gotten. "On the evening of the 15th, Reverend Mother received a visit from Doc-tor Booth, chief-of-staff at the Charity Hospital. He was panic-stricken. He told her that not only the wards but even the corridors were full; men were lying on the floor, and the nurses had fled in terror."[15] He had already sent his own family to safety and was about to depart himself. A few New Orleans physicians and African American women joined the sisters in caring for the sick in the hospital. After the crisis passed, the city entrusted management of the Vicksburg Charity Hospital to the sisters, a role they filled for nearly thirty years.[16] This saga was by no means novel. From mid-century, Chicago Sisters of Mercy, hailed by *The Chicago Daily Democrat* as "among the choicest blessings for our city,"[17] had con-ducted the Illinois General Hospital of the Lake.[18] And members of the San Francisco Board of Supervisors, in the aftermath of an 1855 cholera epidemic, invited the Sisters of Mercy, whom they described as "philanthropists who re-fuse all pecuniary reward for their self-sacrificing devotion to the care of the Sick & destitute,"[19] to conduct the county hospital for the poor. As such experi-ences became increasingly common, Catholic perspectives on the need for sepa-ratism in philanthropy began to modify slightly.

Fears that bureaucratic methods and emphasis on efficiency and reform were incompatible with the spirit of religious giving underlay much of the Catholic resistance to collaboration in the 1870s. The Catholic press sharply at-tacked an 1879 proposal by Boston mainstream agencies to form an umbrella charity organization in that city. A decentralized organizational style was less costly and therefore preferable. In any case, one writer concluded, "we have enough of Bureau charity already."[20] A year later, Rev. William Byrne provided the official Catholic view in an address before the new organization, the Associated Charities of Boston. Although he praised as "judicious philanthropy" its efforts to rehabilitate the poor and eliminate abuses in almsgiving, he warned that undue concern that relief go only to the worthy poor was "not only unchristian but inhuman." The Associated Charities could easily become "a heartless, economic bureau" where almsgiving would be eliminated by "over-nice regulations" and the principles of "mere social economy."[21]

The incorporation of the New York Charity Organization Society in the 1880s evoked similar objections among Catholics there. But, in contrast to Byrne, the chancellor of the New York archdiocese, Thomas Preston, warmly supported the new organization and joined its ranks as a regular member in 1885. A few years later, the Charity Organization Society eulogized him for his cooperation "in every delicate and difficult negotiation which the Society desired to open with authorities of the Catholic Church."[22] Preston's involvement was significant in that it effectively announced that New York's archbishop, Michael Corrigan, approved greater contact with mainstream benevolent groups. It was the initiative of Thomas Mulry, a layman, however, that brought the issue before grassroots Catholics in the 1890s. Until Mulry took the helm of the St. Vincent de Paul Society in New York in this decade, that large benevolent society had worked in complete isolation from mainstream charities and had shown no interest in their activities.[23]

Like Preston, Mulry joined the Charity Organization Society and, from 1896 until his death twenty years later, sat on its Central Council. Archbishop Corrigan summarily dismissed a public protest by St. Vincent de Paul Society members that Mulry, by serving on a Protestant charity committee, had lost all credibility in their society. The controversy strengthened Mulry's influence in Catholic charity circles, since he now not only headed the largest lay benevolent society in the church, but also represented the archbishop. Mulry argued eloquently and at every opportunity that separatism was seriously hampering Catholic social work. "The strange spectacle was presented of charitable societies working, each in its own way, for the good of the poor, and yet violating every principle of charity and religion in their intercourse with each other."[24] As long as Catholics refused to attend charity conferences and speak for themselves, they ought not to complain that speakers at mainstream conferences disparaged Catholic benevolent efforts. After all, Mulry observed, the National Conference of Charities had been meeting for twenty-five years before the first Catholic representatives appeared in 1898.[25]

With strong backing from Mulry, Thomas Ring, leader of the Boston Vincentians, and John Farley, vicar general of the New York archdiocese, the 1895 general convention of the St. Vincent de Paul Society voted formally to cooperate with mainstream charities to the extent its rules allowed. Two years later the convention passed a more far-reaching resolution: "It is the sense of this body that the several Councils and Conferences, under the jurisdiction of the Superior Council of New York, should cooperate, wherever practicable, with the societies of other denominations or of no denomination, which have for their object the permanent improvement of the social condition of the poor."[26]

Efforts by laymen like Mulry to promote Catholic collaboration with mainstream groups had as a critical outcome a decline in defensiveness among Catholics about their own benevolent strategies. At the 1900 meeting of Baltimore's Charity Organization Society, Mulry emphasized that separatism in philanthropy contradicted Catholic benevolent values. "The platform of charity is broad enough for Hebrew, Protestant, and Catholic to meet upon and work together for the amelioration of God's poor. We are no less earnest in adherence to our particular belief because we work with those of other creeds for the common good."[27] Exploration with citizens of other faiths of the strengths and weaknesses of various approaches to charity allowed Catholics to assess objectively their own philanthropic style. A matter of great concern was whether charitable institutions ought to continue to monopolize the benevolent resources of the church.

Debates about government funding, closely related to the question of institutional dominance, also drew Catholics into the wider social arena. While California and Louisiana, with their large Catholic populations, had reimbursed church charities for the care of public wards for some years, and New York had allotted funds for the support of children in orphanages, most states provided no regular support for Catholic charitable institutions in the 1880s.[28] Acrimonious debates in state legislatures on the subject aroused religious tensions almost everywhere in the 1890s. Conceding that Protestant charities also sought and accepted government support, mainstream critics contended that, unlike Catholic agencies, they did so only reluctantly, preferring "to have each tub stand on its own bottom." In contrast, the Catholic church lobbied aggressively for public funds for "its numerous so-called eleemosynary institutions and its army of non-producing priests, monks, and nuns, and its Brothers and Sisters of various orders."[29] Church spokesmen minced no words in response to these outbursts. Vicar General Byrne of Boston, for example, noted that only 3 percent of Catholic charitable funds went to administrative salaries, while Protestants allotted 30 percent for this purpose. Therefore, he concluded, the contributions of benevolent Protestants were going "to swell the hoard of the fat officials."[30] In time, more states and municipalities appropriated funds for the care of state wards placed in Catholic institutions, but only after extended and usually bitter political debate.

Because of their traditional propensity for institutions, Catholics, more than members of other religious groups, were open to the charge that their interest in per-child contractual allowances rather than lump-sum legislative appropriations was more mercenary than philanthropic. As evidence, critics contrasted the low expenditure per child by the orphanages with their per-child public allowance. That the disparity arose almost entirely from the fact that the sisters managing the institutions received only minimal salaries was overlooked. Heated debates on the matter, covered in vivid detail in the press, brought to the attention of ordinary Catholics the social issues raised by their proclivity for the institutional approach to benevolence.[31] The size and number of the institutions kept an emotional issue alive, even though most of their support came from private donations, and state investigating committees acknowledged that public allotments were generally well spent. The New York Committee on Charities, for example, concluded in 1894 that "the public has received adequate return for all moneys paid to private charitable institutions. . . . The expenditures made have been, in most instances, far less than if the institutions had been conducted by the public."[32] The New York constitutional convention of that year voted that no state funds should benefit parochial schools, but that the subsidies that had traditionally been paid to sectarian charity institutions might continue. At this time, these payments accounted for about 25 percent of the annual incomes of New York Catholic orphanages.[33]

The mutual suspicion engendered by such controversies slowed progress toward collaboration with mainstream benevolent agencies. Church members nonetheless learned from these disputes that their traditional priority for the poor would atrophy if it continued to be expressed in complete social isolation. Participation in public debate about the merits of cooperation with mainstream charities aroused among middle- and upper-class laity, at least, a determination to become full partners with other citizens in forming the American social fabric. While grassroots parishioners, for the most part, were content with the separatist approach of the past, bishops and charity leaders recognized that it had already become a serious hindrance to effective social action.

Philanthropy was unquestionably a safe forum in which Catholics could unite with other citizens for the public good and, at the same time, ameliorate their own advance into the mainstream. Unlike the efficient, well-organized structure of Protestant charities, however, Catholic dioceses of the 1890s still had no commonly accepted policies on fundraising and professional standards of social service. At the same time, the heavily working-class composition of church membership and the autonomy of bishops in their own dioceses deterred development of a national perspective in the field of philanthropy. But as the needs of "new immigrants" from Central and Eastern Europe expanded at the turn of the century, the importance of finding ways to cooperate with mainstream agencies was brought home more forcefully. Middle- and upper-class parishioners, already mixing professionally and socially with their mainstream neighbors, were open to collaborating with them in community welfare programs. However, the extremely decentralized character of Catholic charity organization remained a major stumbling block to real progress.[34]

By mid-nineteenth century, as mainstream benevolent groups were turning their attention to social reform, the material need of poor immigrants was strengthening Catholic commitment to relief. Benevolent resources flowed almost entirely to the construction of charitable institutions, open to persons of all faiths but serving mainly Catholics. Debate over the place of reform in religious philanthropy heightened among Catholics after the Civil War. It represented the first serious intellectual challenge to the traditional monopoly held by direct relief in their collective altruism. Working-class parishioners had little doubt that the plight of poor immigrants eminently and patently justified this benevolent focus, and they dismissed proposals that at least some charity resources be diverted to reform agendas. Until the 1870s, extended and widely publicized mainstream debates on the subject were largely ignored by Catholics. The Catholic press continued to depict the economic system as immutable, its flaws attributable to the greed and social indifference of some individuals. Therefore, the alleviation of the social distress occasioned by unemployment and low wages was the responsibility, not of the business sector, but of benevolent private citizens. Such reasoning discouraged criticism of the free-market system and the prevailing social-class structure.[35]

Severe social distress accompanying industrial development in the next decade, however, led more Catholics to challenge the venerable view that poverty and class differences were inexorable conditions. Even conservatives like journalist James McMaster conceded that assisting the poor ought not to be left to private benevolence alone: "Organized society is bound, in natural justice, to keep its needy members from starvation by hunger and cold."[36] Bishops, on the other hand, trod cautiously, lest too radical a social message alienate wealthy donors and affect the funding of diocesan projects. In the face of increasing immigration from Italy and Eastern Europe and mounting labor unrest, they discouraged proposals for social reform activities and continued to discuss reform in individual rather than social terms. In the main, their strongest reform statements were bland exhortations to business leaders to honor the mandate of Christian stewardship.[37]

In the 1890s, more charity leaders were publicly endorsing the mainstream position that social reform was a philanthropic value and asking why Catholics were not allocating funds and labor to it. "Reform as well as relief" became a rallying call for radical rethinking of benevolent priorities. This provoked some serious confrontations within the church community itself, the most notable between Archbishop Michael Corrigan of New York and Edward McGlynn, one of his priests. An eloquent proponent of the view that religious philanthropy had to be more than simple almsgiving, McGlynn publicly challenged Catholic practice. "Charity is a noble virtue," he maintained, "but to make the whole world an almshouse is carrying it to the absurd. The noblest charity is to do justice—not only to procure, at the sacrifice of self, in an unselfish spirit, some improvement in the condition of mankind, but to compel tyrants to do justice to the victims they have wronged."[38] McGlynn supported the Irish Land League, backed Henry George's political campaign, and termed parochial schools an unnecessary burden on local congregations. A furious Corrigan reported to his Rochester counterpart: "Our people are terribly worked up, particularly the better classes. Many say they will go to Church no more."[39]

McGlynn was not alone in his views. Progressive laity as well were working to incorporate social reform in the definition of church philanthropy. At the first Catholic Lay Congress in 1889, Peter Foy addressed the issue. Without public welfare programs financed by income taxes, he argued, private charity could only begin to address massive and growing social need. He advised temperance reformers, who attributed the miserable living conditions of the poor to their excessive drinking, to reverse the causality.[40] The first years of the twentieth century saw general agreement among progressives, clerical and lay, that state aid to the poor was not altruism. When the state provides funds to address social ills it is simply carrying out one of its primary duties, explained Rev. Peter Yorke. "Its motive is not philanthropy or charity, but strict justice."[41] The cadre of social pioneers that had emerged in the 1890s enlisted support for its reform ideas by arguing from material rather than religious values. The disproportionate presence of Catholics in prisons and poor houses suggested that unless the church joined forces with mainstream reformers, the rapid socioeconomic advance of its members was in jeopardy. While this pragmatic message had some short-run success, it could not generate commitment to social reform as an enduring philanthropic value.

Bishops at the turn of the century continued to contend that too much emphasis on justice and social reform, especially on the rights of labor, would destroy the religious spirit of charity. If justice took precedence over charity, its achievement would render charity unnecessary, proclaimed John Ireland. "There are those who say that we need no charity. They say let the rich give what is due of the poor and there is no need of charity. . . . Where is the justice for the orphan baby? The orphan baby has no labor."[42] Bishops, for the most part, ignored Pope Leo XIII's 1891 encyclical, *Rerum Novarum*, that called explicitly for social action. John A. Ryan lamented in 1909 that "the bishops who have made any pronouncements in this matter could probably be counted on the fingers of one hand, while the priests who have done so are not more numerous proportionally."[43] While spreading poverty had led Protestants to focus even more on legislative reform and on social agencies like settlements and cooperative societies, their Catholic counterparts, as a result of episcopal ambivalence, remained reluctant to add social reform to their benevolent priorities.

Although they admired mainstream ideals and practices in secular matters and braved episcopal disapproval to join labor unions, Catholics agreed that, in the philanthropic sphere, extra-ecclesial benevolent values ought to be viewed cautiously. Recent mainstream efforts to deny public funding to their orphanages buttressed resistance to diverting funds from these institutions to unproven and Protestant-inspired reform programs. Because mainstream children's programs retained their sectarian identity longer than did family programs, Catholics were particularly suspicious of pressures to cooperate in this important area of social service.[44] Thomas Mulry tried, with little result, to soothe their ruffled feelings by attributing criticisms to "difference of opinion as to the best means of dealing with the poor"[45] rather than to anti-Catholic sentiment.

As early as 1876, the St. Vincent de Paul Society had proposed the development of child placement programs similar to those of the Children's Aid Society, but society members in the Midwest, envisioning the arrival of hordes of children who would strain their limited charity resources, objected loudly to the idea. Nonetheless, by the 1880s, the New York Foundling Hospital was regularly sending children west on "orphan trains." Writing to a western pastor, the sister-director of the hospital inquired: "Will you please Rev. Father send me the description & age of the boys your parishioners desire, & again if they would meet them at Toledo as it would be quite a risk to let them travel alone."[46] This program was not a short-term experiment, and it was occasionally emulated in other eastern cities. In 1916, John Crimmins, a member of the hospital's board of directors, recorded in his diary: "Called at the Foundling Hospital to see the start of forty-four of the prettiest and healthiest children for adoption in homes in the West and South."[47]

Until the 1890s, the majority of orphanages had simply cared for the children sent to them and remained aloof from the institution versus foster home debate. This stance was now no longer an option. Exacerbated by the controversy over allocation of public funds to Catholic establishments, the issue had become a major public concern. Charges by prominent reformers, like Charles Loring Brace of the New York Children's Aid Society and Josephine Shaw Lowell of the Charity Organization Society, that Catholic institutions were so large and crowded that their managers could not possibly provide the children with "any individual love"[48] hit close to home. By 1899, a St. Vincent de Paul Society member was sitting on the Committee on Dependent Children of the New York Children's Aid Society, and New York City had become the site of the nation's first Catholic Home Bureau, modeled closely on the local mainstream agency.

Even as more progressives recognized that reform programs would benefit the poor, they realized that diversion of resources from the institutions, many of them already seriously underfunded, would not be easy. Benevolent Catholics had to be convinced that their traditional understanding of religious charity embraced such programs as old-age pensions, the correction of slum housing, occupational safety legislation, sanitation improvements, and programs allowing the working poor to "become independent and able to help themselves."[49] Indifference to the growing social movement, warned reformer Rev. William Kerby, would soon reduce the significant influence of Catholics in the public arena. "The tendency is growing by force of circumstances to restrict the Church to action of a secondary kind, and to leave to secular power, leadership in reform work. This is the more marked since religions still divide men while their social interests are identical."[50]

Reform projects remained controversial, however. Catholic settlements had taken hold in a few cities in the 1890s, but the clergy was generally unfriendly toward them. St. Helen's Settlement in Brooklyn, the headquarters of the Catholic Settlement Association, was purposely situated in close proximity to the mainstream settlement, Maxwell House. Unlike Maxwell House, however, it functioned under the direct supervision of the local pastor and a year after its founding still had no resident workers.[51]

Ethnic benevolent societies had never shown much interest in social reform. An exception was the German Catholic Central-Verein. By the 1870s, it had expanded its interests to include national social problems, the situation of African Americans and Indians, Catholic schools, and the media. As a result, it was "*the* organizational vehicle" for Catholics of German heritage by 1900.[52] While Germans had taken a conservative position in the recent Americanist controversy, in the realm of charity organization, labor issues, and social policy, they were far more progressive than other ethnic groups, in large measure because of the Central-Verein. Its magazine, *Central-Blatt and Social Justice*, established in 1909, was the first Catholic publication in the nation to focus on broad social issues.[53]

The message of social reform was finally being heard, although not widely implemented, by 1910. The National Conference of Catholic Charities, formed in that year, boldly stated its intent to wage "a war on the causes of poverty whether that cause is a disease germ lurking in a dark corner or a merchant prince grown rich on defrauding laborers of their wages."[54] Changing the social structure was now seen as a philanthropic value and Catholics were to allocate their benevolent resources to it.

As a group, Catholics never opposed reform per se, and they endorsed the social programs that marked the political agendas of the progressive era. But they continued to believe that, in the face of immediate distress, relief should take priority in distributing the philanthropic resources of religious groups. These sentiments were to endure. In the 1960s, Dorothy Day underscored them again: "I must confess that it is more reasonable a work to help the poor to help themselves, as the saying is, or to work for justice rather than charity. But we are taught in the New Testament to go beyond reason, and live by faith—faith that it is Christ Himself in the poor whom we are helping and loving."[55]

Proximity to large numbers of co-religionists in critical need was, of course, a powerful force motivating nineteenth-century Catholics to contribute to their relief. But as a community, they had never demonstrated much interest in ameliorating the situation of the nation's two poorest populations. The circumstances of newly freed African Americans in the late 1860s again raised the question of how Catholic benevolence should be extended to them, as well as to Indians in the West. The enduring debate that ensued eventually enlarged Catholic philanthropic horizons and led to tentative efforts at cross-diocesan fundraising.[56]

Heavily concentrated in northern and midwestern dioceses, Catholics found local calls on their benevolence invariably more than their limited means could address. As a result, their benevolent vision focused rather narrowly on their own regions. The needs of geographically remote and heavily non-Catholic populations received far lower priority. By the turn of the century, more donations were being made in one day at a single Protestant missionary meeting for work among African Americans than Catholics nationally were giving for the same cause annually. The bishop of Nashville, Thomas Byrne, attributed such an amazing disparity to Catholic indifference to missions, domestic or foreign: "We are not really a missionary people, nor have we the spirit and zeal which should inspire and characterize missionary work."[57]

But this was by no means the complete explanation. Racial antipathy played a critical role as well, and this moral failing was not limited to poor and working-class laity. In May of 1833, Bishop John England of Charleston informed Pope Gregory XVI that his fellow bishops were doing nothing about the Indian and African American question, a matter of critical importance for the national church, not simply for a few southern dioceses and western territories. He asked the pope to appoint a committee of bishops sympathetic to the needs of Indians and African Americans to oversee and encourage benevolent work among these groups. In October of the same year, however, the bishops at the Provincial Council of Baltimore instead gave this responsibility to the Jesuits, a move which England took as a strategy to delay real action on the matter. Archbishop Samuel Eccleston of Baltimore gave the standard public explanation, a shortage of clergy and religious, for his neglect of African Americans in favor of whites.[58] In private, he was unsympathetic to the cause.

The attitude of religious orders toward African Americans was not much better, and it certainly encouraged lay apathy toward them. White sisterhoods routinely turned away African American applicants throughout the nineteenth century. With the help of a local priest, an African American sisterhood, the Oblate Sisters of Providence, was established in 1828 in Baltimore by three Santo Domingo immigrants. They opened St. Frances Academy for Coloured Girls, a small free school, and an orphan asylum. Some academy students were daughters of plantation owners, "the Negro blood in their veins barring them from the schools for whites."[59] In contrast to the strong encouragement given white sisters, these women, for the most part, were mainly ignored by clergy and bishops. Few lay parishioners gave them financial aid, and many challenged their right to wear a religious habit. The same Archbishop Eccleston who had complained of a shortage of personnel a decade earlier proposed in the 1840s that these sisters disband, dismissing them with the query: "What's the use?"[60] The women continued, nonetheless, adding a boys' school in 1852 and supporting themselves and their works by taking in laundry.[61]

Debate over the obligation of Catholics toward African Americans heightened in the 1860s, and exploration began of ways to raise funds to assist them. At the Second Plenary Council of Baltimore in 1866, Martin Spalding drafted a proposal that a national office be formed to direct this work. Although on the agenda, his proposal was not taken up by the bishops. They preferred to settle instead for a general call to Catholics to contribute to the cause. Spalding then called a secret meeting to discuss his proposal, but with the exception of Augustin Verot of Savannah and Richard Whelan of Wheeling, it elicited little episcopal support.

On the contrary, some bishops considered it a serious challenge to their episcopal autonomy. Peter Kenrick of St. Louis threatened to resign as archbishop if it were implemented. John McCloskey of New York reflected popular sentiment when he declared that "in no way was the conscience of the bishops of the North burdened in regard to the African American."[62] Northern bishops were reluctant to consider any project that might threaten diocesan fundraising, and this one certainly could.[63] More surprising than the reaction of northern and western bishops was the notable lack of interest in the issue among most southern bishops. John Odin of New Orleans made the astonishing announcement at the council meeting that his archdiocese needed no more charitable programs for African Americans. Hearing that a New Orleans priest was going to preach a charity sermon on behalf of an African American female benevolent society, the Louisiana Association for the Assistance of Colored Orphans, that was attempting to raise funds for an orphanage, Odin asked him to cancel the event because the timing was inauspicious. In return, Odin promised to support the cause in a less public way.[64] His attitude was no different from that of most Catholics of the day. Not for another forty years would Spalding's plan become a reality in the Board for Mission Work Among the Colored People.[65]

Spalding proceeded to do what he could within his own archdiocese. In 1867, he encouraged pastors to open separate schools, praising local African Americans as "invariably liberal and generous, in proportion to their means, in aiding in the establishment of schools and churches for their benefit.... The pastors who will determine to labor zealously in their behalf will always find them willing cooperators."[66] Progress was slow in southern dioceses, however. Two decades later, there were ninety Catholic schools for African American children in eighteen southern dioceses; these schools were staffed by sisters and lay teachers. "No Catholic brotherhood has charge of a colored school," reported an 1889 observer.[67]

Catholic philanthropy toward African Americans lagged far behind that of Protestants in the 1860s and 1870s. The church had no organization resembling the American Missionary Association that was vigorously constructing and supporting churches and schools throughout the South. Northern bishops routinely refused permission in the 1870s to priests from southern dioceses to collect funds for work among African Americans. Some, like James Wood, who headed the large Philadelphia diocese, announced a blanket proscription on all requests to collect for that cause there. The huge New York archdiocese did not allow such collections either, because it was completing a cathedral and, in any case, its parishes had their own debts to pay. Cardinal John McCloskey not only showed little interest in the cause, but, in fact, by stating publicly in 1877 that "the Negro mission is not permanent," did it immense harm. A priest seeking contributions for the work reported the immediate chilling effects of McCloskey's words: "Our former admirers, for instance, in New York are now very cold."[68]

McCloskey's sentiments were widely shared. In 1871, at the request of Pope Pius IX and Martin Spalding, Herbert Vaughan, the founder of the Mill Hill Missionaries, an English community of priests, commissioned four members of the group to work in Baltimore's African American neighborhoods. Although forewarned, the Englishmen were shocked by the reactions of American Catholics to their enterprise. Commented Vaughan: "Priests and religious whom I meet look upon us with the same kind of wonder that we should, perhaps, entertain for an order of men who had made a vow to live in the wards of a smallpox hospital. The Catholics, as yet, have done next to nothing for them."[69] Vaughan recorded Peter Kenrick's unfriendly response to his application for permission to collect in the St. Louis diocese: "The Archbishop thought all my plans would fail; could suggest nothing for the Negroes, and refused permission to collect, and declined to give a letter of approval."[70] Southern bishops like Napoleon Perché of New Orleans, who wanted to take action, could do little without financial help from Catholics in the North. "While the protestants [*sic*] of the North were sending continually larger sums of money for protestant schools and protestant churches for the colored populations of the South, Catholics have done nothing,"[71] he told Vaughan in 1872. In times of crisis, however, Catholics set aside racial distinctions. Yellow Fever Sufferers Committees, formed in 1878 in most dioceses across the country to aid victims in a New Orleans epidemic were assured by the local Catholic relief association that the funds were distributed "without regard to creed, color or nationality among all the Asylums, giving to each a pro-rata amount according to the number of inmates."[72]

Using their philanthropy as a proselytizing agent had never attracted American Catholics. Efforts by benevolent Protestants to indoctrinate those whom they aided had long antagonized Catholics, and they had little interest in imitating them. Mission collections were less popular and less generously supported by grassroots parishioners than appeals for various charitable institutions. Typical were Catholic laborers working in Utah mines in the 1860s. They simply opened small charitable institutions for orphans, the aged, and the disabled of their own community, although anyone else who sought assistance received it. Unlike their Protestant neighbors, they exhibited no interest in converting the Mormons.[73] This denominational difference was commented upon by mainstream writers. "There is no mission work, that familiar feature of evangelical Protestant churches," remarked one, "no reaching out and gathering in from the by-ways and rejoicing over the sheep that was lost and is found."[74] This characteristic discouraged benevolence toward African Americans, most of whom were not Catholic. As late as the 1920s, bishops were emphasizing that those in "the household of the faith" should take priority in church benevolence. Only as Catholic charities received substantially more government funding and as more Catholics advanced to middle-class status was this message abandoned.[75]

At the Third Plenary Council of Baltimore in 1884 the hierarchy took two steps to stimulate greater national interest. It formed a Commission for Catholic Missions Among the Colored People and Indians, and it introduced a national, annual collection for this work to be held on the first Sunday of Lent in every parish. But since most bishops were unenthusiastic about this collection, it was a failure. American Catholics nationally gave only $82,000 in the first collection in 1887 and gave much less in succeeding years: $76,000 in 1888; $69,000 in 1889; and $66,000 in 1892.[76] This abysmal record stood in embarrassing contrast with the generosity of Protestants at this time. Had Catholics matched the $1.50 per capita gift made by Congregationalists in 1893 for their domestic missions, the collection for Indians and African Americans would have totaled about $12 million, rather than $80,000, or an average per capita donation of one cent. Even taking into account that as a group Catholics were considerably less affluent than Congregationalists, that sum was far below what their numbers and means allowed.[77]

Continued bleak returns in the annual collections prompted an unusually strong and public admonition by several archbishops in 1903. In that year, the nation's Presbyterians, richer on average, but vastly fewer in number than Catholics, had contributed $60,000 to missions in New Mexico alone. This sum nearly equaled the total contribution of American Catholics for all Indian and African American missions. James Gibbons, Patrick Ryan, and John Kain laid much of the blame for this disgraceful situation squarely on the nation's bishops and pastors. What was called for was more enthusiasm and far less provincialism: "Parish and diocesan needs cannot justly be pleaded as a reason for lack of generosity to the missions," they maintained, "any more than a man who owes two debts could be relieved of the duty of paying one because he had paid the other. If the people give liberally to the missions, they will be more generous to their parish churches, because turning a deaf ear to worthy appeals dries up the fountains of the heart."[78] A decade later, their successors continued to beg the laity not to be "a narrow sect, limited to a tongue, race or land," reminding them that, given their numbers, their collective national gift could be truly immense. Such messages continued to fall on deaf ears, and in the 1920s, the average contribution in the national collection for the domestic missions remained at the 1893 level, about one penny per year per American Catholic.[79]

By the turn of the century, the hierarchy had about given up hope that the growing number of rich Catholics would take up so unpopular a cause. "If we have any Rockefellers in the Catholic Church in these United States," lamented the archbishops of Philadelphia, Baltimore, and New York, "they are not establishing munificent foundations for this Apostolic work."[80] Ida Barry Ryan, wife of financier and American Tobacco Company founder Thomas Fortune Ryan, was representative in the causes she favored of most very wealthy donors. In recognition for the millions of dollars she gave to support church construction and schools, Pope Pius X in 1907 named her a Countess of the Holy Roman Empire. But the scope of her charity had always been far less comprehensive than her papal title implied. At the turn of the century, Richmond bishop Augustine Van de Vyver advised a priest seeking financial support for his work among African Americans: "*Do not visit* and *do not write* to Mrs. Ryan, New York. She will not give to colored work."[81] Contributions from ordinary laity in "one, five, and ten dollars" allowed only limited funding of charitable and mission work among African Americans.[82] The aggregate annual collection was so low that "individual missions received as little as $100.00 and some got nothing at all."[83]

A major reason for the continued lack of interest among the wealthy in extending help to African Americans, according to one veteran missioner, lay with ineffectual leadership by bishops who preached on the matter, but were afraid to take strong action. In a trenchant letter of 1903 to his cousin, Cardinal Van Rossum, head of the Congregation for the Propagation of the Faith, Josephite missioner Joseph Anciaux analyzed the "lamentable" American scene: "We have decrees of the Council of Baltimore and synodal rules ordering the greatest charity with regard to the Negroes, but on account of American prejudice it often comes about that those decrees are without force. . . . Excepting the noble-hearted Archbishop Ireland and Bishop Durier (Natchitoches) and the very saintly deceased prelate, Archbishop Janssens, I know of no one who had the audacity to protect and defend the rights of the Negroes openly."[84] Anciaux's charges reached Pope Pius X, who, after an investigation, ordered the American bishops to take immediate remedial action. They responded by forming a new agency, the Catholic Board for Mission Work Among the Colored People, to raise funds to supplement contributions in the annual national collection. Six bishops and archbishops sat on the new board, and Rev. John E. Burke of New York was named its first director in 1907. The board's task was an unenviable one. Burke's special appeal to rich Catholics in 1924 for individuals or benevolent groups to sponsor one African American church or school demonstrated painfully that Ida Barry Ryan's sentiments were not unique. "After all our pleas for parishes or societies or rich Catholics to assist, to the extent of $250. a year," lamented Burke, "we have found so few willing to do this regularly, that they may be counted on the fingers and toes."[85]

Rev. John LaFarge experienced similar disappointment in his efforts to advance African American work at this time. In 1922, with the help of two Jesuit colleagues, he opened an industrial school, the Cardinal Gibbons Institute, for African American youth, male and female, in Ridge, Maryland. Its administration and faculty were entirely African American. Although he had an initial $8,000 gift from Cardinal James Gibbons, and some funding from the General

Education Board, James Byrne of New York, the Knights of Columbus, and the diocese of Pittsburgh, LaFarge's efforts to mobilize Catholics nationally to provide operating funds for the school did not materialize, and it soon failed. A leading lay supporter of the school summarized a bitter fundraising experience. "I ran immediately into a very hard and unpalatable fact," wrote George Hunton. "Nobody was in the least interested in doing anything for the Negro, or at least practically nobody."[86]

The vast majority of Catholic orphanages and schools of the nineteenth century refused admission to African American children, and the small orphanages conducted by African American sisters were not included in the benefactions of white benevolent societies. In the 1880s, for example, St. Francis Colored Orphan Asylum in St. Louis was pointedly excluded in the distribution of charity funds raised in the numerous fairs and subscriptions for children's institutions of the city. Nearly two decades later, the sisters were supporting twenty-four children by cultivating a vegetable garden, begging, and doing all the work of the institution "without any financial recompense whatever."[87]

Baltimore in the 1880s was no different from St. Louis. African American sisters caring for forty children at St. Frances Female Coloured Orphan Asylum reported that they received little help from white Catholics and, like their St. Louis counterparts, did not benefit regularly from the annual archdiocesan charity collections. They supported the children by conducting a tuition school for a few African American children and by taking in sewing and laundry. One of the sisters assessed their situation: "We would be glad to do more, but our means are limited and we must wait until better days dawn."[88] Conditions in southern dioceses were even worse. In Mississippi, for example, there were no Catholic charitable institutions for African Americans in 1881 and although 125 sisters and brothers taught in Catholic schools in the state, "until very recently only one taught a colored school."[89]

In the 1920s, Catholic hospitals were far more likely to maintain strict racial segregation in staffs and patient populations than mainstream hospitals. Of 540 hospitals listed in the 1922 *Directory of Catholic Charities in the United States*, not one was for or admitted African Americans.[90] It took eligibility requirements for government funding in the 1930s to stimulate change in this regard. Hospitals discriminating by race in the admission of poor patients did not qualify to receive government subsidies for their care. An ironic result of this regulation was that impoverished African Americans were now gaining admittance to Catholic hospitals, while those able to pay for their care were not. In 1933, pressure from city officials finally integrated the 65-year-old St. Mary's Maternity and Infant's Home in Brooklyn, New York. A Sister of Charity's report on how the accommodation was made reflects little enthusiasm for the change: "We had quarters on the 5th floor which were used to quarter the maids. We had this section thoroughly renovated, and fully equipped to handle this class of patients."[91]

Their strict discriminatory policies regarding race contrasted sharply with the willingness of Catholic hospitals to admit patients of all religious denominations. A comparison of seven New York City hospitals in 1921–22 reported that 48 percent of patients in St. Joseph's Hospital, Brooklyn, were Catholic, 26 percent Protestant, and 26 percent Jewish, whereas in St. Mary's Hospital the respective proportions were 65 percent, 18 percent, and 17 percent. Differences did not reflect religious discrimination, but rather the religious affiliations of neighborhood residents.[92]

Fraternal organizations, for the most part, allowed local councils to discriminate at will against African Americans. An important exception was the St. Vincent de Paul Society which had formed separate city-wide African American conferences in St. Louis and Boston by the late 1880s. Although a few of its parish conferences in northern and western dioceses were integrated, "colored conferences" soon became the norm, reflecting the racial segregation that marked urban parishes. The Central-Verein and the Kolping Society took a public stand for racial integration in the wider society and contributed to projects assisting African Americans. However, their requirement that members be of German origin shielded them from the charge of discriminating on the basis of race. Until the mid-twentieth century, in fact, the large male societies remained segregated, even when local bishops urged them to reform their policies. In 1954, for example, the Supreme Council of the Knights of Columbus dismissed the request of Cleveland bishop Floyd Begin that it grant a charter to an integrated council. A blackball system, whereby only five negative votes, a very small fraction of votes cast in local elections, would exclude a candidate for membership, allowed this very large society to remain white until 1972.[93] In general, it was the civil rights movement of the 1960s, rather than moral conviction, that motivated the Knights of Columbus, and societies like it, to integrate their memberships.

Despite a generally dispiriting picture, the final decades of the nineteenth century saw several important positive initiatives. In 1881, four English Franciscan sisters arrived in Baltimore from Mill Hill, England, to collaborate with Mill Hill priests who had been working among African Americans there for a decade. At this time, two American religious communities were established for this work, the Sisters of the Blessed Sacrament for Indians and Colored People, established by Philadelphian Katharine Drexel, and the Mission Helpers of the Sacred Heart, which developed from a lay benevolent society founded by Anna Wattleworth Hartwell to do settlement work among Baltimore African Americans.[94]

While Katharine Drexel's community was to benefit significantly from her immense inheritance, the Mission Helpers were soon begging door-to-door for their unpopular work. Anna Hartwell contended that the sisters should rely totally on voluntary gifts, an idea that was impractical in the best of circumstances and entirely unworkable given the nature of their undertaking. They received few contributions and succeeded mainly in alienating local pastors whose support they so badly needed. Many idealistic young women who had joined Hartwell's sisterhood soon left because they disliked having to spend most of their time begging. James Gibbons, who opposed the practice of begging by religious, proposed that they "live by subscription" like other sisterhoods. He overlooked the fact that almost no one was willing to subscribe for their work.[95]

Katharine Drexel and her sister, Louise Drexel Morrell, gave their fortunes to ameliorate the conditions facing African Americans and Indians. Their banker father, Francis Anthony Drexel of Philadelphia, who died in 1885, bequeathed ten percent of his $15.6 million estate to twenty-nine Philadelphia charitable institutions. With the remainder, he established a trust fund for his three daughters. Each was to receive one-third of its annual net income. Should a daughter die without children, her share would go to her surviving sisters equally. Should all die childless, the $14 million principal of the trust would be distributed among the twenty-nine charities designated in his will. His eldest daughter, Elizabeth Drexel Smith, died in 1889, leaving no children. Louise Drexel Morrell had no children, and Katharine Drexel in 1891 founded the Sisters of the Blessed Sacrament for Indians and Colored People.[96]

Louise Drexel Morrell contributed heavily to the support of numerous Catholic churches and schools for African Americans. In 1895, she founded and endowed St. Emma's Agricultural and Industrial School, a boarding school for boys in Belmead, Virginia, conducted by Benedictine priests. The Josephite Fathers, whose members worked only among this racial group, counted her as their major supporter, and she generously financed the efforts of John LaFarge and George Hunton to establish the Catholic Interracial Council in 1934. She was a loyal supporter of the work of her sister Katharine's sisterhood.[97]

As a young laywoman, Katharine had by 1890 established fourteen boarding schools for Indians and funded a Philadelphia school for African American children. Long attracted to the religious life, she sought the advice of her mentor and long-time family friend, Bishop James O'Connor of Omaha. His unexpected suggestion was that she not join an established sisterhood, but instead form a new one dedicated exclusively to the welfare of Indians and African Americans. He explained why this was the best course. "The next thing for you to determine is, whether you shall establish a new order for the Indian and Colored people, or, leaving your income for their benefit, enter an order already established, which will take more or less interest in these races. If you establish the new order, you will need all your income, and ten times more, to make it accomplish its object partially."[98]

Benevolent projects to aid African Americans still remained a low priority for most American Catholics in the 1920s, with exceptions like the Drexels only proving the rule. The church press editorialized that "their indifference to the mental and spiritual welfare of the Negro is nothing short of scandalous."[99] African American Catholics acknowledged the help of a number of priests, but national African American congresses saluted only two bishops between 1890 and the 1920s, John Ireland of St. Paul, Minnesota, "champion of the race," and William Elder of Cincinnati.[100]

Most religious orders remained unwillingly to commit a significant proportion of their resources, financial or human, to work among African Americans. A summary by the general superior of the Jesuits of his community's history in this matter applied to most other groups as well. While he acknowledged that many individual Jesuits had done exemplary work on behalf of African Americans, the religious order as a whole had never made a corporate commitment to help them. Instead, he observed, "as the immigrant groups advanced economically, educationally, politically and socially, the Society of Jesus tended to become identified more and more with the middle-class, white segment of the population."[101]

Religious communities had always been relatively more willing to conduct charitable institutions for Indians than for African Americans, but their record was unimpressive in this area as well.[102] Although European benevolent societies had been financing Indian missions since the early nineteenth century, there were still in 1874 only seven Catholic Indian schools. The hierarchy at that time established the Bureau of Catholic Indian Missions to raise money nationally for the cause. When in 1877 the federal government commenced offering contracts to religious denominations to conduct Indian schools, many religious communities applied for them. Although student allotments were small, $30 annually for a day student and $150 for a boarding student, they were sufficient to allow the schools to function without having to rely much on private charity. Between 1886 and 1891, government appropriations increasingly favored Catholics, a trend not lost on their adversaries. While allotments to Protestant schools, "which recognize allegiance to our Constitution and laws, and which are devoted to American principles and institutions," were warranted, awarding public funds to "an ecclesiastical body which represents no national church organization in America, and avows no allegiance to the American Government"[103] was quite another matter. Heated political controversy led to the phasing out of federal funding for all contract schools, a process completed in the 1890s.

Katharine Drexel kept twenty-two Catholic Indian schools open as government payments declined during the phase-out period by providing the difference between their annual operating costs and the government allotments. As Catholics generally ignored appeals for Indian schools, Drexel was nearly singlehandedly subsidizing them when government funding ceased entirely in 1900. She channeled most of her donations through the Bureau of Catholic Indian Missions, concerned that if the extent of her personal largess become known, grassroots contributions would decline even further and the church would be publicly embarrassed. When in 1897 she provided a group of Indians with the bond for an appeal to the Supreme Court, her instructions to the Indian Bureau revealed her benevolent style: "If the thing should get in the newspapers, or in any way public, don't let my name, or the name of our community be mentioned. Let it be understood as coming from the Catholic Church."[104] At this time, nearly half the Indian Bureau's funds were coming from her.[105]

Although she worked behind the scenes, Katharine Drexel was fully in charge of her money, efficient in her methods, and more politically astute than most of her episcopal and clerical colleagues. In the 1890s, for example, when an act of Congress allowed religious denominations to purchase the government land on which their Indian schools stood, she knew that the offer would be short lived and pressed the hierarchy to revise the Bureau's charter so that it could hold such land. Religious orders that she judged able to raise funds for their Indian schools received no financial support from her. She denied requests for a Jesuit school at the Flathead, Montana, mission, for example, because she believed that this order had the financial means to support the school.[106]

The influence of two long-time advisers, Bishop James O'Connor of Omaha and veteran Indian missionary, Rev. J. A. Stephan, is reflected in this stand. O'Connor had cautioned her in the 1880s never to subsidize financially secure religious orders. He made special mention of the Jesuits who had "so many rich congregations in the eastern and middle States. There is not as far as I know a single Jesuit from the eastern province on an Indian Mission. If they will not go themselves to such missions, the least they may do is to send some material assistance."[107] Stephan reinforced these observations. As the first director of the Bureau of Catholic Indian Missions, he had endeavored for many years, with little result, to coax established religious communities to manage Indian schools. "Old religious orders in our day are mostly on the lookout for fine money-making and profitable places," he informed Drexel. "My sad experience compels me to tell it frankly to you. My poor Indians are mostly looked upon and treated as lepers."[108]

Stephan did have the support of a few prominent laywomen who in 1875 organized a benevolent auxiliary for the new Indian Bureau. Although its aggregate financial support from all sources totaled only $8,600 between 1873 and 1876, its first four years, the ladies' auxiliary was responsible for raising 70 percent of it. They had followed a three-part strategy in soliciting funds for their unpopular cause. First, they bluntly reminded American Catholics of their deficient record relative to Protestants in aiding the Indians. Second, they directed their appeal heavily to women. And third, they employed, to their advantage, their social position and their husbands' titles in approaching donors. The auxiliary's first resolution bore such impressive signatures as Mrs. Admiral Sands, Mrs. General Sherman, Mrs. General Ewing, and Mrs. Ex-President Tyler.[109]

In 1905, Rev. Henry Ganss, chagrined that Katharine Drexel's contribution of $100,000 for Indian missions and schools that year exceeded the total given by the rest of the American church, decided to present the issue as one of justice, not charity. To this end, he asked the St. Vincent de Paul Society to establish a society that would focus on the Indian cause. As an affiliate of the large parish-based society, the Marquette League would be able to solicit funds for Indians at the grassroots level. Men were asked to pay the $2 annual league subscription "not as a matter of sentiment, even charity, but as an act of national reparation."[110] The first national appeal for the Indians by the American Federation of Catholic Societies in 1903 had emphasized the fact that one person was doing most of the Catholic benevolent work in this area. "Shall *she alone* offer her life as a vicarious reparation for the national crime, which makes the Indian an alien, an exile, a pauper? . . . Here we have a *national issue*—one that will reveal the faith that is in us."[111] By 1907, funds raised nationally from all sources for Indian schools and missions totaled about $231,500. Of this sum, 28 percent came from the annual Lenten Collection; 12 percent from Indian Tribal Funds; 55 percent from Katharine Drexel; and 5 percent, collectively, from the Marquette League, the Preservation Society, bequests, and other individual contributions.[112]

With the introduction of the federal income tax in 1913, Katharine Drexel's large annual income from her father's trust fund was taxed, even though she was using almost all of it for philanthropic purposes. In 1924, in recognition of this unusual circumstance, Congress passed the Income Tax Reduction Bill, soon known as the Philadelphia Nun Amendment, exempting from payment of federal income taxes persons who for each of the immediately preceding ten years had given 90 percent or more of their incomes to philanthropy.[113] Pennsylvania Senator George Pepper explained his rationale for proposing the bill: "In spite of the fact that Mother Katharine devoted her income to charity she was taxed just as if she had spent it upon herself. Obviously, the result was to take the amount of the tax she paid away from the very charities upon which she desired to bestow it."[114]

The long struggle to direct the attention of Catholics toward the needs of Indians and African Americans revealed clearly that without strong national leadership results would continue to be unimpressive. Ethnically diverse, working-class congregants preferred to focus their benevolence on the relief of the poor in their own local communities. Such a restriction ran directly counter to the teaching of the church on the nature of religious charity. Inattention to this critical matter for so long by church leaders and charity reformers weakened the traditional understanding that the needs of society's poorest members, whatever their race or religion, held priority in the collective philanthropy of Catholics.

4

The Charity Consolidation Movement

System does not mean the lack of charity, *method* does not mean less of a
desire to be helpful, but they mean the conserving of all energy and the
condensing of all interests which are vital to the cause.

—Adelaide Walsh, 1912

O VER THE COURSE of the nineteenth century, laity, religious, and clergy had
worked in partnership to develop a large and diverse system of charities
marked by considerable lay control and disproportionate reliance on female initiative and management. These features were certainly extraordinary in the society of the day, and particularly noteworthy in a hierarchical church. But by
1900, modern social values and needs were challenging traditional views about
charity organization and the place of voluntary service in religious philanthropy.

The questions of whether and how the church should reorganize its charitable structure and fundraising strategies in order to join other benevolent
groups in the development of social policy had simmered, with little tangible
result, for several decades. Church leaders were convinced by 1900, however,
that without significant structural reform, collaboration with highly organized
mainstream and community agencies would never be realized. The cohesive
philanthropic platform they needed to function effectively in extra-ecclesial forums could not possibly develop as long as autonomous charitable institutions
proliferated, each setting its own policies and raising its own funds. Charity
consolidation not only promised lower costs and higher quality services, but it
would have the added benefit of softening the internal ethnic antagonism which
had long hampered the development of a united American church.[1]

The matter came into sharper focus at this time when a contingent of bishops, clergy, and lay social workers launched a crusade to restructure the philanthropic sector at both the diocesan and national levels. The immediate impulse behind the "charity organization revolution" was the frustration bishops
felt at their inability to develop policies binding on charitable institutions
within their own dioceses. They wanted to be able to articulate the Catholic po-

sition on social issues, and they could not easily do this while institutional charities functioned independently.

Charity reformers assured benevolent laity and members of religious orders that the charitable institutions they were supporting independently would benefit appreciably if they were consolidated under diocesan bureaus. Criticism of orphanages, the key feature of the Catholic charity network, was becoming more heated, and efforts were underway to replace them with a "family system" of adoptions and foster parent placements. At the 1909 White House Conference on the care of dependent children, one speaker after another denounced the institutional approach to child care. "Their words went far and wide and carried weight," reported one witness. "And so, many kindly friends of the orphan have come to look on the institution as an unmitigated evil, believing that the sooner it is out of existence the better will it be for the child and for the community."[2] The controversy at the grassroots level, fanned by extensive press coverage, was bitter, since discussions of the merits of orphanages were usually laced with denominational rhetoric. Typical were Mrs. Don C. Seitz's 1903 remarks before a Protestant Brooklyn women's organization, published verbatim in the *Brooklyn Daily Eagle.* "Here in New York," she declared, "we are running pauper factories, breeding helpless and hopeless human beings. The chanting of a litany does not induce thought nor the saying of a mass inculcate morals and progress."[3] Opposition to public funding of Catholic orphanages had continued in New York ever since it was approved at the state's 1894 constitutional convention. It came to the fore again in 1915 when the Strong Commission, appointed by the governor to investigate the state board of charities, commenced its work. Testimony critical of Catholic orphanages received full press billing; anonymous "exposes" circulated; and ordinary Catholics, dismayed at the virulence of the criticism of their charities, became more convinced than ever that separatism in philanthropy was the only sensible course.[4]

Nonetheless, educated, upper-class laity recognized that beneath denominational bombast lay a number of valid criticisms. They were open to a rethinking of traditional approaches and to drastic reform where it was needed. Journalist Humphrey J. Desmond, for example, termed church reformatories, orphan asylums, and homes for the mentally handicapped merely "end houses," and called instead for more "half-way houses," such as clubs, settlements, and homes for working girls.[5] Another observer supported this judgment, typically contrasting the complex operations of the large charitable institution unfavorably with the "simplicity of the machinery [of settlements and clubs] by which the most far-reaching results are obtained."[6] A popular preacher of charity sermons took the occasion of the dedication of a Philadelphia orphanage to criticize established church practice in child care. Catholics were wrong to justify institutional child care over foster homes on economic grounds, he insisted. "It is in families that God intended that children should live."[7]

Other reformers argued that dioceses needed to hire professional social workers and cooperate with municipal and private agencies in assessing needs and in distributing aid. For the first time, the sisterhoods, as a group, came under public criticism from within the church. Many orphanages were admitting children whose parents and relatives could readily care for them, chided reform advocates, and this was because sisters, who had little or no professional training in social work, were easily hoodwinked by frauds. "In my judgment," one charity leader wrote caustically, "we have reached the point where the problem of caring for our poor is too large for individual effort and too complex for the men and women who have not the opportunity to give them special study."[8] The fact that state and local governments in the early twentieth century were developing better institutional care for needy citizens of all age levels, in any case, freed Catholics to turn from a single-minded focus on institutional services to new benevolent causes. St. Louis charity leaders, meeting in 1914, emphatically agreed that the church "had enough of Institutions and should not encourage the erection of more."[9]

A second major argument for central diocesan organization of charitable institutions and agencies was internal to the church. The popularity of particular good works rather than genuine need was dictating which institutions were receiving the financial support of the laity. As a result, some had more than enough operating funds while others, addressing less appealing but more critical social needs, were struggling to keep afloat. A diocesan-wide charity structure would ensure that each institution would be properly supported. While this was a compelling point, it was a sensitive one as well, since bishops themselves had long subsidized favorite institutions generously while basically ignoring the financial straits of others. In the 1840s and 1850s, for example, John Hughes of New York called on Catholics there to finance what he considered a critical work, a House of Mercy where young Irish immigrant women would be sheltered and prepared for employment as domestic servants. Just as strongly, however, he resisted proposals from laywomen for a reformatory for "fallen women" to be conducted by Good Shepherd Sisters. Only when the women promised to take financial responsibility for the institution did he relent and give the necessary approval.[10]

Benevolent causes could be popular in one part of the country and not in others. The education of handicapped children, for example, attracted little support in Chicago in the 1890s. There a group of women founded the Ephpheta School for the Deaf, but could not muster enough local women to form the benevolent auxiliary that was essential for its support.[11] In contrast, a few years later, 230 members of an Ephpheta Society in St. Louis were enthusiastically backing a free school for eighty children, more than half of them boarders. "No drones in our organization," they boasted, "everyone a worker; no remuneration for service of any kind."[12] Even the usually strong interest in the many orphanages waned at times, with extremely serious financial implications. "Time and again," reported a Philadelphia cleric in 1898, "has the Archbishop commended the generosity of the faithful towards other charities, yet the beggarly contributions to the orphans have forced him to complain, even to threaten."[13]

By this time, more Catholics conceded that mainstream critics might be right in charging that their extensive benevolent network was overlooking some critical social needs. "In glancing over this far reaching array of philanthropic works," observed a Protestant writer, "we are amazed to find no provision made for infants under the age of four, and little or no help extended to the man or woman who has fallen by the wayside. For her young from four years old up the Catholic Church is solicitous. For her aged she will beg from door to door. Her sick she will nurse without money and without price, but for the struggling man or woman beyond the pale of her organizations she offers only the word as it is spoken from the pulpit, the counsel of the confessional and the participation of the sacraments."[14]

While grassroots parishioners were not averse to some consolidation of fundraising activities, they were less enthusiastic about proposals to place charitable institutions under the surveillance of central diocesan offices. They saw nothing wrong with the autonomous structure of the charities and the numerous benevolent societies. It seemed to them that the new stress on efficiency and professionalism was threatening the basic religious values which traditionally motivated their giving. Initially, at least, bishops had some difficulty reconciling the religious call to voluntary service with the approach of "scientific philanthropy." While they very much wanted to tighten control over the charities in their dioceses, they did not want to jeopardize in any way the willingness of the laity to support them.

By the 1920s, however, as the push for charity reorganization accelerated, church officials relegated such concerns to a decidedly subordinate place. Instead, they reminded Catholics that, by clinging to the old ways of giving, they were retarding their integration, as a community, into mainstream society. Austin Dowling of St. Paul, Minnesota, for example, disparaged the charity institution as a paralyzing relic that encouraged undue concentration on relief to the neglect of reform, perpetuated Catholic hypersensitivity toward the mainstream, and made it all too easy for laity to abdicate their philanthropic responsibilities to members of religious orders.[15] John Glennon of St. Louis saw "more mobile" charities, coordinated by a central office, that could assist the poor and unemployed in their own homes and neighborhoods, as a vast improvement over the old-fashioned institutions. "What we are going to try to do is to get away from the institutions, back to the parishes, down to where the poor live. In other words, to treat of the poor in their own homes rather than in 'our' homes." What was needed, he thought, was "some kind of rational barricade between the homes where they live and the institutions."[16] Glennon and his colleagues insisted that charity organization and religious giving were fully compatible. After all, the gospel depiction of charity in no way precluded efficiency, since Christ intended that the style of giving be appropriate to the needs of the age. A central diocesan charity office would simply "help to make our little labor the greater and of greater service to those who need it."[17]

Charity reformers and bishops alike emphasized that cooperation in benevolent work with mainstream organizations would advance the American church as a whole, not just beneficiaries of its charities. Rev. John O'Grady presented the case eloquently. He acknowledged that institutional care of the poor and orphans was "the great link that has bound our lay people so closely to Catholic Charities,"[18] but then proceeded to warn that if Catholics clung to their traditional ways of giving, they would lose their influence in the wider society. The Catholic press praised the idea of diocesan collaboration with mainstream agencies as "good all round for our Catholic cause, for our poor and for our city."[19] The Catholic press showed widening admiration for the progressive character of mainstream philanthropy by adopting its maxim: "Not alms, but a friend."[20] Agnes Regan, executive secretary of the National Council of Catholic Women, and a professional social worker, applauded Catholic attention to "the ordinary problems of relief work," but insisted that it was not enough. Collaborative efforts to bring about national legislative reform in areas such as individual rights, eugenics, and government power were just as essential expressions of Catholic philanthropy as local relief projects. Industrialism and rising social disorder demanded that Catholic benevolence broaden its horizons.[21]

Despite all arguments in favor of charity reorganization, the movement proved time consuming and difficult. Laywomen were more open to change than other church members. A participant at the 1916 meeting of the National Conference of Catholic Charities reported that "members of the women's societies present showed themselves distinctly progressive, whilst the men, or at least the laymen, nearly all of whom were Vincentians, were for the most part conservative."[22] Laywomen may have been progressive, but members of sisterhoods were definitely not. Only eight sisters attended the initial meeting of the National Conference in 1910. Thwarted reformers, lay and clerical, castigated sisterhoods as old-fashioned in methods and ignorant of the philanthropic needs of the hour. William Kerby saw them as "the most conservative elements in Catholic charity," and reminded them that "the danger of making a mistake by changing too slowly and by misunderstanding innovation is always present." He criticized them for being unduly rigid, unlike the "ideally progressive" lay-women's benevolent organizations, where "the pressure of tradition is not heavy. Organization is elastic,"[23] he reminded them.

As a result of often intemperate criticism and of strong episcopal pressures, a Sisters' Conference was finally organized in 1920 in connection with the National Conference, an event greeted with considerable relief by Kerby and his colleagues. He described the creation of the National Conference of Catholic Charities in 1910 as the most promising achievement of recent years, but quickly added that the movement of the sisters into the organization "was the next most significant fact in the recent history of the church, without any exception."[24]

The chief reason for the reluctance of sisterhoods to join the crusade for charity centralization under diocesan bureaus was less related to the charges of their critics than to their fear that under centralization they would lose their authority in the charity institutions and be reduced to the status of lay auxiliaries, working under a diocesan board of clergy and professional social workers. In fact, these apprehensions had considerable merit. The structure of the new diocesan charitable bureau was hierarchical and its authority comprehensive. Initiated by the local bishop and answerable directly to him, it monitored the work of all charitable institutions, agencies and benevolent societies in the diocese. Once in place, "institutions and agencies alike become auxiliary organizations."[25] Charity leaders like William Kerby defended a hierarchical structure as essential if presently independent charities were ever to adopt uniform professional standards. Sisters had to learn that the institutions, although private in ownership, were public in function. The new charitable bureaus would ensure that every charity in the diocese honored public standards and could stand up to public scrutiny. For too long, Kerby emphasized, autonomy and separatism had served as "a cloak for defects."[26]

While some nineteenth-century institutional boards had included a priest among their members, most did not. By the 1890s, however, boards were expected to accord a seat to the local bishop. For example, Patrick Ryan of Philadelphia was heading the board of managers of Philadelphia's St. Joseph's Orphan Asylum in 1890, whereas his predecessor, James Wood, had never been elected to the board. "He was *habile* in business affairs, but perhaps the gentlemen considered his spirit a little too dominant and preferred to manage things more for themselves."[27] By 1900, most institutional lay boards lacked the leverage needed to deny the bishop a seat, had they wished to do so. William O'Connell of Boston, typically, did not ask but rather announced in 1908 that henceforth he would preside at the directors' meetings of the St. Vincent's Orphan Asylum and appoint all directors.[28] Germans were more likely to resist this trend than members of other ethnic groups. The German St. Vincent Orphan Society in St. Louis, for example, delayed electing clerics to its board until 1924. Pastors of its parish branches served strictly as spiritual directors; all financial decisions remained the preserve of laity. "Laymen are in control," noted a local priest, "and the Church leaves 'well enough alone.' "[29] However, lay control diminished swiftly as charitable bureaus gained momentum.

In the exceptional cases where a priest served as orphanage superintendent, diocesan bureaus were able to implement their plans fairly expeditiously, even when those plans included closing the institution. For instance, in 1933 St. Joseph's Orphanage, an 89-year-old German institution in Pittsburgh, was caring for 250 children. At this time, the diocesan charities office assumed responsibility for investigating admission applications and for overseeing the placement of children released from the institution. The number of children in the institution dropped immediately, and five years later the transfer of the institution's property and buildings to the diocese was in process.[30]

More often, institutional closures were painful, divisive experiences, initiated and carried out by diocesan officials over the objections of lay directors. A controversy in the 1940s over the fate of a Quincy, Illinois, parish orphanage illustrates the strong attachment of parishioners to their local charities as well as the issues preoccupying their bishop. Benevolent Germans had formed St. Aloysius Orphan Society in 1851 to support a parish orphanage for children left destitute in a recent cholera epidemic. Monthly subscriptions from local citizens and traditional fundraising activities such as annual picnics and fairs had provided most of its income ever since. School Sisters of Notre Dame cared for the children.

In 1944, the local bishop, James Griffin, was determined to close this charitable institution, despite the fact that it had never benefited from a share in the diocesan charity collections. In early June, the priest-director of Catholic Charities, the charitable bureau of the Springfield, Illinois, diocese, paid a "friendly visit" to the orphanage. A month later, the bishop asked the institution's lay board to sign over its building and land to Quincy College, a local men's institution conducted by Franciscan priests. The dismayed directors immediately called a meeting of the orphan society, but, because they did not give an agenda, attendance was poor. Those present at the meeting saw little alternative but to accede to the bishop's wishes.

When news spread that the orphanage was to be closed, great consternation ensued, leading the directors to call another meeting of the society to get a vote of the full membership. At an emotional meeting, parishioners recalled that their forebears had vowed to support the orphanage, and that they had faithfully kept that promise, "despite much opposition at times, whether justified or not, on part of the Hierarchy."[31] In early 1945, the society directors reported a two-thirds vote in favor of keeping the orphanage open. Bishop Griffin responded to that news by ordering the sisters to leave the orphanage at once, a move that effectively closed it. When society officers visited him to discuss the matter, he did not explain his reasons for closing the institution. He simply restated his requirement that the sisters depart and dismissed the men with a curt "God love you!" The sister who penned the final lines in the annals of this venerable institution made it clear that neither sisters nor laity understood what had happened: "With our feeble minds we cannot at present understand the reason for which St. Aloysius Orphanage was closed after nearly eighty years of fruitful labor."[32]

In 1900, Homer Folks of the New York State Charities' Aid Association, noting its 500 conferences and 7,000 members nationally had praised the St. Vincent de Paul Society for disproving the popular turn-of-the-century notion that "charity is a particularly feminine virtue."[33] By 1909, these figures had risen to an impressive 12,500 members in 708 conferences. But aggregate figures concealed growing distress within the venerable society. In 1908, only sixty conferences submitted returns for the society's annual national report, and these averaged only thirteen members. This stood in sharp contrast to the situation four decades earlier when, for example, Boston alone reported eight conferences, some with memberships of between seventy-five and one hundred.[34]

Several factors account for the society's malaise. Harvard professor Thomas Dwight, a leader of the Boston society, attributed falling membership to the fact that the society was parish-based. With pastors interfering in every point of society business and treating society men as "practically a body of under-sextons,"[35] it was hardly surprising that well-educated, young professionals were not interested in joining. A second factor was the trend among more affluent men to prefer exclusive organizations offering social benefits as well as the opportunity to be philanthropic. A third factor was the increasing migration of Catholics to middle-class suburban parishes where the society had fewer obvious opportunities to carry out its primary benevolent work, the visitation of the parish poor.[36]

To revitalize the society, Dwight proposed that local conferences take up new special works that would benefit American society at large. "Let us not forget, my dear Brothers, that though we are above all things a Catholic Society, our work is by no means limited to those of our faith. It is a perversion of our purpose for a Conference to become merely a parish relief association."[37] Among the special works he proposed was court visiting to monitor the treatment of children in trouble with the law. However, this was time-consuming work that demanded professional training, and so paid agents, who were not necessarily society members, would have to be hired to do it. Such an innovation might further weaken a society that expected members to contribute voluntary service. "There is to my mind a danger in this arrangement," acknowledged Dwight. "It is that we should get to feel that we are doing our whole duty, when a certain part of it is necessarily done by proxy."[38]

Other society leaders thought that tighter organization might reverse declining membership. In 1910, delegates at the society's national conference in Washington unanimously approved a "unification plan," whereby central councils, responsible for large geographical areas, would be established in each archdiocese. Their representatives, in turn, would form a superior council with national jurisdiction, headquartered in New York. The superior council thenceforth would represent the American society in dealing with the international council-general in Paris.[39]

By the 1920s, the effect on the society of the campaign to centralize diocesan charities was dominating discussions. Members agreed that its autonomy as a lay organization was being severely impaired. In 1923, for example, St. Vincent de Paul men in Chicago protested to the archdiocesan charities board that it was not allowing St. Vincent de Paul parish conferences sufficient relief funds to carry out their work and that it was undercutting the authority of the conferences by rejecting cases they judged worthy of assistance.[40] The imposition of yet another level of clerical supervision dealt a blow to lay morale. A sympathetic editor admonished his fellow clerics that "if lay activity is ever to make real progress in America, the priest must realize that his work is that of advice and counsel. . . . Let us assume that the laity have some initiative, some intelligence."[41]

While the metropolitan Chicago society still appeared robust in the early 1930s, with 5,000 members in more than 300 parish conferences, actual personal involvement was at a low ebb. In 1936, for example, one parish conference president reported that no meetings had been held in the past month, because "I'm the only member." He emphasized that it was not prevailing economic distress that explained declining interest, but rather unrest over the society's loss of autonomy. "No doubt you'll be surprised with the answers on the questionaire [*sic*]; however, it's the truth. I think I could reorganize our society if I tried hard enough, but I'll never do it as long as we have to work with the Central Charity Bureau. If the St. Vincent de Paul Society again becomes an independent organization I'll again become interested."[42]

In opposition to this explanation for the depressed condition of this large lay association, John O'Grady, at least initially, blamed its problems on a general erosion of lay benevolence. "Large numbers of parishes that in times past boasted of active St. Vincent de Paul Conferences have practically disbanded their conferences and shouldered their responsibility on central organizations,"[43] he observed in 1930. However, later in the decade he revised that harsh judgment enough to admit that charity reorganization seemed to be undermining traditional commitment to lay voluntary service. "The methods of the large organizations with their full-time and professionally trained staffs appeared to many to be so much more effective than those of the volunteer."[44]

Tensions between St. Vincent de Paul Society men and central charities offices increased over time. In 1948, Richard Condon, an officer of the Boston society, demanded that diocesan bureaus begin to show some respect for lay volunteers. "We have always tried to encourage our volunteers to work with the professional workers, but we have not found it an easy road," he complained. "Too often the trained worker feels that a volunteer group can be 'used' to solve a problem, and they carry out this idea in their relationships with the volunteer. Speaking from the viewpoint of the volunteer, the term 'use' for such a group is offensive, as the volunteers feel they are definitely a part of the Catholic Charities program."[45] By this time, society leaders were glumly reporting that "a young member [is] a rarity indeed."[46]

Although the largest, the St. Vincent de Paul Society was by no means the only lay benevolent society to be adversely affected by diocesan charity consolidation. Clerical authority had been imposed on lay benevolent societies of all sizes from the outset of the movement. William O'Connell in 1918 informed Boston's laity of the new order in their societies: "The Bishop names the spiritual director whose approval will be necessary for whatever action is to be taken. He will act in my name and thus you will labor fruitfully and to good purpose."[47] In Chicago, George Mundelein delivered the same message in the 1930s. Laity had an important, but definitely subordinate, role to play in church philanthropy, he asserted. They should act "as willing, obedient soldiers, not everyone wanting to be a general; no, as humble privates in the ranks, performing a great service for God, for mankind."[48]

Finding such terms intolerable, benevolent laymen turned increasingly to fraternal organizations like the Knights of Columbus, whose charters explicitly protected their autonomy over group funds and activities. Prior to World War I, like most fraternal organizations, this one had served its members mainly through insurance programs and social events and had supported local Catholic charities. But during the war years it broadened its interpretation of the term "charitable causes" in its charter in order to undertake new works. After the war, rather than revert entirely to prewar benevolent practice of supporting local institutions, the Knights developed their own social reform programs. Supreme

Knight John Reddin called on them first to open social centers for the poor in major cities. "This means the raising and expenditure of hundreds of millions of dollars for the erection, maintenance and operation of suitable buildings."[49] The idea was never implemented on the grand scale Reddin envisioned, but a $7 million war fund for the retraining of veterans in "skilled manual callings" was already supporting seventy-three night schools in 1920.[50]

Benevolent women, with fewer opportunities for independent activity than men, continued to try to work within the system. However, professional social workers were assuming many of the service roles formerly filled by female volunteers, and men monopolized seats on institutional and diocesan charity boards. Laywomen's benevolent groups were increasingly expected simply to raise funds to be distributed by officers of diocesan charitable bureaus. As fundraising activities superseded voluntary service in their benevolent works, female organizations declined. Charity centralization, without question, had a more negative impact on female than on male philanthropy. "For a number of women's organizations," conceded John O'Grady in 1929, "it marked the end of their active participation in Catholic charities."[51]

In the late nineteenth century, few male societies admitted women, and those that did segregated them in women's branches and accorded them virtually no power. Kate Reilly, elected second vice president of the Irish Catholic Benevolent Union in 1892, commented in her acceptance speech: "I take it for granted that, as you have elected me, you expect me to be more than a mere figure-head."[52] But this was simply rhetoric. She willingly accepted a subordinate role and instructed women members to thank the men for the privilege of aiding in the organization's work: "To them we owe much, and we desire to pay our debt by being as strongly organized as they are; by so doing we will be able to assist them, be able to lighten their burdens."[53] These perspectives were not shared by the growing number of educated, middle- and upper-class women who preferred to form independent female societies rather than to accept limited roles in men's societies or to chafe under the direction of sisters in institutional auxiliaries. Like mainstream women, they were strongly interested in social reform and wanted to undertake projects that incorporated an explicit reform focus.

Although early-nineteenth-century female benevolent societies had as a primary work the visitation of the poor in their homes, this activity was coopted by St. Vincent de Paul Society men in the 1850s,[54] and by late nineteenth century, it was regarded as socially inappropriate for laywomen. The success and popularity of settlement houses founded by Protestant women in the 1880s, however, led some laywomen to question this arbitrary constraint on female altruism. Their Protestant peers seemed to enjoy more opportunities for real leadership in benevolence than they did, and so they determined to copy their approach. Immediately after Protestant women formed the King's Daughters in 1886, for example, Mary Hoxsey organized Catholic women in St. Louis for similar philanthropic purposes in the Queen's Daughters. A few years later, at the Women's Catholic Congress, held during the Chicago Columbian Exposition, Alice Toomy and Eliza Allen Starr founded the National League of Catholic Women to promote Catholic settlements, day nurseries, girls' clubs, homes for working women, and employment agencies. League leaders and settlement pioneers alike met sharp reproofs in the conservative Catholic press and many pulpits for so brashly replicating Protestant methods. Nonetheless, they continued to explore these new approaches to charity. Chicagoan Mary Amberg recalled the impact of mainstream settlement women on the first Catholic settlement workers: "To us shy wrens of social settlement work the advent of a personality like Jane Addams among us was almost Pentecostal. We all took fire from her bravery, her determination, her insistence that her work was one of the most important in America."[55]

Progressive upper-class laywomen saw in settlements and clubs not only ways to incorporate reform into Catholic benevolence, but also opportunities to assume leadership roles in church charity. Sisterhoods, heavily committed in charitable institutions and schools, were unlikely to become involved in these new works, and men were not interested in them. The Catholic settlement concentrated on educational and cultural activities, gave no material assistance, and was directed by a trained social worker rather than a volunteer. Ideally, it was to be a bridge "between the young man and woman of culture and refinement and the young man and woman who have neither."[56] Advocates of Catholic settlements were not optimistic about drawing many members from the ranks of the numerous ladies' auxiliaries. "The typical well-to-do matron," Mary Amberg reminisced, "while fully social minded, belonged to a very conservative tradition."[57] Rank-and-file Catholics, for the most part, were content with the institutional approach to charity and viewed the settlement movement as regrettably Protestant in spirit and method. As a result, settlements were small, poorly funded, and often short lived. In 1914, they numbered twenty-seven nationally, with ten located in New York City.[58]

By the early twentieth century, more laywomen in major cities were organizing in city-wide female benevolent societies that were independent of sisterhoods and male societies alike. These new organizations charged relatively low dues, and provided social and cultural programs to their memberships. Representative was the Guild of Catholic Women, formed in St. Paul, Minnesota, in 1906 to assist the poor and to raise the intellectual horizons of the Catholic population through monthly programs which were "literary, musical and in-structure."[59] Like mainstream women's clubs, the projects of new societies like the Guild had a reform component, and they supported most of the settlement houses, kindergartens, day-care centers, and homes for working women that opened under church auspices at this time.

Such organized initiatives by laywomen met resistance from bishops and clergy, who took the position that women should carry out benevolent work under their direction, not autonomously. Many considered progressive, independent women to be more of a nuisance than an asset. Yet they could not simply ignore them, lest their considerable property and financial resources drift to causes ranking low in diocesan priorities. William O'Connell ordered members of Boston's Infant Savior Guild to be sure to elect docile officers. At all costs, "strong-minded women" were to be shunned. "The Guild was not intended for them and we will not have them in it."[60] Even though his fellow bishops used more diplomatic language, they proclaimed the same message. Thus tension and controversy marked efforts by laywomen to initiate and direct, rather than simply support, philanthropic projects.

Pioneer members of the Guild of Catholic Women in St. Paul proposed to address two popular female causes, visitation of the poor and maintenance of a home for infants. The Guild soon had 2,000 active members. It followed progressive methods in working among the poor, became affiliated with the city's Associated Charities, and warmly supported benefits held by the League of Protestant Women. Its president reported regularly to the Associated Charities, and its representative attended meetings of the State Conference of Charities and Corrections. In 1910, in order to join the State Federation of Women's Clubs, it amended its bylaws to admit members of all religious denominations.[61]

When Guild women in 1917 took steps to open a home for infants, they soon discovered how illusory their organization's autonomy was. Archbishop John Ireland summarily rejected their plans. He told them that he wanted a large home conducted by sisters, knowing well that they did not have the financial resources to support a large institution and that they wanted their home be conducted by laity, not by sisters. Ireland died the following year, leaving the matter unresolved, and so the Guild proceeded to open the home with some financial assistance from other women's societies. The victory was short lived, however. Within five years, the infants' home was managed by sisters, aided by an advisory board of twelve men who provided "business and experienced advice at times."[62]

Since Guild women had loyally participated in the National Conference of Catholic Charities since its founding in 1910, and had supported steps to centralize diocesan charities in St. Paul, they anticipated that their society would play a major role in the new archdiocesan charities bureau that got underway in the early 1920s. Instead, disagreements arose almost immediately between the Guild and the bureau's priest-director. Alarmed by his autocratic style, the Guild's officers informed Archbishop Austin Dowling of their fears that the Guild might be "eliminated by the Bureau." They received little reassurance when Dowling simply enjoined them to cooperate with the bureau and to act only "on Father Doherty's plan of case work and relief."[63]

Bureau directives soon required the Guild to shift its focus from benevolent works chosen by its membership to fundraising for the new charitable bureau. It complied, and within a few years was mainly engaged in fundraising among middle- and upper-class Catholics. Even though a plummeting membership accompanied this shift, male charity leaders lauded the new focus. In the late 1920s, for example, a priest advised the Guild to follow the example of many exclusive private clubs and tighten its admission standards. By welcoming only socially ambitious, wealthy women, he insisted, its contribution to archdiocesan charities would increase significantly.[64]

Guild officers labored hard to reverse the membership decline, but since they were not allowed to undertake benevolent projects without episcopal approval, and since few women were interested in joining an organization that simply raised money for a central bureau to distribute, they had little success. By the 1970s, Guild meetings, cut to only four annually, always incorporated "a style show or other gimmicks"[65] in an attempt to boost attendance. Yet in 1973, a special meeting, called to arrange for the sale of the Guild's hall, attracted only twenty-five women.

To minimize confrontations with female societies, bishops, by the 1930s, preferred to form new women's groups that functioned under the bishops' direct surveillance. In 1933, for example, Archbishop John Murray established the Archdiocesan Council of Catholic Women to carry on "Catholic Action" in the St. Paul archdiocese. Council members sat on community chest committees and on boards of civic organizations.[66] Direct service to the poor was not among Council priorities. This episcopal strategy soon dampened laywomen's benevolent initiative. Detroit's Catholic Settlement Association was transformed within a decade from a dynamic social reform organization to a cultural and social club.[67] Such chronologies marked the history of numerous female benevolent societies. Encouraged in the nineteenth century, as long as they could fund their benevolent projects, they were seen as hindrances to diocesan charity consolidation in the twentieth century.

Benevolent women did not relinquish their chosen good works without a struggle, however. An experience of the Catholic Ladies' Aid Society, established in Oakland, California, in 1887, with branches in other cities throughout the state, reveals the challenges they faced. In the early twentieth century, this society opened the St. Margaret's Club, a settlement house in San Francisco. A popular and progressive cause, the settlement was supported generously by society members. In 1922, however, at the time that the San Francisco archdiocesan charities bureau was being established, society members decided to expand their settlement work. Archbishop Edward Hanna proposed that they purchase a $75,000 estate for the project. If they would pay $25,000 in cash, he would borrow the rest of the money on their behalf. Although the women agreed to the arrangement, they were extremely concerned about the fact that the archbishop held title to the property. For this reason, they passed two resolutions: one stipulating that when the $50,000 was paid, the title would be transferred to the society, and the second stating that should the society be dissolved, the parishes in which society members had been active, not the archdiocese, would receive its assets.[68]

Five years later, their apprehensions became reality. Hanna took possession of the attractive property and forbade society members to enter the St. Margaret's Club. He maintained that the Hibernia Bank had advised this action, a claim that the bank denied. The women took their case to Rome, asking that the name, property, and funds of the St. Margaret's Club be returned to the society. They pointed out that while society members had spent $250,000 in rents, interest, and purchase of property for the club, no archdiocesan funds had been contributed to its support. Rome backed the women, and in December 1927, Hanna delivered to them an unconditional deed to the St. Margaret's Club property.[69] He remained convinced, however, that the valuable resources of the St. Margaret's Club would have been used far more efficiently under his control and that independent philanthropic groups, like the Ladies' Aid Society, represented serious obstacles to effective archdiocesan charity work.

The victory of the San Francisco Catholic Ladies' Aid Society in this dispute was something of a milestone. However, unlike that society, most female benevolent groups were much smaller and lacked prominent, wealthy members to protect their interests in disagreements with bishops. They resembled the Ladies' Catholic Club Association of Boston, founded in 1894 and the first Catholic settlement house in that city. The women were particularly interested in helping the many single young women who worked in the factories of the city's South End. Their clubhouse, located in the cathedral parish, was paid for entirely by the members, and they also owned a vacation house for city women on Cape Cod. They covered their operating expenses from private contributions and membership dues. The club's agenda of sports, academic classes, sewing, embroidery, and dressmaking instruction, conducted by a staff of nine paid workers and seven volunteers, was attracting an average daily attendance of 170 in 1914. In the 1930s, the priest-director of the archdiocesan charities bureau, at

the cardinal's order but without the women's knowledge, investigated the financial condition of the association and judged that it was "dying a slow death."
He proposed that either the charitable bureau assume supervision of the clubhouse or that the women relinquish their desirable property to the diocese.[70]

At the time of its establishment in 1901, Brownson House, a Los Angeles
settlement founded by Mary Workman to assist Mexican and Italian immigrants, had the endorsement of the archbishop, George Montgomery. But when
the archdiocesan Catholic Welfare Bureau was formed in 1917, Bishop John
Cantwell unilaterally placed the settlement under the direct control of that organization. When Workman's objections to this step went unheeded, she resigned, observing to a friend that "as a consequence of the 'autocratic regime'
our Catholic women are losing interest and going into non-sectarian organizations."[71] By 1931, settlement houses located in Los Angeles were being praised
in the Catholic press for "the manner in which they combine the work of the
Sisters with professional lay workers."[72] No mention was made of the fact that
this was a development that their lay founders would neither have sought nor
approved.

Catholics took it for granted that sisterhoods would continue to subsidize
and staff most of the charitable institutions that appeared in response to the
needs of "new immigrants" arriving in large numbers in the last decades of the
nineteenth century. Despite flourishing memberships, however, the communities found it difficult to satisfy increasing demand for their services. In states
like New York where city and state subsidies were allotted for the care of public
wards, institutions had expanded at a rate well beyond what Catholic financial
means alone could ever have supported. In New York City, for example, Sisters
of the Good Shepherd in 1894 were caring for 1,700 women in their reformatory;
Little Sisters of the Poor nursed 610 destitute persons in a home for the aged;
Sisters of Mercy provided for 585 homeless children in an industrial orphanage;
and Sisters of Charity received 2,705 infants in the New York Foundling Hospital.[73]

By this time, any sisterhood wishing to undertake benevolent work outside
the institutional setting was certain to meet stiff objections from bishops, since
its labor was so badly needed in institutions. Not uncommon was the experience of New Orleans Sisters of Mercy whose Newsboys' Night School for 150
children was endangered because of a priest's complaint to Rome that such
work was inappropriate for sisters.[74] In addition to heavy managerial responsibilities and work loads, late-nineteenth-century sisters had also to deal with
more restrictive church regulations limiting their contact with "the world."
Most found their social and geographical spheres narrowing to the institutions
in which they lived and worked. Continuing efforts by bishops and clergy to

control their labor were buttressed further by a 1917 revision of the code of canon law governing women religious.

These developments adversely affected the charitable sisterhoods and eroded the spirit of partnership which for so long had marked relations between sisters and benevolent laywomen. Sisters were now frequently charged with being domineering and overly directive toward lay volunteers, an "irritating consequence" of the heavy reliance of charitable institutions on the sisters' contributed services. The problem was widely discussed, but most agreed that it had no easy remedy: "Not only do they bring to these works the spirit of religion and the expert training, they also reduce the expense probably by one-half. Consequently they are so popular as to shut out lay work, except as tributary and submissive to their methods."[75] Younger lay women especially felt stifled by the subordinate status sisters accorded the ladies' auxiliaries and were offended at the sisters' expectation that the laywoman's role was to raise funds for institutions but not to participate in discussions of programs and policies.

For their part, sisters found arguments that the institutional approach to charity was now outmoded very hard to accept. For over a century, church leaders had insisted that the most efficient way for them to contribute their services to charity was through institutions. As demand for their services in all kinds of institutions increased over time, the hierarchy had pressured them to abandon early commitments to visiting the poor and sick in their homes and to evening schools, in favor of greater concentration in institutions. They had acquiesced to these requests with considerable misgiving, especially at first. Some had agreed that rising professional standards by the 1880s in teaching and social work necessitated more study and less home visiting, but others considered this a poor excuse for retreating from radical charity: "It is laziness, and not necessity for study, that makes people neglect visitation," wrote one Sister of Mercy to a colleague at this time. "How can they forget that we bind ourselves by vow to the service of the sick? We can do this without neglecting that—All the old stock were devoted to the sick."[76]

Because churchmen of the 1920s, for the most part, shared William Kerby's assessment that the sisterhoods were out of touch with modern philanthropic trends, new diocesan charity organizations swiftly and permanently relegated them to subordinate roles in charity decision making. Cardinal O'Connell of Boston depicted them as naive in the ways of scientific organization and unaware of the links between charity and justice. He deprecated them as vulnerable to the importunities of frauds who could well afford to pay for service. Their glaring shortcomings called for direct episcopal intervention in their work. He stripped them of their authority by requiring the sister-directors of all charity institutions to make monthly financial reports to him in person. "That

really is the simple secret of the success of our institutions today,"[77] he concluded. By the 1950s, sisters were not consulted on any regular basis on matters
affecting the diocesan institutions they staffed. In 1951, for example, when Sisters of Charity managing a St. Louis girls' orphanage protested their exclusion
from archdiocesan meetings about its future, the central charity board, headed
by the archbishop, simply ignored them. With no sisters present, the board proceeded to pass a resolution to close St. Mary's Female Orphan Asylum "as soon
as conveniently possible."[78]

Sisters' control of hospitals was being challenged across the country by
mid-century. Catholic Charities, the Brooklyn diocesan charities bureau, for example, requested in 1955 that, in the interest of efficiency and better quality care,
two local hospitals merge, and Sisters of Charity assume the management of the
consolidated institution. In preparation for this change, but without consulting
the sisters involved, Catholic Charities had already acquired the necessary per-
missions from the Hospital Council of Greater New York and had made its decision before the sisters were approached.[79] Because they did not have enough
sisters to conduct another hospital, the Sisters of Charity were forced to withdraw from Holy Family Hospital, a local institution that they had subsidized
and staffed for forty-six years. "The thought of leaving a work into which our
Sisters for a long period of years have put so much hard work and self-sacrifice
was a cause of painful regret," wrote the sister superior to her community. "We
knew that the staffing of another hospital in addition to Holy Family would be
out of the question. We could continue what we were doing but we could not
take on additional obligations."[80]

Precursors of central charitable bureaus were diocesan offices for the placement of children in foster homes and orphanages that began to appear after
1900, first in Boston and Newark in 1903, in Hartford a year later, San Francisco
in 1909, Philadelphia and Pittsburgh in 1910, and Detroit in 1913.[81] Progression
from these single-focus agencies to full-fledged charitable bureaus followed the
same general path, with episcopal personalities accounting for diversity in implementation. At one extreme were bishops like William O'Connell of Boston
who likened himself to the head of a well-managed corporation. As such, he
knew more about its work than any single employee, and so logically he was
uniquely qualified to supervise the charities and distribute funds contributed
for their support.[82] In 1916, he announced without preliminaries that he intended to federate all charitable institutions and organizations. "All will be under the direction of the Catholic Charitable Bureau," his secretary informed the
priest-director of the bureau, "and the heads of all charitable organizations in
the archdiocese may be responsible to His Eminence through you as head of the
Bureau."[83]

Most bishops took a less autocratic approach by initially consulting the larger parish conferences of the St. Vincent de Paul Society in their dioceses. These overtures were not always very fruitful, however. John Glennon of St. Louis, for example, had asked society officers there in 1912 whether society rules allowed a parish conference to aid poor persons residing outside parish limits. He was told that while this was technically possible, it was likely that the rank-and-file membership would disapprove. He then suggested that the society hire a professional social worker to help members carry out their charities "more scientifically," not an unprecedented proposal, as councils in other dioceses had been employing paid agents on a limited basis since the 1880s. However, it met very strong resistance in St. Louis. A society committee told him that hiring paid social workers violated the spirit and rules of their society, but if he wished to establish a new association that permitted the practice, the men of the St. Vincent de Paul Society would cooperate with it. At this, Glennon moved quickly to form the Central Bureau of Catholic Charities and Kindred Activities of St. Louis. Half of its forty-member board were his personal appointees; the other half represented the ten charitable agencies of the archdiocese.[84]

Immediately following his appointment as archbishop of Chicago in 1915, George Mundelein inaugurated the consolidation process there. Like Glennon, his first step was to approach the St. Vincent de Paul Society's central office, the agency responsible for child placement in the archdiocese. Within three years, the society's central office was subordinate to an archdiocesan charities bureau headed by Mundelein's appointee.[85] In the archdiocese of Baltimore, the St. Vincent de Paul Society had supervised all non-institutional charity work since 1864. In 1906, it established a central office headed by society president Robert Biggs and, with the approval of Cardinal James Gibbons, introduced cross-parish family welfare work, an unprecedented step that encouraged middle-class parishes to aid poor parishes. The society's Baltimore central office served as a model for similar offices in other dioceses and gave impetus to the movement for a national charity organization. However, in 1923 its work was taken over by the newly formed archdiocesan Bureau of Catholic Charities, headed by a priest. Archbishop Michael Curley appointed the same priest to serve as "spiritual director" of the lay society, now classified as "an associate of the Family Department of the Bureau of Catholic Charities."[86] Within a decade, the role of the St. Vincent de Paul Society had narrowed to "giving temporary relief in the parishes."[87]

This autocratic approach allowed diocesan charitable bureaus to develop rapidly. While before World War I, only five dioceses had full-fledged bureaus, seventeen were in place by 1918, sixty-eight by the late 1930s. Their organizational structure was fairly similar across the country. The bishop, as chief administrator of the diocese, appointed a priest as deputy-director for the bureau and designated members of a central charity board. Appointees to the board were men, a reflection of the belief that wealthy professional and business laymen, when complemented by a strong clerical representation, formed an effective board.[88]

Professional training in social work was becoming a prerequisite for employment in public and private social agencies, and the new diocesan bureaus were eager to meet the highest standards in this regard. Paid social workers were soon playing important roles in enforcing bureau policies and standards. However, their introduction raised serious questions among Catholics about how this step affected religious charity. A speaker at the 1916 National Conference of Catholic Charities meeting voiced the reservations of many. "We are beginning to drift away from the methods which have been in vogue these centuries, that of personal service. Benevolent associations composed only of donors who pay workers to do charitable work are not true charities. . . . Volunteer service has always been integral to the Catholic definition of charity; it permits all, regardless of social class, to give."[89] Defenders of the innovation brushed aside such worries by pointing out that social work is simply a means to an end, and that end is charity.[90]

Lay volunteers, nonetheless, felt marginalized as paid social workers appeared in larger numbers. John O'Grady acknowledged in the 1920s that the dissatisfaction of lay volunteers was a potentially serious problem, since it was "fairly typical of the viewpoint of the rank and file of our people, and it is also fairly representative of the viewpoint of the rank and file of the clergy."[91] Nonetheless, social workers, nearly all of them women, continued to be in high demand in diocesan charitable bureaus and agencies. Catholic colleges and universities began to offer degrees in social work, and in 1921, the National Catholic Welfare Council established the National School of Social Service in Washington, D.C. Since its student body was female, the National Council of Catholic Women agreed to finance the new school, pledging $500,000 for its initial three years. A 1924 grant from the Laura Spelman Rockefeller Memorial Foundation of $15,000 annually for three years significantly boosted the founders' morale as well as the school's financial situation.[92]

Although a few reform proponents proposed to bishops that the charitable institutions be invited to choose their representatives for diocesan charitable boards, this modest concession to democracy was largely ignored. In fact, directors of the charitable institutions were forced to surrender considerable authority to the diocesan bureau, since "any other method of procedure would lead to confusion, discord, and disunion."[93] Directors of many large, urban institutions were not averse to this development. They were already introducing progressive features of mainstream charity organizations, expanding the number of seats on institutional boards from the customary ten to as many as fifty, and actively recruiting wealthy businessmen for them. These new board members tended to be less committed to preserving an institution's traditional autonomy than older members and were less likely to demur at episcopal orders that an institution close or merge with another.[94] The language of early diocesan bureau reports reveals the growing influence of mainstream values. In the 1920s, for example, the San Francisco Affiliated Catholic Charities bureau stated that its purpose was to help Catholics meet their "social responsibility in a manner which is Christ-like as well as scientific."[95] This meant more active collaboration with mainstream agencies, since, as William Kerby put it, "poverty is no respecter of persons or of religions."[96]

Board members of small, ethnic institutions, which far outnumbered the large establishments, did not share the progressive sentiments of diocesan bureaus. Most of them had struggled against odds to keep their institutions open, sometimes undertaking door-to-door solicitation, and they were deeply committed to preserving their autonomy. Ironically, however, their institutions were usually the first to lose their independence under charity centralization. Representative was a hospital and home for the elderly founded in 1891 by the German farming community of Aviston, Illinois, and staffed by German sisters. Although its income had always been uncertain, since it fluctuated with the price of wheat, its directors were able to finance it independently by charity fairs and especially by an annual door-to-door begging tour conducted by the sisters. Local citizens gave the sisters cash donations and valuable in-kind gifts, usually wheat ground free by the local milling company. In this way, the institution was able to play an essential role in the local community for nearly three decades. However, it lost its autonomy in 1919 when the Belleville diocesan charities bureau prohibited the sisters' annual begging tour.[97]

With diocesan financial support came diocesan appointees to institutional boards. This development was all to the good in the eyes of reformers like John O'Grady because it promised to reduce "the chasm separating the different nationalities,"[98] a major barrier to the rationalization of charity work. Ethnic groups and sisterhoods, in contrast, saw merit in the independent institution, and so they resisted taking diocesan funds as long as possible. If buildings and land of the charitable institutions were owned by religious orders, they were legally free from diocesan control. But to keep their independence, the sisterhoods had to be able to support themselves, and that became impossible for most in the depression years of the 1930s. The experience of Baltimore's St. Vincent's Infant Asylum is exemplary of these independent establishments. Owned and conducted by Sisters of Charity since 1856, its charter required that "this

Corporation shall at all times be composed of females devoted to works of benevolence."[99] The 1930s placed heavy financial pressures on the sisters, and although they created a lay advisory board in 1938 to help them raise funds, the
move proved futile. By 1949, their asylum, like many others, was finally "consolidated or merged with the Associated Catholic Charities, Inc."[100]

Hospitals, more than other institutions, resisted oversight by central charitable bureaus. But they, too, had to bow in the face of financial exigency. When,
for example, the St. Louis charitable bureau announced in the late 1930s that it
was creating a special office to supervise local hospitals, some of the institutions
declined to share their accounts with the new officials. These archdiocesan officials immediately informed the recalcitrant directors that, until they complied
with the request, their hospitals would not share in the annual distribution of
the archdiocesan charity collection. A bureau emissary reported that his visit to
DePaul Hospital with this disturbing news proved "very fruitful."[101]

From a financial standpoint, the centralization movement significantly
benefited most institutions. Payments from relatives, friends, or government for
the care of orphans were made directly to the diocesan charitable bureau, which
then distributed monthly allowances to the various homes. While these institutions were not compelled to accept bureau policy recommendations, it was
definitely understood that they would. At the same time, responsibility for institutional maintenance, improvements, and debt remained with individual orphanage boards.[102] Directors of the German St. Vincent Orphan Association in
St. Louis in 1928 applauded the new Department of Children of the archdiocesan charities bureau for assuming responsibility for the investigation of applicants to its orphanage.[103] The price of that assistance was a significant loss of
lay authority over the institution, however. In the mid-1960s, Cardinal Joseph
Ritter wrote to the president of the same orphan association to admonish him
for introducing a policy that the archdiocesan charities office had not approved.
He reminded him that "failure on the part of your Board to conform with Archdiocesan regulations as set forth by the Charities Office will result in the with-
drawal of my approval of St. Vincent's as a Catholic children's institution."[104]

Tensions between charitable institutions and diocesan bureaus were ongoing and common. Diocesan bureaus were able to work harmoniously with government and civic organizations, but found it hard to collaborate with their own
Catholic institutions. By the 1950s, the situation was indeed discouraging. "In
many places we still find a wide chasm between our central diocesan organizations and the institutions," wrote one observer. "In some places the relationships are quite strained and in very few places is there a truly close democratic
relationship."[105]

Charity reformers and the hierarchy concurred that resistance to charity centralization by grassroots laity and religious orders was simply the result of lack of education and the lingering effects of ethnic separatism. "No solidarity between the various groups. No consciousness of any union except that union of the Faith,"[106] grumbled Archbishop Austin Dowling. But these assessments seriously underrated popular objections to organizational change. Ordinary congregants much preferred to tolerate some inefficiency in giving than to adopt criteria which could possibly result in aid being denied to worthy persons. If givers did not see in the needy the person of Christ, they noted, then the material benefits of their philanthropy will have no lasting value. Centralized charity organization might encourage Catholics to view charity as a civic obligation, motivated only by community pride, "a mere department of civil service that elicits from those who follow it no greater interest than one may reasonably expect from a hireling."[107] They pointed out that when faced with a need, parishioners had traditionally addressed it and worried later about whether their approach had been efficient. While philanthropic resources might occasionally go to unworthy recipients, this approach was still preferable to that of "scientific charity," where those in genuine need might be turned away.[108] Adoption of secular standards and the introduction of professional social workers, many concluded, placed Catholic giving in grave danger of losing its personal character and spiritual vitality.

Lay reformers had long found these arguments galling and unenlightened. Robert Biggs, president of the Baltimore St. Vincent de Paul Society, emphasized at the first National Conference of Catholic Charities in 1910 that in large cities benevolent people simply cannot know who is most in need of help or what their most pressing requirements are. "Unintelligent," casual giving may not just unwittingly benefit charlatans but may also result in less support for those truly in need. "A Catholic doing an act of charity as he sees it, is looking at the spiritual benefit flowing back to himself rather than to the amount of practical benefit he confers upon the dependent. This conception to my mind is distinctly unfortunate."[109]

Biggs's message resounded from every quarter at later conferences. Tighter organization would eliminate overlap in the services of independent benevolent agencies and expedite investigation of those seeking assistance. Charitable resources would, therefore, reach more of the worthy poor than the current decentralized system allowed. William Kerby begged for a more intellectual and less emotional approach to giving: "We cannot dismiss with a gesture proposals which we do not like. . . . System, science, formula, method have their advantages. If they do not frighten in theology, why should we fear them in charity?"[110]

Objections from the grassroots persisted, nonetheless, centering mainly on the threat of charity consolidation to the democratic values that made the Catholic giving style distinctive. Because they did not organize a response, their statements were often simply emotional calls to preserve old ways. As such, they were easily countered by articulate social reformers. Ordinary parishioners possessed neither the academic training nor the inclination to challenge bishops and clergy who were so wholeheartedly crusading for charity centralization. Thus, they were at a definite disadvantage in public debates on the topic. Generous in doing good, they found it hard to explain why they found the new approach so troubling. As a consequence, their arguments for the preservation of small scale, local control, and community commitment fell before the overriding claims for centralization: its promise of greater efficiency, higher professional standards, and more rapid progress toward collaboration with mainstream and government agencies.

Although they had long participated in the support of independent charity institutions, ordinary laity found few places for themselves in the new central bureaus. Institutional lay boards and auxiliaries were losing their authority to central charity boards dominated by priests and wealthy laymen. As more Catholics in the 1920s moved from inner-city parishes to the suburbs, their personal links with the urban charities weakened. Meaningful service opportunities contracted, and new benevolent projects originated more often in central bureaus than in local initiatives.

The typical charity sermon of the 1930s resembled that of preceding decades in its rhetoric, but it no longer fit the modern context. Reminders that charity was not the "begrudged giving of material things" that marked the bureaucrat, but rather the opportunity to "perform a direct personal service for Our Lord Himself"[111] had a hollow ring, as opportunities for significant voluntary service diminished.

In 1910, more than 500 diocesan charity leaders and social workers had assembled in Washington, D.C., for the first meeting of the National Conference of Catholic Charities. Inaugurated by Rev. John O'Grady, Rev. William Kerby, and Bishop Thomas Shahan, rector of the Catholic University, in collaboration with Thomas Mulry and Edmond Butler of the St. Vincent de Paul Society, the conference aimed to evaluate Catholic efforts relative to the "drifts" in modern charity. "The practical outcome will be the discovery of defective methods where they may be found or of the lack of organization, if such there be."[112] From its inception, it gave priority to social reform agendas and challenged Catholic philanthropists to do more than simply relieve material distress. Meetings of the National Conference soon became major forums in which bishops, diocesan charity directors, and professional social workers strove to develop national policies on charity and to devise more effective benevolent-fundraising strategies.

The World War I crisis encouraged Catholics to cooperate at the national level with other religious groups. The National Catholic War Council, made up of the nation's fourteen archbishops, supported by an administrative committee of four bishops, commenced its work in 1917. Two sub-committees, the Knights of Columbus and the Committee on Special War Activities, collaborated closely with their counterparts, the War Time Commission of the Federal Council of Churches and the Jewish Welfare Board. In 1920, the War Council became a permanent organization, renamed two years later the National Catholic Welfare Council.[113]

The first priority of the new council was to consolidate lay benevolent societies under episcopal jurisdiction. Bypassing the lay-led American Federation of Catholic Societies, the bishops established two new departments, the National Council of Catholic Men and the National Council of Catholic Women. Their approach was in full keeping with their view of the place of the laity in church affairs. A sympathetic priest summarized lay-clerical interaction at this time: "Every time that a practical plan is formulated, at the last minute some eccles. authority either takes it out of the hands of the laity, or highhandedly, and not at all acquainted with the preceding discussion, at which they were not present, they give us their enlightened opinion, and force recognition of their immature suggestion."[114] Not surprisingly, neither the National Council of Catholic Women nor the National Council of Catholic Men prospered. The men's organization was a failure. And in 1923, despite minimal individual membership dues of one dollar per year, only twelve thousand of four million eligible women had joined their organization.[115] A decade later, although it counted fifty councils in 104 dioceses, the women's council continued weak.

By the mid-1930s, even the leaders of the National Conference of Catholic Charities felt that their authority was threatened by the National Catholic Welfare Conference. Under dispute was who should present the official Catholic view on federal legislation dealing with social welfare issues. William Montavon, of N.C.W.C.'s legal department, complained of "a spirit of hostility toward the National Catholic Welfare Conference" among the directors of the National Conference of Catholic Charities. "In a lobby conversation . . . [they] have said that they believe that the National Catholic Welfare Conference should have no voice in the field of charity, but that it should accept the voice of the National Conference as final in this field. . . . They do not seem to admit that the National Catholic Welfare Conference is the Hierarchy."[116]

Bureaucratic organization, public funding of private charity agencies, and a rapid introduction of paid professionals in institutional charities combined to diminish opportunities for lay voluntary service by the mid-twentieth century. The St. Vincent de Paul Society, still committed to the principle that personal service was integral to the practice of charity, was already profoundly weakened by the 1930s. By the 1950s, women's organizations, for the most part, were reported as having "little or no contact with Catholic charities."[117] A benefactor's remark to the sister in charge of the House of the Good Shepherd in St. Paul, Minnesota, at this time, captures the long-run danger to religious giving in these developments: "I, of course, knew what good work you were accomplishing out at the House but, like everything else, one does not pay much attention to those things until one comes in actual contact."[118]

Hierarchically imposed, bureaucratic in structure, and heavily clerical in administration, central charity organization did not win warm support from ordinary laity or religious orders. As a consequence, the strong sense of personal ownership of the charities, so long a characteristic of the American Catholic community, began to wane. Resistance by parishioners to changes in charity organization took many bishops and reformers by surprise. They had foreseen few problems, since the bureaucratic model seemed to fit well with the hierarchical style that marked other areas of church life. However, the economic distress of the 1930s buttressed their confidence that, despite all difficulties, the new approach was a positive step forward.

Directors of the new diocesan bureaus and national offices were well-educated professionals, eager to collaborate with other private and civic benevolent groups. Government funding for Catholic charities was increasing, allowing the church to provide more and improved services. Most important, Catholic charity was in a better position to identify those in real need and to marshal its considerable benevolent resources quickly and effectively. By "working expertly," diocesan bureaus were significantly extending the scope of Catholic philanthropy. This was, without doubt, the best way to practice the corporal works of mercy intelligently,[119] they concluded.

Bureaucracy, however, was not easily compatible with volunteer service. In the single area of church life where personal initiative had flourished, hierarchy was replacing local decision making, and avenues for voluntary participation by ordinary laity were shrinking. Those who argued that the benefits of centralization, in terms of the numbers aided and quality of services provided, justified these costs overlooked a troubling statistic. Despite a growing church membership, lay volunteers in 1930 were fewer in number than they had been in 1900.[120] Charity reformers had not taken seriously enough their own initial reservations. "It is undoubtedly true," William Kerby had acknowledged in 1909, "that system in charity work does at times chill the free and buoyant impulse to service which is the crowning glory of Christian character, and does rationalize where feeling loves to have its sway."[121] Centralization had clearly undermined traditional understanding of personal service as a necessary complement to monetary giving in religious philanthropy. By the late 1930s, even charity leaders were noting its effect. "One wonders why the old-time crusading spirit has disappeared from our charity," commented one. "How far is it part of the spirit of the age? The institutions are there. The charitable organizations are still doing good work, probably better work than ever before. The people contribute their support more than ever, but they don't want to be bothered any further."[122]

5

New Strategies in Fundraising

If Almighty God wishes us to be charitable, He wants us to be enlightened in
charity. That is to say, charity should be guided by the light of intellect.

—James Blenk, 1910

BY THE 1880s, despite episcopal protests that congregants should support
their parishes without having to be amused, pastors had begun to introduce
fairs as a way to supplement inadequate Sunday collections. Pressed to construct and maintain parochial schools, as well as to meet ordinary parish expenses, they saw no other recourse. "They are all in the same boat," observed
a Detroit pastor in 1886.[1]

This development immediately affected charitable institutions. As pastors
now saw charity collections as threats to the success of parish fairs, they denied
permission for charity appeals in their churches. This precipitated a dramatic
increase in separately organized institutional fairs, bazaars, and festivals. By
the turn of the century, Catholics were barraged by solicitations. To control them
somewhat, bishops assigned a "donation day" to each institution, on which it
could make a public appeal for funds, free from competition from neighboring
institutions. The typical institution held an open house on its appointed day,
convinced that if people saw first hand its needs and the quality of care it was
providing, a generous response would be more likely. "If you will visit the Asylum and come face to face with the orphan, and in touch with our needs, nothing more will be required,"[2] wrote sisters at a Philadelphia orphanage to the
general public. While "donation days" alleviated the problem of incessant appeals somewhat, the number and needs of institutions in urban dioceses made
them nearly continuous throughout the year.

Indeed, funding of charity institutions had become a serious problem by
the 1890s. Although dioceses assumed responsibility for financing some institutions, the majority still relied on returns from their own subscription drives
and fairs to meet operating expenses. Since individual subscriptions ordinarily
cost only 25 cents per year, a drive's success depended upon convincing large
numbers of laity to take a personal interest in a particular institution. The

democratic nature of subscription collections, which were "not the work of the few, but the charity of the many,"[3] bolstered strong local commitment, but their expanding number strained the patience as well as the purses of many parishioners.

On the diocesan level as well, the need for more revenue sparked reassessment of fundraising techniques. In order to finance construction of seminaries and other major diocesan projects, bishops looked to the large Christmas and Easter collections, long sacred to the cause of charity in many dioceses. Since 1833, for example, both of these collections in the New York archdiocese were assigned to the Roman Catholic Orphan Asylum. In the 1870s, a few hardpressed local pastors decided to withhold some of the money contributed in these collections to meet parish expenses. Episcopal censure was so memorable that the violation never recurred. Yet only three decades later, bishops were themselves reassigning the charity collections to less lucrative Sundays.[4]

By the 1890s, social criticism of gambling motivated bishops to discourage it in charity fundraising. St. Paul's John Ireland banned it outright and instructed his clergy to enforce the order strictly: "Public sentiment has become so pronounced, and rightly so, against lotteries and chance games, that we deem it our duty to prohibit altogether, as we now do, the raising of money for religious or charitable purposes by the sale of chances, the use of wheels of fortune, or by any method savoring of lottery or gambling. This rule, which we now make, admits of no exception; it applies to countries as well as to towns, to convents as well as to parishes."[5] Such prohibition of a staple ingredient of the charity fair made fundraising a greater challenge than ever.

Because they were popular with their mainstream counterparts, benevolent middle-class Catholics turned to card games, especially euchre, and lawn fetes, although these devices were considerably less remunerative than the typical fair. The cost of running a 1908 euchre for a Baltimore boys' asylum, for example, absorbed 37 percent of total receipts, leaving a meager $600 for the institution. While the institution's directors blamed low gross receipts on competition from other benefits, they did not explain the high administrative costs. They customarily held several of these fundraisers yearly to supplement revenues from subscription drives and parish collections.[6] Most institutions depended on fairs, however. As these events multiplied, they faced more competition and fared less well financially. At the turn of the century, some began to reach beyond their immediate environs for subscribers, using city directories to get names. Volunteers would distribute thousands of flyers, and "lady solicitors" would travel door-to-door to collect pledges. Should returns be disappointing, paid collectors might be hired to continue the work, but this was still a fairly unusual step.[7]

Because few charitable establishments had significant savings or endowments, fluctuating private contributions meant that revenues did not routinely cover operating costs. The sight of sisters begging in the streets disturbed bishops of the late nineteenth century, and they made the provision of financial security for charity institutions a priority issue. Although, in good times, marginal institutions might survive from day to day on small contributions, they were extremely vulnerable to economic downturns and natural disasters. People responded generously in these crises, but those conducting the institutions recognized that support would decline as memory of the calamity faded. In 1905, for example, Sisters of Mercy appealed for subscriptions for a Raleigh, North Carolina, home for boys, explaining that while they were grateful for the "outburst of charity" after a recent fire at the orphanage, the impulse had been very short lived.[8] A destructive 1915 hurricane left sisters managing a New Orleans orphanage in dire financial straits. Already begging daily to support eighty children, they now were obliged to give even more time to this activity. Fearful that ordering a special collection in the parishes for one institution would inspire many others to seek a similar favor, the archbishop hesitated for three years before approving a special collection for the orphanage, making clear his disappointment that voluntary action had not long since resolved its financial woes. "I regret that we have to resort to this method of supporting the little ones of Christ. God grant that we may be able at no distant date to provide other sources of income."[9]

His colleague, Cleveland bishop John Farrelly, had taken a step toward this goal in 1911 when he appointed the city's seven pastors to a Board of Charities to consider the whole issue of how to fund properly the charitable institutions of the diocese. The board proposed that all Catholics in the diocese, rather than just those in parishes where orphanages happened to be located, assume responsibility for their financial support. To this end, the diocese designated the first week in November as Orphans' Week and assigned a quota to every parish. Results were surprisingly good. While under the old system of independent institutional fundraising, Cleveland citizens had provided only one-fourth of the funds needed annually for the establishments, contributions increased 150 percent within two years under the new approach. News of the extraordinary success of consolidated collections spread, and other dioceses quickly introduced them. Most built on their traditional orphans' collection. For example, while Chicago parishes had long reserved the Pentecost Sunday collection for the children's institutions, because the collection was not mandatory, not all parishes participated. When "Orphans' Day" evolved into Charity Sunday, however, the collection became obligatory.[10]

Seemingly endless appeals from independent charities led wealthy Chicago laity to inform Archbishop Mundelein in 1918 that they would contribute more if they were solicited less. After consulting St. Vincent de Paul Society leaders and other prominent laymen, Mundelein determined to replace indiscriminate collecting with a single annual subscription drive to benefit all archdiocesan charities. He was convinced that Catholics of every social class would prefer to give in this modern, efficient way, especially since the new collection promised that the institutions would be better funded. Bishops generally concurred that a diocesan charity collection would allow all to give, raise more money for the charities, and cost little to administer.

Nearly half the $438,000 raised in Chicago's first archdiocesan charity collection in 1918 came from the parishes, the rest from special solicitation of wealthy individuals and corporations. The average parish subscription in the first few years was relatively low: $9.48 in 1918, $7.22 in 1919, $8.20 in 1920, and $8.46 in 1922.[11] In contrast, forty-five individuals alone accounted for 29 percent of the 1920 collection. This persuaded the diocesan charity committee to propose concentrating more attention on soliciting the rich. But Mundelein disagreed. Greater parish cooperation, he believed, was the essential element for the collection's lasting success. "Time and again, there have been collections promulgated for different purposes, and they have all failed because of the fact that the parish organization was not used."[12]

Pastors, however, disliked the new collection, since they saw in it a major challenge to their cherished parish autonomy. Forty-two of Chicago's 350 parishes boycotted the second collection in 1919, with the pastors of the Polish and German parishes notably uncooperative. The archbishop retaliated in 1921 by directing that the allotment from the diocese for the city's Polish orphanage not exceed 80 percent of the money contributed by the Polish parishes. If the parishes did not choose to give generously, then Polish children would suffer. In the same year he instructed the executive committee of the charities bureau to table a request for $27,000 from a German orphanage until contributions from the German parishes in the annual collection reached at least 80 percent of that amount.[13]

Pastors objected that charity officials, without consulting them, were aggressively soliciting donations from their more affluent parishioners. Some tried to exact, as conditions of cooperation, promises that the central office would send no letters "of any nature" to their parishioners[14] and that they be allowed to conduct the new collection in their own way. They particularly objected to the imposition of parish quotas for the collection. Instead, in 1922, Mundelein placed his chancellor on the charity executive committee and instructed the committee to draw up directives for pastors and see to it that they were fully implemented. These instructions were explicit. Each parish was to meet its assigned quota for the collection. Pastors were to compare lists of donors in the

Easter collection and in the new collection to discover those who were not supporting the charities and appoint a visiting committee of parishioners to urge the delinquents to give. Should a pastor resist, the central charity office would step in to form the visiting committee.[15]

In an effort to engender greater parish cooperation, the chairmen of parish drives, most of them business and professional men, were named directors of the diocesan charities bureau, the Associated Catholic Charities. In 1920, directors numbered an unwieldy 274, plus the archdiocesan chancellor. They generally agreed that more efficient methods in charity fundraising were long overdue and that the church had much to learn in this area from other religious groups. In 1923, for example, director David Shanahan called for adoption of the no-nonsense approach of the Jewish community, which denied admission to important clubs to applicants unable to demonstrate that they had supported Jewish charities in accord with their means. He lauded Jews generally for their willingness to give money directly to charity rather than wasting both time and money in sponsoring elegant charity balls.[16]

The fact that large numbers of parishioners were contributing nothing at all in the new charities collection seemed to diocesan officials to justify stern measures. In 1920, they estimated that while about half of Chicago's one million Catholics could afford to give something, only 150,000 did so. "There are over four hundred thousand Catholics who are escaping us each year," concluded the chancellor. He predicted that once the new quota system was operative, parish contributions would immediately increase by at least 125 percent. Indeed, by 1922 most parishes were meeting their quotas.[17]

While quotas brought impressive short-term financial results, their long-term effects were less clearcut. Pastors knew that if they did not meet their assessments they would be billed for shortfalls by the chancery. At the same time, the diocese frowned upon parishes holding fundraising events, such as benefit games and concerts, to meet quotas because they violated the new goal of a single, annual charity appeal. Given this situation, if returns from the annual collection in parishes fell short of their quotas, pastors were expected to hold a second collection for the cause. However, as the need to make a second appeal for the same cause would be publicly humiliating for pastors, they instead quietly and unhappily made up deficiencies from general parish funds.[18] Diocesan officials, by overlooking this prevalent practice, begged the question of whether the single charity collection was fostering grassroots participation in the corporate charities of the church. It did not appear to matter to them whether parish quotas were being met from contributions intentionally made for charity or from other parish resources.

Although the practice of taxing Catholics collectively for the support of diocesan charities through parish quotas spread quickly, personal tithing never did, although rural parishioners of the nineteenth century had traditionally pledged shares of their farm produce to local charitable institutions.[19] Catholics were simply asked to give proportionately to their means. A few dioceses, however, did introduce tithing. The Des Moines, Iowa, diocese, in the 1910s, wrote a tithing requirement into its diocesan code based on net income of all owners and earners, married or single. "Tithes and first fruits are sacred and precious before the Lord, because they are his portion, are used for his service and because in them he beholds the industry and honesty of his faithful stewards."[20] The diocese of Elkhart, Indiana, followed suit in 1915. In the 1920s, St. Cloud and Seattle Catholics were invited to contribute 4 percent of their annual income to the church. The Superior, Wisconsin, diocese called for a 5 percent contribution, Cincinnati for 7 to 10 percent.[21] These initiatives generated hope in some quarters that the practice would spread nationally and eliminate the "execrated money-talks which only too frequently have replaced the Sunday sermon."[22] This was a vain hope, however, as the huge urban dioceses, populated by many poor parishioners and few property owners, showed no interest in tithing. A 1987 study found that while 22 percent of Protestants pledge a percentage of their annual incomes to the church, only 8 percent of Catholics do.[23]

The first central charity appeal in the archdiocese of New York differed in approach from the Chicago collection. Soon after assuming the post of archbishop, Patrick Hayes formed the Archbishop's Committee of the Laity, which was composed of 25,000 parishioners who agreed to conduct a one-week campaign in April of 1920 for $1.5 million from 100,000 fellow Catholics, who would pledge to give five dollars annually for the next three years. The response surpassed all expectations, with pledges of $1 million annually made by 233,000 Catholics. A week after it ended, the new archdiocesan charities bureau, Catholic Charities, commenced operations.[24] The remarkable response to this campaign, and to a collection for the Catholic War Fund a year earlier, was attributed by expert observers directly to professional organization: "The New York campaign was put in charge of professional money raisers. . . . The Catholic authorities of New York had the perspicacity and the enterprise to realize that the professional organizers of money-getting 'drives' really have the power to bring out, extend and supplement the latent possibilities of the diocese and the parish."[25]

The structure of New York charity fundraising soon became more elaborate. Hayes divided the archdiocese into sixteen districts with approximately twenty parishes in each. A priest served as manager and a layman as chair of each district. Each parish formed a team of ten to solicit funds in the appeal. Catholic Charities officers supervised all districts. Before the actual appeal

week, press and pulpit emphasized the needs of the charities and prepared parishioners for visits by solicitors to their homes. After the appeal, parish trea-
surers remitted to the central office all funds collected, with a list of donors and
the amounts of their gifts. The archbishop personally acknowledged every contribution.[26]

In the short run, at least, the New York approach proved encouraging in
terms of numbers participating as well as in financial donations. Hayes had
asked for $500,000 in each of the first three appeals and received an average of
$867,000 annually, 73 percent more than the target. Although the average gift
was small, the total number of donors was large. This "democracy in giving"
pleased Hayes. He saw central organization as a way to involve every Catholic
in the works of charity and stressed at every opportunity that he was more interested in how many contributed than in the amounts they gave. The charities
collection, he insisted, allowed the laity to become "a potent factor in the work
of the Church, assuming a large share of the burden which had long been borne
by the religious alone." Participation in the annual appeal would "make every
Catholic in the diocese a real, live, and earnest friend of the Catholic Charities,
and therefore, a better Catholic in the highest sense of the term." Hayes had less
to say about contributions of voluntary service in the traditional sense, taking
the excellent response in the charities collection as evidence of a new "apostolic
sense of Christlike service" among the laity. "Service," in his definition, meant
giving generously in the charities appeal.[27]

Advocates of a consolidated charities collection presented as their strongest
argument the same one they had used to promote diocesan charitable bureaus.
With thousands of poor in every sprawling city, it was virtually impossible for
benevolent individuals to independently identify those most in need. They
could not even decide intelligently which of the charitable institutions were
most worthy of assistance at a particular time or place. By delegating the dis-
bursement of their contributions in an annual collection to bishops and their
professional staffs, benevolent laity could feel certain that their donations would
be equitably and scientifically allocated. "In this way there can be little worry
as to where to give one's alms."[28]

Hierarchical control of the distribution of the charity collection seriously
dampened local interest in it, however. Bishops constantly rejected the suggestion that pastors be able to retain a fraction of the collection for distribution to
local charities, a concession that would acknowledge parish autonomy. The time
had come, bishops and reformers maintained, to replace local loyalties with a
"diocesan spirit." Only thus would Catholics unite in truly corporate giving.
"While the parochial spirit has accomplished great things for the Church, we
all know that it has its limitations."[29]

This position affected the work of the numerous lay associations and auxiliaries attached to specific charities. Not only did it limit the revenues they could raise, but, more importantly, it placed a wedge between benevolent laity and the religious orders.[30] For instance, in 1921, Chicago's Associated Catholic Charities, eager to boost its annual contributions record, instructed the South Side Catholic Women's Club to surrender the funds its members were planning to present to sisters at a local hospital. The bureau rather than the laywomen would distribute their gift to the hospital.[31] Because they feared that parishioners who contributed a small sum to one charitable institution might feel they had no obligation to give in the annual diocesan charity collection, bishops severely restricted independent institutional appeals after 1920.[32]

Proponents of the diocesan charities collection acknowledged that it could weaken personal ties of individual givers to benevolent institutions, and they also knew that donors liked to decide for themselves which charitable institutions they wanted to support. On the other hand, they argued, centralized fundraising would ultimately raise more money for charity and strengthen the religious spirit of giving as well. The purchase of raffle tickets, after all, had little spiritual merit. And most fair goers were more interested in winning prizes or in being entertained than in assisting the poor. Was it not more Christian, as well as vastly more efficient, to unite with other church members in one annual collection for charity, than to continue to use the poor as an excuse for having a good time?[33]

The emotional ties of parishioners to individual charitable institutions remained strong, however, and directors of the establishments continued to call on their traditional benefactors. This deeply distressed those responsible for the success of the annual diocesan charity collections. But the charities, in fact, had little choice in the matter. Their financial worries did not disappear with the introduction of the diocesan charity collection because bishops often reserved a large share of it for their own priority projects. For example, in 1923, Archbishop Hayes earmarked the entire $2.6 million raised in a recent three-year archdiocesan charity appeal for the introduction of new activities, the expansion of some others, and the implementation of professional standards in charity work. All other charities, he warned, "hospitals, nurseries, orphanages, etc., must still continue to raise their own funds as they did prior to the establishment of the Catholic Charities."[34] The intense publicity and frequent sermons about the importance of giving in the archdiocesan collection, however, had led many New York Catholics to reason that they had done their duty by giving during that collection, a perception that made fundraising more difficult than ever for charitable institutions.

In their eagerness to attract donors, especially wealthy ones, in the early diocesan charity collections, a number of dioceses promised that Catholics would be asked to give to charity only once annually. In 1918, the Chicago charities bureau went so far as to write to persons who had recently donated at least $50 to a charitable institution to say that if, instead of contributing directly to the institution, they would donate the money in the diocesan charity collection, they would receive a certificate from the bureau exempting them for a year from annoying "miscellaneous solicitations."[35] Within a few years, however, hard-pressed institutions were again appealing directly to individuals, leading annoyed certificate holders to complain loudly that the archdiocese was reneging on its promise to end "promiscuous solicitation of funds."[36] Archbishop Mundelein was at first ambivalent in his response. He pointed out that because the direct needs of the poor consumed the contributions in the charity collection, the institutions had no recourse but to conduct separate appeals to meet building maintenance and construction costs. Thus, it was unreasonable for donors to the diocesan collection to expect to be completely insulated from independent appeals. Two decades later, however, he virtually guaranteed a single, yearly solicitation. "You may help those less fortunate than yourself and fulfill your Catholic duty of charity by *one* annual donation."[37]

This assurance was soon incorporated into most diocesan fundraising campaigns. It was taken so literally that even members of the hierarchy met indifferent response when they appealed for contributions for a particularly pressing need. Three years after his appointment as archbishop of Los Angeles in 1948, James McIntyre established the Los Angeles Archbishop's Fund to assist very poor persons, especially those living in places without community chests, whose needs were not being met adequately by other private or public social programs. The Fund held an annual subscription drive, asking parishioners for two dollars in membership dues, paid through the parishes.[38]

McIntyre was sure that this special fund would greatly stimulate the benevolent spirit of ordinary parishioners, but he was mistaken. After four years of mediocre parish membership enrollments, he resorted to more coercive strategies, requesting pastors to send him names of "preferred donors" who could give at least one thousand dollars and assigning parish quotas for the Fund. Despite his insistence that the quotas were not assessments, both pastors and people saw them as exactly that.[39] Local foundations, benevolent societies, and individuals of other faiths, impressed by its focus on society's most neglected citizens, contributed generously to the Fund, but the response from Los Angeles Catholics remained poor, both in dollars contributed and number of participants. Only 5 percent of more than one million Los Angeles parishioners subscribed in 1959, and very few large individual gifts were received.[40] The average contribution was small, since a significant proportion of donors were very poor. The poor, more than others, appreciated the Fund's intent, as one individual indicated in his letter to the cardinal in 1967: "Inclosed please find five dollars 5 dollar Bill as my contribution to the Archbishops fund for Charity. . . . I know what it is to be poor and to be with[out] any means, but still I am a little more fortunate than some. I am at least getting Welfare help. . . . But there was a time when I had nothing."[41] Most parishioners, however, accustomed to giving to charity only once a year, did not want another appeal, not even for the Archbishop's Fund. By the 1960s, the Fund's original focus was being lost as applications for financial support poured in from directors of charity institutions and agencies. Although they were receiving United Fund support, they maintained that, since requests for aid exceeded their resources, the Archbishop's Fund ought properly to make up the difference.[42]

Most workers in the diocesan charity collections of the 1920s were volunteers. Catholics were still uncomfortable with the idea of paying professional campaign managers, although the practice was common in nonsectarian charity appeals. Archbishop John Glennon, for example, termed the professional campaign a last resort for the St. Louis archdiocese, a sign of failure in "spontaneous charity." If parishioners would simply give generously in the annual collection, there would be no need for "the drive or campaign for funds."[43] By the 1940s, however, indifferent returns convinced bishops that more professional approaches to fundraising were in order.

Circumstances leading the St. Paul and Minneapolis archdiocese finally to shift from a volunteer-based collection to one directed by a professional fundraising firm were typical of those faced in other dioceses. During the 1960s, approximately 20,000 volunteers had visited every Catholic home in the archdiocese yearly to solicit for the collection. However, the average amount collected per volunteer per year was less than seventeen dollars. Archbishop Leo Byrne, therefore, consulted a professional fundraising firm. It promised him that it could transform his volunteers from amateur into expert collectors, able to "sell" the cause and present various giving options capably. Professional campaign literature and media publicity would prepare "prospects" for visits from volunteers, and appeals would be tailored to the social class of those being solicited. The firm would give high priority to early acquisition of "special gifts" from the wealthy in order to "set the tone of the program and raise it up from the ordinary to the extraordinary."[44] Finally, the volunteers would be instructed to reassure parishioners that their pledges would be painless, representing "a sacrifice of only 'pennies a day.' " By following these strategies, the firm maintained that it could raise $35 million for archdiocesan charities over a ten-year period.

Since the primary objective of professional fundraising firms was to meet or surpass financial targets, they ranked strategies according to their relative effectiveness in advancing that goal. Thus their staffs wooed the rich aggressively, appointing them to campaign committees and encouraging them to sponsor benefits patronized by other rich persons. Since professional firms expected contributions from this group and from local businesses to account together for at least 25 percent of a campaign's goal, they gave extensive publicity to big givers. This did not distress church officials, who averred that it was fully in keeping with tradition. Annual reports of charitable institutions of a century before had regularly included lists of benefactors and the dollar amounts of their gifts. However, an important difference was immediately apparent to grassroots parishioners. Because there were so many independent charitable institutions in urban dioceses of the nineteenth century, and because the benevolent rich typically contributed to a number of these annually, it was virtually impossible to know how much any single individual was giving to church charities in a given year. On the other hand, the public commendation being accorded major donors in modern, professional campaigns seemed to many to be simply an offensive, high-pressure fundraising maneuver. By singling out upper-class donors for so much praise, the church appeared to be exalting the financial contributions of the rich over the more modest gifts of ordinary Catholics.[45]

Catholic understanding of religious charity had traditionally included an expectation that donors would do more than simply give from their surplus. "The phrase 'give until it hurts' should become true in our contributions to our charities," wrote one editor in 1920. "It was on this principle that our institutions were founded. It is on the sacrifices of the present generation that they must be maintained and enlarged."[46] But instead of the message of sacrificial giving, that of "painless giving" was increasingly preached by professional fundraising firms.

Since aggregate returns from professionally conducted campaigns exceeded those from volunteer-managed collections, delighted diocesan officials did not initially pay much attention to another statistic, the proportion of congregants participating in the drives. However, as financial targets of drives became larger, the pledge system had to be relied upon more heavily. This presented a considerable challenge, since pledging had never been popular among Catholics.[47] In the 1960s, Cardinal Richard Cushing of Boston confronted the problem when he inaugurated a "Jubilee Fund Drive" for $50 million. This was the first appeal for so large an amount in the history of the archdiocese, but with a population of about two million Catholics, the target did not seem unreasonable for a major campaign. However, total contributions in cash and pledges reached only $42 million, and, more significantly, only 48 percent of that amount had been received by 1969. Cushing ruefully acknowledged that the drive's heavy reliance on pledges was a serious flaw. "We are now feeling the pinch from some well-intentioned Catholics who made a pledge and have been unable for one reason or another to make payments as promised."[48]

Professional firms challenged Catholic philanthropic traditions in their publicity and literature, as well as in their solicitation techniques. When the J. Walter Thompson Company donated its advertising services for the 1968 Chicago charities campaign, the archdiocese gratefully accepted the gift. The firm proposed that accepted symbols of Catholic charity be replaced by modern, eye-catching literature, an idea that the director of the charitable bureau heartily endorsed. "For years, we have used a photograph of a nun with an orphan," he noted. "We need something a little more shocking to get across our message." The slogan settled on for that year, "Take Abe to Mass," aimed to generate more contributions of at least $5.[49]

The language of efficiency, reform, and civic responsibility increasingly dominated the literature of diocesan charity drives. A 1975 Chicago cover letter and campaign brochure, for example, informed parishioners that only 1 percent of their contributions would be used for administrative expenses and emphasized that, since Catholic Charities assisted all in need, regardless of race or creed, they were fulfilling a civic duty by participating in the drive. However, the campaign materials made no mention of the religious precept to give, Catholic traditions of giving, or why church charities should take priority among Catholics over other good causes. Except for a *pro forma* "May God bless you" in closing, the cover letter did not differ from the appeal of any secular philanthropy.[50] Chicago was by no means exceptional in this regard. The Rockville Centre, Long Island, diocese decided to strike a bicentennial note in its 1976 charity-campaign literature, urging donors to thank God for their freedom and to commemorate the nation's anniversary by sharing their means with those who had less. It touted a dinner-dance for charity as "the greatest social event on Long Island each year" and promised to list donors of more than $200 in the souvenir program. As in the Chicago case, campaign materials nowhere alluded to the religious call to give.[51]

By the 1940s, the annual campaign, whether managed by the diocese itself or by a professional fundraising firm, was the charity fundraising technique of choice. It was by no means always successful, however, as an experience in the Baltimore archdiocese in the late 1940s illustrates. On arriving in the archdiocese in 1947, Archbishop Francis Keough found a seriously inadequate fundraising system. The latest archdiocesan campaign, conducted by the Archbishop's Confraternity of the Laity, had dragged on for two years, although original plans were for a much shorter campaign. Contributions were designated for a comprehensive array of projects, but campaign planners soon realized that they had not taken into account sufficiently the rundown condition of older charitable institutions, a result of deferred maintenance during the war years. Thus, they decided to delay distribution of contributions to designated projects until they had adequate funds in hand to repair the older facilities as well. Parishioners, however, observed only that no charities were benefiting from their contributions in the campaign. They concluded that the money was not going to charity at all and complained vehemently when rumors surfaced that another campaign was in the offing. Clergy and laity alike called for a respite from solicitation and for some tangible evidence that funds already contributed were being used for the purposes for which they had been given. Since dismal contributions in campaigns had forced pastors to make up large shortfalls in quotas from parish revenues, they were as opposed to another drive as their parishioners.[52]

For all these reasons, Archbishop Keough found extraordinarily staunch support when he proposed radical changes in the way the archdiocese raised funds for its charities. He had two basic difficulties with the professional campaign. First, the philosophy behind it seemed to him to violate the meaning of religious charity, because it eliminated personal links between giver and beneficiary. "Charity, I feel, comes from the heart," he explained, "and the hearts of our good people can and will be moved to regard our youth, our orphans, and our aged and infirm as brothers and sisters committed to our loving care by Our Blessed Lord, Himself."[53] Second, he believed that religious giving ought to be spontaneous, and this, of course, was impossible in professional campaigns based on future pledges and parish quotas.

Determined that the 1949 charities appeal would be both religiously rooted and personal, Keough directly challenged prevailing practice. He asked all employed persons to contribute a day's pay, or at least ten dollars, in an archdiocesan collection. The funds contributed would be entirely applied to two very popular causes, a home for Baltimore's orphans and a home for the elderly poor. To ensure that the funds reached their destinations, he promised that only he or his delegate would write checks on the charity-fund account. The ten-day Catholic Charity Fund Collection, set for May 1949, promised to differ markedly from the two previous drives. "It will be an appeal, not a drive," promised Keough, "a personal contribution, not a defined quota; an action, not a promise; an opportunity, not a requisition."[54] In contrast to the large paid staffs of most professional campaigns, the 1949 appeal would have a payroll of only three clerical workers. Lay volunteers would do all the work.

Mainstream citizens, as well as the Catholic population, warmly welcomed Keough's plan. The *Baltimore Sun* editorialized that raising money for charity should not require a vast bureaucracy and a slick hard sell. Straightforward publicity outlining particular needs and explaining how to make contributions for them should suffice. "Why not announce the opportunity and let the public respond without high-powered salesmanship and urging? Archbishop Keough has had the courage and indeed the faith to try the ideal way," the *Sun* concluded.[55] Cash contributions of $658,000 in the 1949 appeal exceeded all expectations, registering 267 percent of the 1948 total.[56] More significant to Keough was the fact that the number of donors was also strikingly higher than in earlier drives. The success of the 1949 Baltimore appeal suggested that parishioners responded more generously to charity appeals that asked them to give immediately, in accord with their means and conscience, than to highly structured campaigns based on quotas and pledges. However, most church leaders by this time were convinced that the scientific approach promised superior results for Catholic charities in the long run. The success of professional fundraising campaigns for secular agencies seemed to them to provide incontrovertible evidence for that position.

Collaboration with mainstream agencies in the provision of social services had accelerated significantly during the World War I years. But bishops remained dubious about the advantages of participating in community fundraising drives, like the community chests, which were appearing in the 1920s. The St. Louis charities bureau in 1923 declined to participate in that city's inaugural community chest drive since it would require modifying approaches that "have long prevailed and have been found generally, very well suited to the needs of the various charities."[57] The bureau's director reflected the Catholic mood generally in his question: "Why should we be changing horses in the middle of the stream?"[58] Within a decade, however, the hardships of the depression years provoked a complete about face. Now the same priest warmly endorsed archdiocesan membership in United Charities, which he termed a "modern, co-operative plan of securing money."[59]

Reliance of Catholic institutions and agencies on community chest funding increased substantially during the 1930s. In financial terms, the charities clearly benefited. At the onset of the Depression, for example, the benevolent society supporting the German St. Vincent's Orphanage in St. Louis had four thousand members. Within a year, its membership had declined by 35 percent, leaving the institution to depend for operating income on a ladies' auxiliary and the community chest. In 1930, returns from Cleveland's diocesan charity collection covered only 10 percent of the $2 million budget of its eighteen charitable agencies. They survived only because the diocesan charities bureau belonged to the city's community fund. In the 1940s, charitable bureaus were routinely participating. Between 1942 and 1948, for example, annual community fund allotments to the

Catholic Charitable Bureau in Boston increased by 56 percent from $147,000 to $229,000. In the latter year, the community chest was providing 90 percent of the funding for New Orleans Catholic Charities and its member child-caring institutions.[60]

The argument that more poor people benefit when Catholic charitable institutions and agencies pursue large government contracts overrode some serious concerns that this course of action could adversely affect the benevolent initiative and generosity of the church membership. By the late 1940s, there already were indications that participation in community chest campaigns had diluted enthusiasm for church charity. "One of the greatest disadvantages has been the falling off of interest on the part of Catholics in their own agencies," reported one observer. "In many cities we now lack that deep, vibrant interest in the welfare of dependent, neglected, and delinquent Catholic children that has been the basis of Catholic Charities for more than a hundred years. . . . In Chest cities there seems to be a lessening of interest in active lay boards in Catholic Charities." He concluded that "easy money from the Chest has made us musclebound."[61]

For charity officials of the 1930s, Catholic participation in community chests proved convincingly that religious and "scientific" charity were fully compatible. Without question, the charitable institutions were in better financial condition than when they had to raise all their funds on their own.[62] Some observers wondered, however, whether this fact, in itself, justified Catholic participation. They suspected that it could negatively affect giving by parishioners, since agencies supported by community chests had to agree to refrain from independent fundraising. This substantially reduced the number of charity raffles, fairs, and bazaars organized and patronized by grassroots laity. At the same time, because community chests funded only the operating costs of institutions, dioceses focused more attention on the wealthy in their search for funds for construction and renovation.[63]

In 1920, funds from subscriptions, donations, legacies, and benefits accounted for 44 percent of the total receipts of the Affiliated Catholic Charities of San Francisco. In 1923, the charity bureau's first year as a member of the local community chest, these private donations comprised 31 percent, and community chest funds 13 percent of total receipts. Although aggregate revenues from all sources were higher in 1923 than in 1920, dollars given in private subscriptions and donations declined absolutely by 13.6 percent. This unsettling fact was overshadowed by delight at the increase in monies from all sources for the charities.[64]

The role of government in promoting the common good came to center stage in the 1930s, as it became very obvious that private benevolence, and state and local resources, could not begin to relieve the unprecedented distress. The hierarchy, through the National Catholic Welfare Conference, formally endorsed massive federal intervention as the only way to effect a speedy economic recovery. Bernard Sheil, auxiliary bishop of Chicago, reminded opponents of government programs that those in need had "an inalienable right" to public assistance and added that if employers had paid fair wages, there would be less need now for either public or private charity. "Those who dare to proclaim these principles . . . have been branded as Communists by many. We might say to them—'If that be Communism, make the most of it.' "[65] Church leaders nonetheless took steps to ensure that new government social programs would not displace private charities. John O'Grady presented the position of the National Conference of Catholic Charities: "Without active support and participation by private agencies, public welfare is liable to become harsh, rigid and even cruel. . . . Any law granting Federal funds to the states for medical care, should provide for the use of not only public but also private agencies in the program."[66]

By the end of the 1930s, most diocesan charitable bureaus were actively pursuing opportunities to collaborate with all levels of government in social welfare programs, since government contracts guaranteed that church charitable facilities would be fully utilized.[67] In 1938, for instance, government contracts and other payments represented 48 percent, the community fund 22 percent, and private contributions 31 percent of the $1.7 million annual income of Chicago's charitable institutions and agencies.[68] In accepting public monies for the support of its charitable institutions and agencies, proponents insisted, the church was in no way rejecting its voluntary benevolent tradition. After all, the charitable institutions had been seeking and accepting state funding for over a century. Extra-ecclesial funds, whether from federal, state, or local government, or from community chests, simply enlarged the scale and quality of Catholic philanthropy. At the same time, by contributing to community chests, Catholics were supporting other private and civic agencies in addition to their own.[69]

The experience of the depression years brought to the fore the place of reform in the definition of religious charity. The hierarchy, in 1940, explicitly linked justice and charity in a call for social and political reform. Now that government at all levels was finally providing welfare programs, more Catholic benevolent resources could be diverted from relief to reform projects. At the same time, the bishops emphasized, justice ought always to be tempered by charity. "Unfortunately there has been a tendency among too many to dissociate the virtue of justice from the virtue of charity, with the result that life has been made even more selfish and heartless. Charity is no substitute for justice, but it cannot be ignored or derided without failing utterly to comprehend its meaning and its potent influence in regulating and sublimating our social relations and responsibilities."[70]

As tax-funded social welfare programs expanded significantly in the 1940s, some laity began to question the need for separate church charities. After all, they were already contributing to the poor through their income taxes. Archbishop Richard Cushing considered this development an ominous sign of advancing socialism: "It is always harder to collect charity dollars—and it becomes increasingly hard, almost to the point of impossible, in a socialist state when so many tax dollars are being collected from the same people to finance increasing state-subsidized and state-controlled community works. . . . The charity dollar, freely given, must lose out to the tax dollar, legally required, and, if need be, taken by force."[71] Others recognized the absolute necessity of government social programs, but called for a reasonable "balance of power" between public and private benevolence. "As the tax dollar increases in quantity," warned an Illinois bishop, "the charity dollar decreases in quantity."[72] John O'Grady predicted that religious philanthropy would soon be narrowed to programs serving the middle class, if the belief spread that the government was solely responsible for the poor.[73]

As diocesan bureaus moved swiftly to collaborate with government agencies in aiding those in need in the 1930s, an alternative response was developing at the grassroots level. In this decade, the traditional understanding of Catholic charity found radical expression in the Catholic Worker Movement. Founded by Peter Maurin and Dorothy Day, it held that government welfare agencies and programs would be unnecessary if private citizens responded as they should to the needs of the poor. Catholic Workers took little satisfaction in the immense number and variety of their church's charitable institutions, since they testified so eloquently to the inequities of "a social order which made so much charity in the present sense of the word necessary."[74]

The first Catholic Worker House of Hospitality opened in New York City in 1934, and, within five years, twenty-four more had been established in the nation's major cities. The houses were resident communities where lay volunteers shared housing, food, material resources, and companionship with the local poor. Houses were autonomous in structure, small, and committed to the avoidance of bureaucracy and the cultivation of a democratic spirit and mutual respect among residents. They served also as forums where reform-minded laity and religious could consider critical social problems and ways to address them. Financial support for the houses came from voluntary donations and from "canvassing" to meet rent and maintenance costs. House residents appealed to local markets and restaurants for food for their breadlines and soup kitchens.[75]

Catholic Worker houses relied on benevolent individuals rather than on diocesan charitable bureaus or government funds for financial support. Explained Dorothy Day: "We do not ask church or state for help, but we ask individuals, those who have subscribed to *The Catholic Worker* and so are evidently interested in what we are doing, presumably willing and able to help. Many a priest and bishop sends help year after year."[76] Catholic Worker houses never adopted professional fundraising strategies, seeing in them evidence that the spirit of religious charity was eroding. The eager acceptance of government funds by Catholic charitable bureaus in the 1920s was, in Dorothy Day's view, wrongheaded: "More and more, they were taking help from the state, and in taking from the state, they had to render to the state. They came under the head of Community Chest and discriminatory charity, centralizing and departmentalizing, involving themselves with bureaus, building, red tape, legislation, at the expense of human values."[77] These trends were a matter of mounting concern to sisterhoods as well, who found themselves conducting more institutions and agencies heavily subsidized by government and community agency monies. Less often were their members addressing critical social needs not yet being met by state or private agencies. Indeed, by the 1960s, they seemed to be concentrated in "tasks no longer clearly needed."[78]

Despite such concerns, bishops continued to encourage diocesan charitable bureaus to apply for government and community agency funding. These monies, they argued, allowed them to apply a larger share of contributions in charity collections to projects that could garner no extra-ecclesial support. Given that the chief means bishops have to acquire financial resources for diocesan and national causes has always been to order special collections in the parishes, their perspective is understandable. In 1873, New York Catholics were giving annually to five archdiocesan collections and one national collection. These were in addition to regular Sunday collections for parish support. The special collections included an archdiocesan collection for the poor; an Easter collection for the orphans; a Christmas collection for the orphans; a collection to liquidate the archdiocesan orphanage debt; a collection for seminarians; and the Peter's Pence collection, a national appeal introduced in 1866 to benefit the Vatican. A representative parish was that of St. Vincent de Paul in Brooklyn where, in 1873, contributions to the special collections totaled about $2,700. Of that sum, 70 percent went to orphans and their needs, 13 percent to the poor, 8 percent to the support of seminarians, and 9 percent to the pope.[79]

By 1930, the special collections numbered six; two were for diocesan needs, four for extra-diocesan causes. Diocesan collections were for local charities and for the diocesan seminary. In addition to the Peter's Pence collection, the national collections included one for the Home and Foreign Missions, another for the support of the church in the Holy Land, and a third for the Catholic University of America. Episcopal conferences regularly discussed the progress of the national collections, but early-twentieth-century bishops, caught up in funding their own diocesan projects and protective of their autonomy, often gave them only cursory attention. When, for example, Cardinal James Gibbons of Baltimore, dean of the American hierarchy, pressed his colleague, Thomas Beaven of the Springfield, Massachusetts, diocese, to remit returns from the 1915 collection for the Catholic University, Beaven replied that he had suspended that particular collection for a while in favor of local charities. His response had a typically provincial character: "I do not believe it will be of any harm to the University.—The Collection was [not] growing at all with our people—and they gave as niggardly as they give for the Pope's Collection."[80] A Pennsylvania pastor gave a similar report: "I always 'whoop it up' for the Annual collection for the University. But my congregation, composed almost exclusively of farmers, does not seem interested in higher education. And mores [sic] the pity. I am simply stating a fact."[81]

At their 1919 annual meeting, the bishops returned to the intractable question of how to raise more funds for missions, especially those among African Americans and Indians. At that time, the Catholic Church Extension Society served as the collecting agency for domestic missions, while the Society for the Propagation of the Faith played a similar role for the foreign missions. In addition, numerous benevolent associations and religious orders collected independently for specific missionary enterprises. The hierarchy decided that donations to the annual national mission collection would increase appreciably if all mission appeals were brought under its direct control. To this end, a governing board of bishops was formed to oversee fundraising and to distribute the funds collected. Henceforth, the laity would be solicited for the missions only once a year in the national collection. While foreign missionaries might still preach, they could not collect funds in the parishes for their work without episcopal permission.[82]

The expectation that this consolidation would inspire larger contributions to the missions did not materialize, and the financial situation of southern and western dioceses continued to deteriorate. Therefore, in 1927, the bishops agreed to establish in each diocese a Society for the Home and Foreign Missions. Adult subscriptions were ten cents monthly, or $1 per year. The rate for children was half that of adults. These subscriptions would supplement contributions in the annual mission collection.[83] Of total receipts from both sources,

60 percent would go to the Society for the Propagation of the Faith for foreign missions and 40 percent to the American Board of Catholic Missions for home missions. This restructuring did not evoke any substantial increase in support of the missions, and the national collection continued to languish. Josephite priests, responsible for 140 churches and 80 parish schools in African American parishes, benefited in the 1950s from the national mission collection, from funding by the American Board of Catholic Missions, and from scattered contributions from dioceses. Together, however, these sources provided only ten percent of the annual cost of their work. Yet many Catholics took offense when the Josephites appealed to them for contributions. The superior general of the order described a typical response at this time: "The writer asked why we seek financial help in view of the fact that only the previous week there had been the annual collection for the Negro and Indian Missions."[84]

In response to international distress accompanying World War II, the American bishops established, in 1943, the War Relief Services, soon renamed the Catholic Relief Services of the National Catholic Welfare Conference.[85] A new annual national collection for the Bishops' Relief Fund funded the work. Catholic Relief Services collaborates closely with the government and with other private agencies in distributing food, medicines, and supplies in the wake of wars and natural disasters. Although initially focused on relief, it now provides strong support for self-help community projects in underdeveloped countries. The world's largest relief and development agency, it reported a total program value of $286 million in 1992. Over 75 percent of its funding comes from federal agencies.[86] While this allows it to provide far more services than reliance on private charitable contributions alone would permit, it also introduces a danger that the government will enjoy more influence than the Catholic community in determining Catholic Relief Services program priorities.

The Campaign for Human Development addresses the same issues, but on the domestic level. A national collection instituted in 1969, it supports self-help projects among low income groups. More than most of the national collections, it has aroused lay interest because, from its inception, it has allowed each diocese to retain 25 percent of the collection for local poverty projects. The campaign has awarded more than $175 million to several thousand projects since 1971, and recent collections average about $12 million, making it third highest of the twelve national collections. Its funding of local, congregation-based projects has steadily increased over the years, representing 35 percent of grants in 1992.[87]

The annual diocesan-wide charity appeal that had replaced most independent institutional fundraising by the 1940s had several untoward outcomes. First, heavy emphasis on financial donations in diocesan and national collections weakened traditional Catholic appreciation of voluntary service as philanthropy. Second, centralized fundraising reversed a highly personal approach to giving and reduced lay participation in the distribution of charitable monies. Third, while the single collection brought welcome relief from constant solicitation by individual charities, it was deleterious to the local autonomy of these institutions and agencies. By the mid-1980s, strict rules governed all forms of charitable fundraising. Illustrative was Green Bay, Wisconsin, where no agency could collect funds or advertise independently. The Diocesan Services Appeal would do the former and the diocesan communications department the latter.[88]

Although the parish remained, as in the past, the basic structural unit for fundraising, by the 1940s pastors and parishioners had little discretion in raising and distributing charity funds, and their segregation from the charitable agencies was nearly total. The director of Chicago's Catholic Charities reported gloomily at that time that the average parishioner knew little about the largest private philanthropic agency in greater Chicago.[89]

The very rich, who gave individually, endowed institutions, and set up charitable foundations, and the Catholic Workers, who challenged the injustices of the existing social order in inner-city neighborhoods, had at least one common characteristic. Both maintained autonomy in benevolence by operating outside diocesan structures. The vast majority of Catholics, however, who endeavored to continue their traditional support of charitable institutions and programs, were far less successful in maintaining a personal focus in their philanthropy. In consequence, their willingness to fund church charities began to fade. Veteran missionary and fundraiser Bishop Harold Henry aptly expressed their position when he advised a friend in the 1970s: "I have found that people do not like to donate to a *general* fund, but to specific projects; so they know where their money is going."[90]

6

Social Class and Ways of Giving

If a strong supernatural motive of charity does not inform the various types of welfare activity these degenerate into bureaucracy or into mere good will performances.

—John LaFarge, 1955

CATHOLICS AGREED MORE often early in the nineteenth century than later upon the best approaches to religious giving. In the 1840s, they still carefully distinguished their benevolence from humanitarianism, which they defined as giving by the middle and upper classes. Their charity, they insisted, was more democratic, since parishioners of all social classes united to support the good works of their church. Because they came at greater personal sacrifice, the offerings of the poor received special recognition. Directors of St. John's Orphanage in Philadelphia expressed a mid-century consensus when they noted in 1845 that although individual bequests that year were small, "yet are those small sums in the eyes of God fully equal to thousands given by others."[1] Rapid changes in American society and in the church community itself soon tested that perception in critical ways.

Women continued to take responsibility for the organization of charity fairs: renting large halls, assigning positions for "fancy tables," and arranging flower tables, refreshment stands, and post offices. Patrons purchased food and enjoyed music while shopping at booths offering needlework and household items. The booths collectively raised the most money, but the sale of chances for large prizes generated substantial revenue as well. Fair organizers of the 1850s stressed that all, even the very poor, could help support Catholic charity simply by purchasing a ten-cent admission ticket. Since the fair usually continued for some days, those working long hours had a chance to enjoy its entertainments at least once. Fair attendance increased in proportion to the value of prizes offered. While the grand prize at an 1862 Milwaukee fair was a depiction of Peter the Great and his mother, embroidered by the orphans, by 1870 it was a $600 piano. The 1889 fair, offering a grand prize of a $400 horse and 240 acres of land,

lasted ten days and attracted approximately forty thousand citizens of every religious denomination.

While the charity fair of the 1850s was a relatively modest event, by the
1870s it had become, in many cases, a mammoth affair. Large aggregations of
Catholics still provoked occasional confrontations with other citizens. A crowd
of thousands attending a drawing to benefit a New York children's home led
distressed neighbors to demand that police disperse the gathering. The crowd
cried bigotry and ignored police orders to disperse. Only an order from the
priest directing the event brought reluctant compliance. The publicity attending
the incident generated national sympathy in Catholic communities, but upper-
class parishioners were chagrined. Boisterous crowds of poor and working-class
fair goers increasingly embarrassed upper-class Catholics, and they complained
that intemperance, gambling, and dancing at the fairs were demeaning the
church before the wider society.[2]

Charity appeals by bishops generally took the impersonal form of sermons
before large congregations or circular letters read in the churches. However,
when the bishops participated actively and personally in charity fundraising
events, attendance and financial returns escalated. St. Paul's bishop, John Ireland, for example, organized a group of his clerical friends in 1885, to collect
attractive prizes for a Minneapolis fair to aid a boys' orphanage. At this news,
sales of chances immediately soared, and public bidding by prominent citizens
for such treasures from the bishop's trove as a $200 silver service became the
highlight of the fair. Criticisms from some wealthy laity that charity fairs were
too time consuming, and that their net proceeds did not warrant the expenditures for materials, advertisements, and facilities' rental that they entailed, were
readily controverted. Aggregate funds raised for charity by this vehicle sur-
passed the record of all others. For most of the 1880–1920 period, for instance,
the annual income of the archdiocese of Milwaukee was lower than the annual
proceeds of local charity fairs.[3]

Charity directors recognized the importance of reaching ordinary parishioners in their appeals for support, since wealthy donors were scarce. Given the
charity fair's immense popular appeal, it continued despite upper-class distaste
for it. "The masses must ever be the main support of all charitable institutions,"
observed one editor in the 1850s. "Ten gifts of a hundred dollars, making a thousand dollars, sounds large, but forty thousand quarters of a dollar tells [sic] a
bigger story." Ordinary parishioners should not be denied the chance to meet
their charitable obligation by engaging in "a season of pleasant and innocent
recreation, at the Fair, in the Music Hall, in viewing the rare collection of articles
of value, beauty and curiosity, which [they] may not be able to purchase."[4]

Because of their unwillingness to rub elbows with the lower classes, very wealthy parishioners were avoiding charity fairs and bazaars by the 1870s. Directors of charitable institutions, unwilling to lose the financial contributions of these individuals, encouraged them to organize separate benefits for members of their social class. At St. Joseph's Orphanage in Washington, D.C., for example, working-class supporters conducted pound parties where, in return for their gifts of food, lard, sugar, or salt, they were entertained by the orphans with songs and recitations. Well-to-do patrons of the same institution raised funds by holding an annual Thanksgiving Ball that by the 1880s had become one of the city's most glittering social events.[5]

In raising funds for capital expansion projects, wealthy supporters of charitable institutions were, by the 1870s, modifying the usual subscription appeal. Rather than solicit subscriptions door-to-door, which they considered a waste of valuable time, they simply formed a committee, established a financial goal, and agreed that each committee member would pledge to raise a fraction of the total by making a personal contribution and by soliciting among his friends and business acquaintances as well.[6] Hailed as a "new departure" in Catholic philanthropy, this innovation did not reduce institutional reliance on charity fairs. The number of wealthy Catholics in any large city was still small, relative to the number of charity institutions. Thus while wealthy prospective benefactors might respond favorably to an institution's appeal for funds, they were just as likely to refuse to assist it at all.

Cultivation of grassroots supporters, therefore, remained essential, and managers of charity institutions not only engaged them in fundraising events that offered lively entertainment for young and old, but also called on parishioners routinely for gifts of service and material supplies. Sisters would simply call attention to some modest institutional need, and local parishioners would organize to meet it. For instance, in the 1870s, Little Sisters of the Poor pointed out that their Washington, D.C. home for the elderly indigent lacked a garden. One hundred men contributed labor, materials, and the use of forty horses and remedied the deficiency in a week.[7]

At its 1866 meeting, the American hierarchy decided to prohibit charity dances, "which, as at present carried on, are revolting to every feeling of delicacy and propriety, and are fraught with the greatest danger to morals."[8] The bishops relied on pastors to enforce the ban. A minority complied zealously. For example, a charity ball organized by Irish immigrants in Sumter, South Carolina, at this time came to an abrupt halt once the parish priest heard that it was underway. Reported an eyewitness: "Lo! he suddenly appeared in the midst of the fun loving crowd and scattered them with a whirl of his stick."[9] Since, for the most part, pastors simply disregarded the edict, the bishops took up the matter again at the Baltimore Council of 1884. Once more they forbade parish dances for charity fundraising. However, in enforcing the regulation in their own dioceses, most of them routinely excepted the upper-class charity ball from the rule.

This distinction irritated those who opposed such events on principle. While dances sponsored by the rich might raise money, they argued, from a religious standpoint that was not a good reason to approve them. In fact, these dances testified more to the urgent need for reform than to a vigorous benevolent spirit. "In the charity ball money is raised for noble purposes; but there is an incongruous combination effected when the gay and well-dressed and well-nourished must have pleasure out of the money that is destined to procure help for the suffering and the hopeless."[10] Critics also had difficulty reconciling a fundraising strategy that purposely excluded most parishioners with the democratic values of traditional approaches. Whatever their shortcomings, fairs and bazaars welcomed patrons of every social class. Exclusive balls and parties, they objected, were distressingly Protestant in tone and just as much "charity with a hook" as charity fairs. The benevolent wealthy strongly disagreed. Elegant balls and lawn parties allowed them to support charity institutions in ways appropriate to their position in society. At the same time, the favorable publicity such refined events engendered served only to enhance the prestige and influence of the church. Although the growing popularity of exclusive charity events signaled a hardening of class distinctions within the church community, Catholics of every social class were still in agreement on benevolent priorities. The elegant ball and the working-class fair alike were to benefit institutions serving the poor.[11]

More bishops of the 1870s recognized that the roots of sluggish giving by upper-class parishioners lay not simply in their dislike for noisy charity fairs and picnics, but also in their minority status within a heavily poor and working-class church. Therefore, besides encouraging them to sponsor their own charity projects, many bishops also endorsed the establishment of exclusive clubs. These organizations would not only strengthen the ties of the rich to the church, but would also improve the public profile of the church community. "It is important that the position of the Church socially should be one of influence," Archbishop Patrick Ryan told members of the Catholic Club of Philadelphia in the 1890s, "and this can be best effected by a united body of lay Catholic gentlemen such as in your Club."[12] When this club was founded in 1876, pioneer officers worried about attracting members, since affluent laymen showed little interest in activities not directly related to their financial or social progress.[13] However, despite relatively high annual dues of twelve dollars, club membership stood at 172 within a decade. Male clubs like this one had appeared in every major city by 1900, offering cultural, intellectual, and social opportunities to members and sponsoring balls, concerts, and lectures that raised large sums for local church charities. Since the charity ball was their most popular benevolent project, some male clubs took the politically expedient step of admitting women. When the Catholic Philopatrian Literary Institute in Philadelphia held its first annual charity ball in 1879, it also admitted its first female members. The event was soon a major social event, attracting several thousand guests who happily paid five dollars for ordinary seats, more for box and special seats.[14]

Exclusive men's clubs, and a few large fraternal societies that were developing at this time, carefully screened the socioeconomic backgrounds of applicants for membership. A description of the Knights of Columbus typifies the social boundaries of these associations at the turn of the century: "The ranks are being cautiously recruited from among the educated and more fortunate, and the intellectual and social standard is confessedly the highest of the secular societies of gentlemen. It is understood that the Chicago Knights will not have to go out of their own ranks for orators, amateur musicians, athletes, or thinkers and executants in any of the arts or pastimes that make refined life polished and restful."[15]

Although an 1877 bylaw of the Catholic Club of Philadelphia had given the local archbishop the right to distribute the proceeds of club charity events, the membership, intent on protecting its financial independence and decision-making authority, had revoked this clause by the 1890s. As dioceses undertook to consolidate their charities in the 1920s, bishops encouraged male fraternal societies and elite clubs to channel their benevolent work through the new charitable bureaus. They met with little success. When, for example, Archbishop Mundelein of Chicago wrote to each member of the local Catholic Order of Foresters for donations to the 1920 archdiocesan charity collection, fewer than one percent responded. A luncheon meeting with the same agenda, arranged for Forester officers and diocesan charity leaders, was similarly unproductive. "All engagements for said luncheon were broken."[16]

The St. Vincent de Paul Society had, from its establishment in the 1840s, counted some very wealthy men among its most active members. However, the society's requirement that members contribute anonymously to its benevolent works, its intensely spiritual focus, and its class heterogeneity in membership had become stumbling blocks for many rich men by the 1870s. The exclusive men's clubs, on the other hand, promised them applause and publicity for their individual benefactions and congenial fellowship among others of their social class. Unlike the St. Vincent de Paul Society, personal visitation of the poor found no place on their charitable agendas.[17]

Working-class and poor Catholics continued, as in the past, to give anonymously in parish collections and to support the many fundraising fairs and picnics held by the charitable institutions. A Protestant writer attending a Sunday mass in a large New York City parish in the 1860s observed that "at the usual time the collection was taken, to which few gave more than a cent, but to which *every one* gave a cent."[18] Debates in the 1870s over the relative generosity of working-class Irish and Germans were common among the clergy but generally inconclusive. According to James Roosevelt Bayley, archbishop of Baltimore, the voluntary system of American church support did not work nearly so well with the Irish as with the Germans, where "no one individual gives much. But all give."[19]

On the other hand, his contemporary, English missionary Peter Benoit, found the Irish, on the whole, to be very generous. He conceded that they might not give as regularly as the Germans, but when they did give, their contributions were usually larger. Contrary to prevailing impression, he reported that they responded warmly to his appeals for former slaves. As an example, he recorded in his diary an 1875 encounter with an Irish immigrant: "On Sunday-afternoon an intelligent working man called on me & insisted on my accepting a dollar 'tho he had only two in his possession, owing to the slackness of trade. Who c'd be hard on the faults of Erin's children, when you find such self-denying generosity among them!"[20] On the advice of a Philadelphia pastor, Benoit took up his collections for the African American cause himself. This somewhat coercive approach had good results. "He was right," related Benoit. "A few people let the plate pass, but evidently it was only because they had it not. I rec'd $370, a large sum from a scanty congregation."[21] Benoit's assessment of Irish benevolence was more commonly heard than Bayley's. Reports from pastors of Irish parishes at this time reveal a generous people. Members of a Pittsburgh parish, for example, were contributing, on average, about 10 percent of their incomes in Sunday collections and "extraordinary fundraising projects."[22]

In most parts of the country, wealthy Catholics of the 1870s still did not enjoy the same social status as their mainstream counterparts. Exceptions were residents of California, who had participated fully in business, the professions, and politics since the mid-nineteenth century, and those living in traditional Catholic strongholds like Baltimore, New Orleans, and St. Louis. Eager for mainstream acceptance and vastly outnumbered by poor and working-class co-religionists, the rich sought to give in ways that would, as they put it, "give dignity, decorum, and stability to our institutions, elevate and refine our social tone, and add a becoming splendor to our civilization."[23]

Until the 1840s, most rich Catholics had made their fortunes themselves. Their working-class roots led them to share the charitable perspectives of other Catholics. But the proportion of the upper class born into wealthy families was already growing rapidly by the 1850s. These individuals had never experienced deprivation or had personal contact with the poor. They responded with much more alacrity to personal appeals for assistance from bishops than they did to charity sermons and episcopal letters addressed to the entire church community. Archbishop John Hughes, seeking funds for the construction of St. Patrick's cathedral in the 1850s, recognized and acted on this characteristic. Separating wealthy New Yorkers into three groups according to their estimated income, he drafted letters requesting donations of $1000, $500, and $250, respectively, and sent one, personally signed, to each person on his list. The *Atlantic Monthly* editorialized tartly on the $300,000 that poured in: "Such requests are never made without due consideration, and they are seldom refused. Nor is the church too particular as to *whose* money it shall accept. . . . All is fish that comes to the church's net."[24] Hughes's successor, John McCloskey, also took a personal approach to acquiring $100,000 to complete the cathedral roof before the winter months of 1875. He invited 100 wealthy men to a special luncheon and presented his case. Each guest, flattered to have been included in so exclusive a gathering, forthwith contributed $1,000.[25]

McCloskey's Baltimore colleague and contemporary, James Bayley, was notorious for his enterprising techniques in soliciting the wealthy. "He was ever aiming not at the sparrows but at rich game," observed Canon Benoit. "He w'd try to interest his hearers by every means serious & jocose." For example, he would bestow his own portrait on very generous donors and record every contribution received in one of the two books he carried with him everywhere. "He w'd present his red book wh contained only big subscribers; when made aware that they intended to offer but a small subscription, he brought out his black book wh was, he said, for the poorer."[26]

One perennially popular way for the rich to acquire social standing, at least within the Catholic community, was to channel their benevolence through the religious orders. These "intermediaries between rich and poor," as John Ireland described them, accepted only nominal salaries, so donors could feel certain that their benefactions would really reach the poor. At the same time, since religious communities were permanent societies, gifts to support their work assumed a timeless quality. "An organization endures," Ireland explained, "the individual drops from the ranks—his place is quickly filled; there is no interruption in the task of mercy."[27] This approach also allowed donors a highly valued opportunity to collaborate closely with superiors of the religious orders. In the 1870s, for example, William Shakespeare Caldwell worked out, in extended meetings with Louisville Sisters of Charity, every detail of what "will suit you and me" for a charity hospital he was planning to build and finance. Despite their reservations about the bishop's reaction, Caldwell pledged them to secrecy about the project and informed the bishop only after all arrangements were completed.[28]

While middle-class laywomen of the 1870s joined benevolent societies and auxiliaries, upper-class women were more likely to carry out their charity work independently. Philadelphian Emma Bouvier Drexel was exemplary of women of her class. She conducted an extensive social service project from her home, distributing money to the poor three times weekly for necessities like rent, food, fuel, and clothing. She managed the enterprise "scientifically," insisting that reform was a "higher charity" than simple almsgiving. More than sixty years later, Katharine Drexel recalled her mother's benevolent approach: "She employed someone to go around and visit the poor and she (the woman employed) made a report to my mother. If the report were favorable and the woman had given the person a ticket, the ticket could be presented to my mother in person. . . . My mother would try to devise means of giving the needed help right then and there—a grocery order or an order for coal or rent, or shoes. . . . Everything given out was noted down in a book, so that Mama knew if the same need was brought to her again very soon it was because the right use had not been made of the thing given before. . . . In this way, Mama took a personal interest in them."[29] To encourage her three daughters to view philanthropy as a privilege rather than a duty, Drexel allowed them to assist her "only on condition that any alms they might give, or anything they might do should be done only at the cost of personal sacrifice from their own funds."[30] These early lessons in giving influenced the adult priorities of the Drexel women and, in consequence, vitally affected the course of Catholic philanthropy.

Like their wives, benevolent upper-class men of the 1860s and 1870s also took literally the admonition to contribute voluntary service as well as money to the poor. They sat on institutional boards and offered extensive professional counsel without charge to bishops and superiors of religious orders. New York building and railroad contractor John Crimmins typifies these men. He began his charity work at the time of his marriage in the 1870s. With his wife he gave to homes for working girls, distributed food to the local poor, and organized charity balls. Widowed by 1888, he took very seriously his duty to encourage a spirit of religious altruism in his eleven children. A diary entry for Christmas Day, 1888, reveals a hands-on approach: "At noon with Miss Julie, my dear children, Susy, Lily, Mary-Christine, John, Martin and Tom we called on Sister M. Irene at the Foundling Asylum. We then visited the Little Sisters of the Poor. We aided the good Sisters in waiting on the old people at dinner, 135 old men and 160 old women. My daughters and sons were furnished with white aprons and attentively served the dishes prepared by the good sisters."[31]

As the number of upper-class parishioners increased after the Civil War, the concept of Christian stewardship was more often incorporated into charity sermons, and pastoral letters reminded the rich that their financial assets were only lent to them by God as "traveling money" for life.[32] Bernard McQuaid, bishop of Rochester, New York, typically warned that "it is a presumptuous assertion that a man's money is his own, and that he can do with it what he likes."[33] Appeals from charitable institutions also promised that by giving "a small portion of his means" the rich individual could "sanctify the remainder of his wealth."[34] Some wealthy parishioners waited until death to contribute to religious causes. However, there was little admiration for those who gave only through bequests. The practice reflected miserliness more than benevolence, since the donors were sharing their resources only when they could no longer enjoy them themselves.[35]

By the early twentieth century, however, major financial contributions, rather than voluntary service, were looked for from the very rich, and bishops everywhere knew that they would not be forthcoming without considerable personal cultivation. Archbishop Patrick Riordan of San Francisco advised a colleague in 1912 that he would discover that there was abundant money available if he simply approached the rich properly: "I have been so many years collecting money for churches and institutions of all kinds that I have come to the conclusion there is no way of getting it except by a personal appeal to those who have it, and that appeal coming from the lips of an enthusiastic speaker."[36]

Making these personal contacts was not always easy, however, as one Colorado bishop pointed out at this time. The church focused too heavily on building up the eastern dioceses, he maintained, and the western church was suffering as a result. Bishops of geographically huge dioceses with scattered congregations could not possibly cultivate the very rich to the extent required for major gifts. As a result, these Catholics were drifting to secular philanthropies. "Poor Denver diocese! In the last six months four Denver Catholic millionaires died. Any one of them would have paid the Cathedral debt of $250,000, if some respected American bishop were bishop of Denver. They left nothing to the Church. . . . One of them, a monthly communicant left $15,000,000."[37]

Social ambition drove the giving decisions of millionaires, as well as the simply rich. Steel industrialist Charles Schwab, for example, already a major donor, informed his bishop that if the church would lift its ban on freemasonry he would become far more generous. "If she would do so, I would think nothing of giving a million dollars to the Catholic University," he told John Shanahan in 1915. "I am not a Mason, and I do not believe in Masonry, but the plain truth is that few men in this country can climb to the top of the social ladder unless they are Masons."[38]

Gender differences in benevolent priorities and styles became more pronounced over time. Diocesan leaders eagerly sought contributions from wealthy women for special diocesan projects, but were far less likely to include them in regular discussions of charity policy and strategy. As a result, wealthy men, in general, became increasingly interested in supporting boys' schools, churches, and seminaries, while women of the same economic class continued to favor charity institutions, especially those benefiting women and girls. The wills of two Pennsylvanians of the 1870s illustrate these divergent preferences. Catherine Madary left her fortune to establish a local girls' orphanage, whereas Thomas Cahill gave $1 million to found a free high school for boys.[39]

Because they preferred to support large projects that would attract public notice to their philanthropy, rich individuals took less interest than lower-class parishioners in the success of routine charity collections.[40] Community recognition was more likely to accompany large gifts to local charities than those made for distant causes. Thus their benevolence not only began at home but usually ended there as well. They agreed with the observation that "the duty of each individual is to do what he can for the benefit of those who are within the sphere of his own efforts or influence. Let him pay attention to his own dependents, and to the poor and suffering who are immediately around him."[41] The expectation of accolades and church honors in return for large financial donations had become a matter of considerable discussion within the church by the turn of the century. If ordinary parishioners were asked to give in accord with their means without looking for personal public commendation, why should the rich demand such recognition for their gifts?

The propensity of socially ambitious laity for civic causes that seemed to promise a more direct route to mainstream recognition than church charities escalated in the late nineteenth century. St. Vincent de Paul Society men denounced as social climbers those who justified their support of secular philanthropic causes and neglect of church charities with the dictum that true charity recognizes no denominational boundaries. "Every virtue is essentially denominational, every virtue is essentially Catholic," they admonished, "and, if you wish to practice that virtue in its true spirit, you cannot go outside of the pale of the One, Holy, Catholic and Apostolic Church to do it."[42] Bishops, too, were troubled by the growing readiness of upper-class Catholics to accept rather than challenge secular benevolent values. Some, like Bishop James O'Connor of Omaha, begged upper-class Catholics to witness to the radical meaning of religious philanthropy. He argued, in 1889, that rich Catholics should concentrate their philanthropy on very poor groups whom church and society alike were ignoring. "Do not help colleges or schools for people who are able to pay for their own education, or whom, if poor, the congregations to which they belong should educate," he told the young millionaire, Katharine Drexel. "The greatest charity will be to go in search of those in whom even the Catholic public cannot be brought to feel an interest or a sufficiently strong interest to provide adequately for them."[43]

Nearly two decades later, John Glennon of St. Louis was, in somewhat milder tones, raising the same question. He did not object if very rich Catholics supported educational, cultural, and civic causes. However, he informed them, their religion called on them to do more than other citizens at their income level. "Let our millionaires found their universities and end on them—they are philanthropists. Let them aid the cities by giving libraries, so that man may read. Let them reward the brave and protect the scientific, and blaze and broaden the pathway of knowledge with their patronage and their money, tainted or otherwise. It is well. But is it enough?"[44]

Wealthy laity joined the debate. John Fitzgerald, a prominent Catholic and mayor of Boston, compared the philanthropic values of the rich with those of the poor in a major speech in 1910. He emphasized that the poor give higher proportions of their incomes to charity, give anonymously, and give faithfully throughout their lives. In contrast, too many rich laity flagrantly disregard these essential principles of Catholic giving.[45] The hierarchy and clergy were somewhat less sanguine than Fitzgerald about the benevolence of the poor and working class at this time. They agreed with him that grassroots parishioners, on the whole, gave more liberally, relative to their means, than did the rich, but this did not necessarily mean that as a group they were unusually altruistic. An Indiana pastor's assessment was widely shared: "Less than one half of our Catholic people support religion in any form, if we except the nickel or dime which they drop in the collection basket when attending Mass on Sunday." He conceded that "the one-half which does not contribute is better able to do so than the one-half which does."[46] With a few notable exceptions, wealthy Catholics continued to give in charity collections as though they were still members of the working class. An annoyed William O'Connell declared that he knew at least one hundred Bostonians who could give five thousand dollars annually and not miss it as much as a poor woman would miss a gift of twenty-five cents a year. Yet she gave, while they did not. "So rare is it to find money left to charity that it is always published as news. We have come to expect little from the rich."[47]

As class differences within the church widened, diocesan officials saw little choice but to accommodate the need of the rich for public acclaim for their benefactions. Thus, after 1900, a variety of church honors and extensive press coverage typically accompanied very large donations. Rich givers actively sought and used honorary titles, and soon every diocese boasted its corps of titled parishioners. Millionaire Martin Maloney was addressed as "Marquis Maloney" after receiving his papal title in 1903. And "Count John Creighton" was both a Count of the Holy Roman Empire and a Knight of St. Gregory. Rich women, too, like "Duchess Genevieve Garvan Brady" and "Countess Annie Leary," reveled in papal titles that accompanied their large financial contributions. In the late 1920s, the Knights of Malta, an international charitable order and the most socially prestigious lay organization in the church, opened its membership to Americans and soon was tapping major donors for its exclusive ranks.[48]

As titles and decorations proliferated, the merits of anonymous giving, still presented in press and pulpit as the Catholic ideal, became decidedly unfashionable in upper-class circles. Rather than name the charitable institutions they financed in honor of patron saints, as had been past custom, donors now preferred to name them for themselves. Prospector John Judge's widow, for example, endowed the Judge Mercy Home and Hospital for Miners in Salt Lake City in 1910. And Josephine Bradburn DeJonghe of Chicago a few years later bequeathed her fortune for several homes for needy women and children, each to be called the Josephine Bradburn DeJonghe Memorial. Such practices spread quickly, despite reproaches that they were self-aggrandizing. "Under the mask of charity, philanthropy has masqueraded among us," thundered one critic. "The man who donates millions to found libraries, to endow institutions, to erect monuments to himself is impelled by philanthropic purposes. The world sees all that he does. Indeed, this is made a condition for the benefactions conferred. The Christian ideal is to bestow charity lavishly but to screen it from the public eye."[49]

Press reports about large benefactions by wealthy Catholics to civic and other secular causes increased in the early twentieth century, prompting church leaders to ask why these individuals were not giving generously in the new diocesan charity collections. They proposed several possible explanations. First, the rich craved public notice, and this was more likely to be satisfied by secular philanthropies. "Every dollar must pander to their egoism or their vanity." Second, the rich did not view their duty toward diocesan charities as "just as binding as church-building and paying the salary of the pastor." Finally, the rich had convinced themselves that by donating to mainstream causes they were doing more good than by contributing to church charities that they judged to be less efficiently managed.[50]

They agreed that the first explanation was by far the most important. The tradition of anonymous giving held no weight with the very rich, and the old custom of making large undesignated bequests for diocesan needs was rapidly losing ground as well. Eliza Andrews of Baltimore, who in 1913 bequeathed most of her $1.2 million estate to Cardinal James Gibbons for application, at his discretion, to archdiocesan needs, was already exceptional.[51] Even donors willing to give to diocesan charities wanted to earmark their gifts for specific institutions, monitor their disposition, and receive public acknowledgement for them. As these inclinations were not readily accommodated by new diocesan charitable bureaus, the benevolent rich continued to contribute liberally to civic causes, but did not increase their giving to church charities. George Mundelein of Chicago reminded them in 1918 that giving to church charities offered more lasting rewards than other types of benevolence: "It is perhaps simple to perpetuate one's memory by giving a library or endowing a university, but to take a boy from the street-corner and from temptation, give him a chance which he may not have had, set him right and show him how when he has made just one youthful mistake,—that means writing one's name in letters of gold in the register where neither time nor eternity will ever blot it out."[52]

Neither Mundelein nor his colleagues in other dioceses discussed publicly a critical reason for the apathy of the wealthy toward the diocesan charities, namely, clerical dominance of leadership roles. By the 1920s most dioceses instructed laity that the approved way to support the charities was to give generously in the annual diocesan charity collection. At the same time, policy decisions about the charitable institutions and agencies and the distribution of all contributions in the annual collection henceforth would rest with diocesan authorities. Such "reforms" did not sit well with the very rich who had long enjoyed complete independence in contributing their money and counsel to their favorite charitable institutions. Behind the scenes, diocesan officials struggled to accommodate class differences in drafting public appeals for annual charity collections. "It is not fair either to the poor or to the rich to put them all on the same plane in our annual appeal for charitable assistance," acknowledged William O'Connell in 1916. "Besides the little donation usually contributed by all alike to the annual collection, those who have abundant and even superabundant means may well be expected to give proportionately."[53] As specialization benefited American business, so it should benefit charity, O'Connell argued. If the middle and upper classes gave generously of their relatively abundant resource, money, and the poor and working classes gave of their relatively abundant resource, voluntary service, then diocesan charities would be amply sustained. For O'Connell, the sisterhoods and upper-class laity represented polar examples of these benevolent roles. With no monetary resources, sisters gave generously of their time in voluntary service. Most of the rich, however, rather than giving generously of their fortunes, continued "to dole out the same half-penny alms of earlier days."[54]

O'Connell's assignment of benevolent responsibilities according to income level marked most diocesan charity appeal literature of the 1920s. In a heavily working-class church, it put the affluent on notice that their monetary contributions ought to correspond to their income levels. But by linking contributions of voluntary service to income level, it gave a second, less constructive message, one that challenged a fundamental principle of Catholic charity. It suggested that, as laity advanced to the middle and upper classes, they might legitimately reduce, even eliminate, their gift of voluntary service relative to their gift of money. This interpretation ran counter to traditional understanding that gifts of money without voluntary service did not fully satisfy the religious mandate to give.

A practical problem, how to incorporate some autonomy for rich givers within the diocesan charity organization, remained. Bishops usually adopted a two-fold strategy. First, they personally assured the very rich that they could designate their contributions in the annual charity collection for their favorite charitable institutions. At the same time, they made every effort to enlist them as special associates in diocesan projects. In archdiocesan charity collections of the 1920s in Boston, for example, the cardinal urged all parishioners to give as much as they could afford in the general collection. At the same time, he selected one charitable institution annually, described its needs in detail, and invited the wealthy to make it their particular priority by making an additional contribution for its needs. He called the Boston School for the Deaf to their special attention in 1923 and in 1929 selected St. Elizabeth's Hospital to benefit from the generosity of those able to give "in a large manner."[55] Despite these strategies, however, the fact remained that donors had to concede considerable discretion to episcopal judgment, and so they remained cool toward diocesan charity collections.

Relative to other religious traditions, endowments and foundations appeared only slowly as important actors in Catholic benevolence. Early-nineteenth-century parishioners had no objection to endowments. Institutional boards, appreciating their merits, allotted budget surpluses to build them[56] or allocated bequests, annuities, and unusually large donations for that purpose. As pressures to address the immediate needs of immigrants intensified, however, these early efforts collapsed. In 1807, for example, the sixty-six incorporators of St. Joseph's Orphan Asylum in Philadelphia intended to endow it expeditiously. But because of demands on the institution, income from the endowment fund supported only 62 percent of the children by the mid-1850s. Economic conditions had led most boards to abandon any effort to endow charitable institutions by this time.[57]

Not only were most charitable institutions spending all donations they received, but an increasing number were also assuming debt and mortgaging

property to acquire operating funds. They argued that if they demonstrated ut-
ter reliance on charity, they would elicit more sympathy and hence larger contributions from the general public. Rare reminders that "in religious and charitable concerns, the virtues of prudence, foresight, a cautious adaptation of
means to ends, have their place"[58] had little effect. By the 1860s, charity institutions were opening with a building and staff, but few other resources. Not unusual was a New Orleans female reformatory that had not a dollar in the bank
on its opening day. The sisters bought everything, food, clothing, furniture, on
credit.[59] Such establishments suffered inordinately during recessions and depressions as subscription lists thinned and proceeds from fairs declined. Even
in more conservatively managed institutions, contributions were expended as
received, and after 1850 most Catholics agreed that this was the authentic religious response in the face of social distress. An exemplary charity appeal of the
1890s indicated the prevailing stance toward endowing charities: "Every penny
raised will go towards the work which it should be given to, not to drawing
large sums in interest, but to the opening of new branches of instruction while
continuing the proper influence of the old."[60]

By the turn of the century, Catholics had developed three arguments
against endowments for charitable institutions. First, as long as benevolent
funds were insufficient to meet present social need, diverting them to endowments violated a basic principle of religious giving. Second, if charities were
routinely endowed, parishioners might neglect to give and thus lose the spiritual merits that accompany benevolence. Third, the charitable institution, by
definition, cannot be financially independent, since if it were fully endowed it
would no longer require voluntary donations. Conservatives and liberals of the
1920s joined in condemning as weak in faith those who "seek the money first
and do the charity afterwards."[61]

Popular sentiment against endowments reflected the heavily working-class
composition of the nineteenth-century church. But the fact that it persisted until
the mid-twentieth century, long after the Catholic community, as a whole, had
begun to move to middle-class status, suggests that religious values played a
critical role as well. Although endowments clearly promised to relieve them of
onerous and incessant fundraising, church officials feared their deleterious effects on grassroots giving. In 1916, although not one of its thirty-two charitable
institutions was endowed, the Boston archdiocese reminded parishioners in the
annual charity appeal that "even if all our institutions were endowed, if the rich
gave so that there would be no need to worry, even then we would not be relieved of our duty to give alms."[62] Even the benevolent rich feared that endowments might be built at the expense of those in immediate need. In drafting the

rule for her sisterhood in 1903, Katharine Drexel stipulated initially that members "should not endow their institutes and works to the neglect and abandonment of the present needs of the Indians and Colored People."[63]

There was one important precedent for endowing a charitable institution, however. Although they usually had a few generous local donors, Catholic hospitals had never enjoyed the same grassroots support as orphanages and homes for the elderly poor because, by admitting paying patients, they seemed to compromise their commitment to the poor. Thus if its donors drifted away, a hospital's ability to care for charity patients was severely affected, since it had only minimal patient fees to rely on. In order to address this concern, hospital boards across the country, following mainstream practice, began in the 1890s to solicit endowments for free beds. Boston's Carney Hospital, for example, that had received only one endowed bed in its twenty-six year history, appealed in 1889 for $100 donations to endow free beds for the poor.[64] Four years later, forty-four-year-old St. Vincent's Hospital in New York City received $5,000 for its first perpetually endowed bed,[65] and, in 1898, St. Mary's Hospital in San Francisco announced its first endowed bed, forty years after its foundation.[66] As the Catholic population advanced economically in the twentieth century, the concept of the endowed free bed gained more support.

Early-twentieth-century bishops occasionally encouraged the endowment of a charitable institution, but only for an exceptional reason. For example, in 1911 a Boston orphanage was in extremely serious financial straits, with annual contributions covering only 40 percent of needed revenue. The usual solution was for the bishop to order an emergency collection in the parishes. However, since a collection would jeopardize the nascent movement toward consolidated fundraising in the archdiocese, the cardinal instructed the orphanage board to establish a permanent endowment fund and solicit wealthy Catholics to contribute to it.[67]

Despite its unquestionable financial advantages and its universal acceptance in other churches, the charitable endowment, although tolerated by the 1940s, was still not warmly endorsed. Lay organizations and bishops alike doubted that it was appropriate for Catholic charities. The St. Vincent de Paul Society, for example, still adhered to its traditional ban on the "perpetual investment of capital, which would be funded, and the interest alone drawn."[68] And in 1944, Archbishop Richard Cushing reflected national episcopal sentiment in his instructions to the directors of Boston's charitable bureau: "All money given for charity in the Archdiocese should be used as it comes along, without undue preoccupation with possible depressions or other future contingencies. Contrary practices . . . may be good business; they are not, however, good charity. Money given for charity should be used and used immediately—

for charity. The Archdiocese is big enough and generous enough to take care of crises should crises come."[69]

While the building of a charitable endowment remained suspect throughout the nineteenth century, its converse, begging for charity by members of religious orders, was routinely accepted. Only the wealthy disapproved of the practice as reinforcing stereotypes of an improvident, foreign church. A French-based sisterhood's proposal to open a home for the elderly poor met strong opposition from rich Catholics of the late 1860s, because the rule of the sisters required them to support themselves and their work by regular begging. "To the thrifty American mind, this scheme of beggary will, no doubt, appear to some as a nuisance, and call for the interference of the laws against begging,"[70] acknowledged one of the sisters' supporters.

Religious brothers also begged to support charitable institutions, but much less frequently than sisters. They found it to be a humbling experience. After a fire in an Indiana industrial school, for example, two Holy Cross brothers undertook a begging tour in 1849 among Irish railroad construction workers. Brother Stephen summarized his day in Galena, Illinois: "This is an un-Christian and uncharitable place. It's been so to me at least."[71] Priests who belonged to religious orders did not beg door-to-door in the late nineteenth century. Instead they applied to pastors to preach and collect contributions for their work at Sunday parish masses. In response to strenuous complaints from pastors everywhere, the hierarchy at the Third Plenary Council of Baltimore in 1884 decreed that clergy collecting for works located outside a diocese could not celebrate mass in any parish without prior permission from the local bishop. As this was rarely granted,[72] indiscriminate appeals by itinerant priests died out.

In contrast to male religious, "begging nuns" were legion by the 1870s, especially in western territories where the poor did not stay long in one place and where benevolent societies were ephemeral at best.[73] Increasing mainstream disapproval and a sense that soliciting by wandering religious was depressing contributions for diocesan needs led some bishops at this time to outlaw "foreign sisters" from their dioceses as "a source of disorder and abuse."[74] By the turn of the century, most of their colleagues had followed suit. Sisterhoods generally welcomed proscription of the practice. Community annals are replete with comments about sisters' "feelings of repugnance" at having to ask poor people for money and their dejection at the meager returns they typically received for long, humiliating days trudging door to door. In the 1880s, for example, a California sister reported collecting only $7.75 during an entire day of begging. "Forty-one houses gave ten cents each."[75]

In contrast to their disapproval of charity endowments, Catholics never objected to endowing academies, colleges, and universities, simply because they did not consider gifts to such institutions to be religious charity in the strict sense of the term. The charitable institution focused on the needs of the poor, while these other church-affiliated institutions did not. Popular sentiment was that tuition schools should call on their own students, parents, and alumni for financial contributions, not on hard-pressed parishioners who could not afford to enroll their own children in them. "Special collections for educational purposes," concluded an observer in 1930, "are not very popular or satisfactory."[76]

For the same reason, nineteenth-century efforts by bishops to build endowment funds for seminaries were disappointing. The case of the American College in Rome, founded by Pope Pius IX in 1859 to prepare priests to work in America, is illustrative. Because the school was in danger of closing in the 1860s for want of funds, the American hierarchy decided in 1866 that a national collection to endow it was in order. This directive had not yet been implemented when, in 1868, the bishops singled out the wealthy for a special appeal for $250,000, "not only to save, but to endow, and render perpetual for all time, our American College in Rome."[77] By 1900, the wealthy were routinely expected to provide for diocesan seminaries. Archbishop Patrick Riordan of San Francisco, for example, solicited a group of rich parishioners to pay for construction of the archdiocesan seminary, hoping that their example would spur other rich laity to come forward and endow it. Why, he asked, should very rich Catholics differ in their disposition toward the seminary from so many rich Protestants who were generously endowing colleges and universities across the country?[78]

The intellectual advance of the church in America had suffered immensely from the poverty of so many of its members during the nineteenth century. Given chronic and severe material distress, most Catholics agreed that relief of the poor should take first priority in their collective giving. The financing of colleges and universities, while philanthropic, was definitely secondary to that primary religious obligation. Among the small minority who included higher education in the domain of religious giving was the Creighton family of Omaha, Nebraska. Edward Creighton, a mining and telegraph millionaire, died intestate in 1874 before he could carry out his plans to build and endow a free men's college. Two years later, his widow, Mary, died, leaving $200,000 for the project, and in 1879 Creighton University was incorporated. In 1900, John Creighton, who inherited his brother Edward's fortune, provided the funds needed to develop the school into a full-fledged university. On his death in 1907, he bequeathed more than $1.5 million to the institution.[79]

In contrast, most wealthy donors accorded higher education a relatively low rank among their favored causes. Typical was rubber magnate Joseph Banigan of Providence, Rhode Island, who contributed $50,000 to the Catholic University in 1896, but gave far more in that year to local institutions serving the elderly poor, working girls, and foundlings. Most Catholics agreed that Banigan's proportions were appropriate. The preacher at the dedication of one of the charities Banigan had paid for commended him for his spiritual astuteness: "The erection of this Home is the best investment you could make of your money, the one that will pay the highest rate of interest . . . You have made, as it were, God and His chosen ones your debtors."[80] More practical than intellectual in their interests, most wealthy parishioners at this time had not attended college themselves. When they supported education at all, they focused more often on vocational institutions than on colleges and universities. Typical was international trader William Russell Grace who, in 1897, established the Grace Institute of New York, an industrial school for girls.[81]

Given prevailing sentiments of the early 1880s, the hierarchy's plan to found a national Catholic university, under discussion at this time, aroused little interest among rich laity. Only two large gifts were forthcoming, $100,000 from merchant and banker Eugene Kelly to endow two chairs and $300,000 from Mary Gwendoline Caldwell of New York. At the Third Plenary Council of Baltimore in 1884, the bishops voted to establish the Catholic University of America and designated Caldwell one of its founders.[82] By 1888, the cornerstone of the first building had been laid, and in 1889 the first students arrived. Members of the episcopal committee appointed to raise funds for the institution appealed, at first, to wealthy Catholics. This strategy proved notably unproductive. Therefore, they determined in 1887 to appeal to the Catholic public nationally. They asked every priest in the country to give at least one hundred dollars for the cause and sought subscriptions from ordinary parishioners as well. This move irritated many bishops who viewed it as a direct threat to diocesan collections. Bernard McQuaid of Rochester, New York, for one, predicted that the next step would be to mandate an annual national collection for the new university. "This will be the next move," he fumed to a Cleveland colleague. "The instance of Belgium will be cited where there is an annual collection in every church and chapel of the country for the support of Louvain University. Mind my words."[83] His prophecy came true in 1904 when Pope Pius X instituted an annual collection for the university's support.

Although there was some consensus by 1900 that higher education was a more appropriate concern for those of high income and social rank than for working-class parishioners, response from wealthy individuals and benevolent societies to appeals for the new university remained chilly. Because the Knights of Columbus had given $50,000 to endow a chair in 1904, university trustees decided to ask them a few years later to establish a $500,000 endowment fund. The Knights complied, but without relish, and took five years to complete the fund.[84] A major supporter of the university, New Yorker George Duval, agreed with its rector, Bishop Thomas Shahan, that a major fundraising campaign, in the planning stage in 1915, ought to be deferred: "I think you are wise to delay activity in collecting now for your great work," he told Shahan. "A few people are prosperous very prosperous but they are not of the class that will be interested in the project."[85] Mary J. Hill, wife of Minnesota railroad baron James J. Hill, declined to contribute for the university at this time on the grounds that local needs were more compelling. Her husband, she explained, "is constantly helping poor struggling new little places and how many of them there are in these new States."[86] By 1930, the university's total endowment remained small, and in dollars per student it registered barely one-seventh the record of Yale University. Why should the Catholic University have only "about half the endowment of a certain Kentucky hill college," queried one journalist, when Catholics comprise twenty percent of the American population and when "at least a hundred Catholic multimillionaires" are in a position to endow it handsomely?[87] Despite all efforts, by the mid-1950s, the university could boast of only ten gifts of at least $100,000. John K. Mullen of Denver, Colorado, had contributed $500,000 in 1923 for the library.[88] Only one contribution, made in 1914 by Theodore Basselin for the education of seminarians, approached $1 million. Interest in supporting higher education rose somewhat in the 1920s as more Catholics graduated from college. Typical of a new generation of donors was oil industrialist Ignatius A. O'Shaughnessy of St. Paul who, in addition to his alma mater, local St. Thomas College, supported several other Catholic men's colleges, as well as Yale and Lehigh Universities.[89]

By the 1940s, wealthy individuals had begun to appreciate that by making major gifts to Catholic higher education they could exercise considerable personal leadership in shaping the direction of church and society. They, not church officials, made the decisions about the institutions and programs that would receive their benefactions. Although most gave for buildings and endowments, some, like Peter Reilly, who in this decade contributed $1 million to Notre Dame University for scholarships for low income students, incorporated traditional Catholic priorities in their gifts to higher education.

Charitable foundations made their appearance as the ranks of upper-class parishioners swelled significantly in the mid-twentieth century. Currently numbering about three hundred, Catholic foundations are, on average, relatively small, most awarding under $500,000 in grants annually. The majority prefer to fund local causes, although very few support parochial schools.[90] Because charitable foundations are not so popular among very wealthy parishioners as direct individual giving, they represent a very small segment, about 1.5 percent, of all American foundations. Nonetheless, within the church they are becoming prominent actors, not simply because of the significant financial support they provide to dioceses, charitable agencies, and educational institutions, but also because they are assuming leadership roles in developing philanthropic agendas and policies.

Until recently, the world's largest private foundation focusing on religious causes was the Milwaukee-based De Rancé Foundation, founded in 1946 by Harry John, a conservative scion of the Miller Brewing Company fortune. Unlike most American foundations, De Rancé had an international focus and was supporting organizations serving the poor in all parts of the world. However, in 1986, after a bitter lawsuit brought by the foundation's two other directors, a Wisconsin court removed the controversial John as trustee and director for reason of gross misconduct. Just before John's death in late 1992, the trustees voted to dissolve the $100 million foundation, naming the Archdiocese of Milwaukee Supporting Fund as chief beneficiary of its funds.[91]

Although older and considerably larger than most Catholic foundations, the Raskob Foundation for Catholic Activities is representative of their character and focus. Established in Delaware in 1945 by John and Helena Raskob, it currently ranks among the nation's one thousand largest foundations. Of its eighty members, half are women, most are descendants of the founders, and nearly three-fourths are under thirty-five years of age. In awarding grants, the foundation strongly favors "projects in which local support and self-help are demonstrated." It also promotes the development of efficient and innovative fundraising strategies at the diocesan level.[92] In recent years, it has disbursed approximately $3 million annually to hundreds of agencies and institutions, 80 percent of which are American, all of which have episcopal endorsement.

In 1976, a group of foundations and philanthropic individuals joined to establish Foundations and Donors Interested in Catholic Activities [FADICA] in order "to undertake selective educational research and other activities and services to improve the effectiveness of private philanthropy in assisting the Roman Catholic church to carry out its mission."[93] FADICA quickly developed into an important forum for national dialogue about church giving and needs. By 1993, membership included thirty-nine foundations and one individual, most of them Catholic. Despite its eagerness to have the public endorsement of the National Conference of Catholic Bishops, FADICA delayed seeking "a formal liaison" with this organization until 1986, by which time it had solidly established itself as an independent lay organization.

FADICA has effectively represented lay philanthropic perspectives and priorities in a number of ways in its interaction with the hierarchy and with leaders of various national and diocesan charity organizations. One notable instance reveals its benevolent perspectives and approach. It was FADICA, not the hierarchy, that in 1983 pressed for resolution of the critical issue of retirement funds for religious sisters. Lack of bargaining power and aging memberships had combined to force most sisterhoods to draw on their retirement savings to meet current expenses. These funds were sparse, a result, in large measure, of the low salaries paid their members by dioceses over many decades.[94]

FADICA members asked the hierarchy to make this issue one of its priorities and, to promote that goal, held a conference on the topic in 1984. In addition, three institutional members, the Raskob, Brencanda, and Koch Foundations, underwrote a three-year study of retirement and pre-retirement planning by the National Association of Church Personnel Administrators and established an emergency fund for sisterhoods in immediate financial distress. In 1985, FADICA proposed that the bishops introduce a national collection to provide adequate retirement funds for the nation's sisters. Describing the situation as "the greatest scandal in the U.S. Catholic Church," they stressed the urgency of strong and immediate action.[95]

In 1986, when an estimate of $2.5 billion in "total unfunded past service liability" received national media coverage, FADICA moved at once to incorporate a lay organization "to raise funds, enlist volunteer professional help, and educate the public to the needs of the retired religious."[96] Under the leadership of the president of the Loyola Foundation, the new organization had more than four thousand volunteers and patrons within three years. Finally, in 1988, the hierarchy instituted an annual national collection, to continue for ten years, for a retirement fund for religious. Contributions in the first annual collection represented "the single largest outpouring of support for any cause in U.S. church history,"[97] and every collection since has at least matched the first-year record of nearly $25 million. FADICA had proved its worth as a significant agent of reform and an astute judge of the lay philanthropic spirit.

An enduring FADICA concern is the fact that "few direct avenues exist for regular contact and sharing of experience between the laity who are leaders in the world of commerce, and the leaders in the Church." Not only does this situation deprive laity of essential moral support, but "church leadership is unable to assimilate the contribution of the lived Christian experience of many of its own people in its discussion of public issues."[98] Nonetheless, FADICA's brief history suggests that the charitable foundation is an effective instrument allowing some members of the laity to participate distinctively and significantly in the good works of the church.

In response to the important question of how general diocesan needs were to be funded, the hierarchy, at the Second Baltimore Council in 1866, decided that each diocese should establish its own procedures. Most dioceses today levy a tax, the *cathedraticum*, on each parish for the support of the diocese, with the amount and terms of payment left to episcopal discretion. However, interest in building diocesan endowments developed only sporadically,[99] with the result that some dioceses today have substantial endowments, while others have none at all. Endowment income covers 97 percent of the annual budget of the diocese of Wheeling-Charleston, West Virginia, for example, while the diocese of Rochester, New York, with no endowment income, relies entirely on an annual diocesan appeal for its needs. As deficits mount, more dioceses see in endowments and foundations ways to augment grassroots donations in annual appeals.

Recent efforts to establish endowments generally focus on wealthy parishioners, who are able to do more than simply contribute in regular collections for diocesan needs.[100] In some cases, however, appeals for endowment support are being made to middle-class parishioners as well. In 1985, for example, the Catholic Diocese of Pittsburgh Foundation was formed specifically to undertake a $30 million capital campaign for endowment funds. The foundation initially appealed to the twenty-three wealthiest prospective donors in the diocese for "leadership gifts." Invitations to approximately 180 individuals to give at least $750,000 followed. In the campaign's third stage, an appeal was made for gifts between $50,000 and $500,000, and in the fourth stage, 2,000 parishioners were asked to give between $5,000 and $50,000. The latter received a videotaped message describing diocesan needs and stressing "that the appeal is a one-time crisis that is not expected to repeat itself." A personal visit from a diocesan volunteer followed. The final stage entailed a mailing to approximately 20,000 parishioners requesting a contribution of $200 annually for five years.[101]

Declining immigration, a lessening of religious tensions, and accelerated movement from city to suburb affected the attitudes of twentieth-century Catholics toward their collective philanthropy. In particular, class differences in giving became increasingly important as more parishioners achieved upper-class status. In the process of modifying its benevolent perspectives to accommodate these differences, the church community confronted more directly than ever before in its history the question of how to reconcile traditional religious benevolent values with the more secular values of modern philanthropy. Its responses to this challenge shaped in critical ways the course and character of Catholic giving.

7

Parochial Schools and the
Social Conscience

Our Catholic school system . . . is the most potent expression of Catholic charity
that exists today, beside which all other forms pale in their significance.

—John Glennon, 1912

COMMITMENT TO "FREE" schools has long distinguished Catholic philanthropy from that of other religious denominations. These institutions, also called parish or parochial schools and, until recent decades, sisters' schools, more than other benevolent works have been viewed by American Catholics as a public and enduring testimony to their democratic and socially progressive values. "Free" schools were among the pioneer charitable works, and these schools continue to benefit disproportionately from Catholic financial and labor contributions today.

Although mainstream citizens took issue with Catholic ways of giving on many points, they applauded the collective benevolence of the working-class community toward the sick and the destitute. By mid-twentieth century, governments at all levels were routinely allocating public funds to church institutions and agencies serving these social needs. In sharp contrast has been an historic opposition to parochial schools and an enduring reluctance to divert public funds to them.

By 1800, a few boarding schools for boys, funded mainly by wealthy benefactors, had appeared in Maryland and Pennsylvania. Philadelphian James White, for example, left funds in 1767 for a Catholic school in that city.[1] And Frederick Brandt bequeathed substantial Maryland property in 1815 to Rev. Francis Neale of Georgetown College "in order to establish thereon as soon as convenient a school or seminary, or any other house of education for the purpose of bringing up youth in useful literature and Christian piety."[2] Female academies accompanied the development of sisterhoods after 1790, although Ursuline nuns had conducted a New Orleans school for the daughters of "the better class" since 1727. Religious orders directing these early tuition schools fared relatively well financially. The Visitation academy that opened in Washington, D.C., in 1790 soon attracted Protestant as well as Catholic girls from across the country, allowing the founding sisters to follow a pay-as-you-go policy in financing the school. Since sisterhoods specializing in boarding academies recruited members from among their graduates, they benefited materially from large dowries and occasional fortunes brought to the convent by novices from affluent families. In the antebellum era, convent annals of southern communities record that recruits occasionally brought "young Negro women as a dower offering; at other times large groups of slaves formed the inheritance of a religious."[3]

Convent boarding schools spread as the number of wealthy Catholic families rose, and by the 1850s they numbered about one hundred. The rich patronized and liberally supported these schools for their own class. Typical was the Academy of the Sacred Heart in New York, which in 1864 was admitting only "young ladies of the higher class" who could afford its sizable annual fees.[4] But schools restricted to the children of the affluent did not address the needs of the poor, and Catholics agreed that contributions to them, while laudable, did not alone fulfill the charitable mandate.

Since benevolent Catholics had as their paramount concern the spiritual welfare of poor children, particularly orphans, the provision of schools for them naturally held a prominent place among early-nineteenth-century charitable works. Clergy and laity alike saw in the education of these children a critical contribution to the nation's well-being. Bishop John England reminded Charleston parishioners in the 1820s that support of the parish school was their civic as well as religious responsibility: "This is the parents' special obligation and the pastors' pressing and elevated duty, as it is also the patriot's and the charitable man's field of active and useful benevolence."[5]

Early strategies to support free parish schools were identical with those employed to fund other charitable institutions. In 1781, for example, Philadelphia parishioners solicited subscriptions to purchase land and pay for construction of St. Mary's free school. They planned to meet operating costs by charity sermons and bequests. By 1805, however, these funding sources were not covering the cost of conducting the school.[6] A continuing heavy debt and the poverty of parishioners led parish trustees to table an 1817 petition from African American Catholics that the parish take their children "under your protecting wing as you have taken the poor of your own colour and to have ours also instructed in a common English education."[7]

Because funding sources remained inadequate and unreliable, early free schools were soon obliged to introduce student fees. Even though they were low, the fees adversely affected the schools. One New York City parish opened its school in 1828, but because parents could not pay the tuition fees, it survived only two years. A second attempt in 1836 failed for the same reason. The parish opened a third school in 1856, on condition that Sisters of Charity and Christian Brothers replace lay teachers the next year, so that eventually the tuition fees could be eliminated. In 1856, with tuition fees still in place, enrollment stood at 500. Six years after the arrival of religious-order teachers, when the parish was finally able to abolish fees, registration climbed to 1,200.[8]

Although most pioneer schools relied on fees for some years, they tried to ensure that poor children would not be denied admission. In 1853, for example, the first parochial school in Minneapolis set a fee of fifty cents per month for children who could pay, admitting others free.[9] Nonetheless, concern that fees were excluding the poorest children increased over time. In 1878, Detroit's Fourth Diocesan Synod emphasized that all parish schools were to be free for poor children. The goal of eliminating tuition fees entirely was difficult to achieve, however, and in Detroit, as in most other dioceses, schools were still charging tuitions nearly forty years later.[10]

Early-nineteenth-century state legislatures permitted lotteries to finance schools, and Catholics took full advantage of them. At a time when John Carroll's lotteries to fund the construction of the Baltimore cathedral met disappointing results, local lotteries for free schools were supported enthusiastically. In 1803, for example, by selling tickets at six dollars each, a German parish in Philadelphia raised the immense sum of ten thousand dollars in a schoolhouse lottery. School lotteries were proving popular in less settled areas of the country as well. As early as 1808, Rev. Gabriel Richard had applied for a lottery in anticipation of opening several schools in Michigan.[11] Benevolent societies that formed to fund early free schools set very low membership dues to encourage laity of every economic class to join. In 1817, for example, men and women in Baltimore's cathedral parish formed separate societies to collect from their Protestant and Catholic neighbors for two parish schools. The laywomen at first staffed as well as directed the girls' school, but soon invited Sisters of Charity to take over teaching responsibilities. As was the usual sequence in other charitable institutions, they yielded management of the school to the sisters within two decades.[12]

Although teaching sisters remained few in number in the 1820s, brothers were nearly impossible to find for boys' schools. New York Catholics in this decade had eagerly subscribed for a boys' school and had even formed an Education Assistant Society for its ongoing support. However, they had to abandon their project because qualified brothers could not be found. Teaching sisterhoods expanded steadily over the nineteenth century, but brotherhoods grew very slowly. Since lay teachers were costly, and since most sisterhoods initially would teach only girls, antebellum free schools tended to enroll considerably more girls than boys.[13]

Until the 1840s, the occasional individual benefaction for free schools was more likely to come in the form of property than cash. As a result, covering school operating expenses remained a preoccupation in most parishes. In 1818 and 1823, for instance, Sisters of Loretto opened two free schools in St. Louis on property donated for this purpose. However, the local bishop, Joseph Rosati, described them as in very poor shape, "without funds, because of the poverty of our Catholics."[14] Few philanthropic individuals, European or American, earmarked their gifts for such schools. The French countess, Felicité de Duras, however, was one who gave them priority in her benevolence in the 1830s. "I have asked our dear sisters," she told Bishop Rosati, "never to refuse admittance to their schools to poor children."[15] A rare American benefactor of the free school was Ann Herron of Norfolk, Virginia, who in 1848 offered to furnish and support a school "for the poorest of the poor" in St. Patrick's parish in Norfolk, Virginia.[16] Most parishes had no such benefactors, and bishops of the 1840s, while favorably disposed toward schools as a way to protect the faith of the children, had few resources to devote to them. They echoed the lament of Bishop Peter Lefevere of Detroit: "But where shall I find the means to support them? . . . We have so many other things to do."[17]

Until 1840, states occasionally allocated funds to the support of parochial schools. Three years after the first such school opened there in 1800, New York State passed legislation permitting denominational schools to share in the School Fund. By 1822, five New York City parochial schools were among twenty denominational institutions receiving assistance from the fund. At this time, however, demand for public schools was escalating, prompting the legislature in 1825 to prohibit the diversion of public funds to denominational schools. It modified this ban six years later to except sectarian orphanages, all of which incorporated some type of school. Other states followed the New York example, and after 1840 only orphanage schools and Indian schools received state or federal funding.[18]

Little interest in the education of African American children appeared in the Catholic community before 1850. Two small schools for free children opened in Charleston, South Carolina, in 1835. They resembled in curriculum the Protestant schools in the city. Seminarians were found to teach the boys and Sisters of Mercy the girls. When eighty children immediately applied to attend, the alarmed white population, already threatened by abolitionist literature, insisted that the bishop close the schools. Fearing violence, John England complied, but only on condition that the city's Protestant schools for this population also close. Six years later, the schools reopened, only to close permanently in 1848.

There were a few other isolated efforts in this area. A wealthy New Orleans African American, the Widow Bernard Couvent, provided in her 1837 will for the education of African American children. To this end, the Catholic Society for the Instruction of Indigent Orphans was formed in 1847 and a free school was opened the next year.[19]

The financial condition of free parish schools in major cities deteriorated as poor immigrants continued to swell the ranks of the church in the mid-1840s. This led bishops to lobby vigorously for a restoration of state support. Archbishop John Hughes of New York pursued a spirited but ill-fated school crusade that succeeded mainly in arousing more religious antagonism. Similarly futile campaigns in other states in the next decade ultimately persuaded Catholics that they would have to finance the schools themselves. This would be no easy task, since bishops of the 1840s and 1850s, anticipating the restoration of public monies for the schools, had left the financing of the schools to the local parishes and devoted their attention to more pressing diocesan needs.[20]

Benevolent societies of the 1840s soon became deeply involved in the relief of social distress, and so the financing of free schools took a secondary place in their priorities. Typical were Baltimore men who had founded the Young Catholic's Friend Society in this decade to provide poor school children with books and clothing. They soon discovered that the provision of clothing was absorbing all their funds. This led them to revise their society's goals to meet basic survival needs, despite the concern of a few members that this shift in focus "would destroy perhaps the greatest sphere of our usefulness. . . . Surely the mind is more worthy of care than the body."[21] By the 1860s, St. Vincent de Paul Society conferences in major cities were abandoning their work for free schools. While the first activity of the New Orleans conference of the society in 1852 had been to provide books for children attending a free school, within eight years, the men were devoting their resources entirely to meeting physical needs of orphans.[22]

As the support of care-giving institutions absorbed more attention, the burden of financing free schools fell almost exclusively on local pastors, parishioners, and the sisterhoods staffing them. Poor parishioners could not raise enough money to operate the schools satisfactorily, and so sisterhoods frequently contributed money as well as teaching services. They did this by adopting the practice of sisters in the first convent academies of using tuition revenues to finance free schools. When Ursuline Sisters opened the first North American convent school for daughters of the wealthy in New Orleans in 1727, they simultaneously opened a separate day school for local white girls. "All the inhabitants who could not afford to send their children to the academy were invited to send them to the day-school, in which the teaching was free of charge. They began with 24 boarders and 40 day-scholars."[23] The Visitation Academy that opened in Washington, D.C., in 1799 had a similar structure, its free school antedating the District's first public school by six years.[24]

By the early nineteenth century, however, Catholics saw the free school as an essential benevolence rather than simply a casual foundation that appeared only in places where a girls' academy happened to be located. The new perspective was greatly encouraged by the enterprise of Elizabeth Seton, a young New York widow, and members of the sisterhood she founded in Emmitsburg, Maryland, in 1808.[25] The Sisters of Charity were the first community to make the education of poor children a priority work. Their democratic example was followed by most of the many teaching sisterhoods that appeared over the next century. Chicago Sisters of Mercy, for example, who in 1846 opened simultaneously a free parochial school for girls and a "select school" for boarding and day pupils, clearly considered the latter as a way to earn money to support the former. Teaching the children of the poor was their priority work and the select school was definitely secondary to it.[26] Indian schools in Minnesota, Dakota, and Oklahoma Territories served a similar function in the 1850s. Much of the $40 monthly federal salaries earned by Sisters of St. Joseph teaching Winnebago children at this time was used to subsidize poor parish schools the sisterhood was staffing in the diocese of St. Paul, Minnesota.[27]

Although parochial schools were opening in every diocese in the 1840s, they were especially in demand in places where public school systems had not yet developed. In 1849, for example, Galena, Iowa, residents, Protestant and Catholic alike, applied to Bishop Mathias Loras of Dubuque for a school. They pledged to provide a school building and operating funds if he would use his influence to convince Sisters of Charity to send a faculty. He agreed, despite considerable private misgiving: "If I am so fortunate as to succeed in procuring some of those excellent educators of youth, I shall bring them with me next summer on my return from the Council of Baltimore; but what great expense it will entail on me!"[28] In sparsely populated western territories, pioneer schools were not necessarily parish-based. Since they knew that their new hospital would be filled to capacity only during epidemics, Minnesota Sisters of St. Joseph in the 1850s devoted a wing of the building to a free school for girls. As school would be closed during epidemics in any case, the hospital easily expanded to accommodate increased demand during these crises.[29]

The financial contributions of sisterhoods were critical for the survival of early urban parochial schools as well. Congregants of a new Philadelphia parish, St. Patrick's, formed in 1839, were Irish immigrants, so poor that their first church, dedicated in 1841, had "no pews, nothing but benches free to all." Special collections, supplemented by fairs and benefit lectures, had provided the money to build the church. Plans for a parish school got underway eight years later, with contributions at the first parish meeting on the project amounting to $300, given "in sums of five and ten dollars." Although donations of labor kept construction costs down, it was another three years before the school opened in 1852. Its faculty of six laywomen received annual salaries of $150. While low, these salaries represented a heavy burden for a poor parish, and so a search for religious-order teachers was soon underway. It took five years to find Sisters of St. Joseph to teach the girls and thirteen years before Christian Brothers were finally engaged for the boys.[30]

A rising class consciousness precipitated new problems by the late 1840s. Until that decade, orphans and neighborhood children alike had attended free schools opened by sisters near the orphanages. However, working-class parents now complained that their children should not have to mix with orphans in these free schools. Parental complaints in 1848, for example, forced sisters conducting St. Mary's Free School in Charleston, South Carolina, to teach the orphans separately in the orphanage building.[31] By the 1860s, middle- and upper-class parents were demanding that all physical links between the select tuition schools their daughters attended and the "free schools" conducted by the same sisterhood be severed. When Sisters of Mercy announced the opening of a tuition academy and a free school in Wilmington, North Carolina, in 1869, its opponents attempted to defeat the project by labeling the academy "half free." The convent annalist explained that "the name 'free school' was associated in the minds of the people as something low."[32] About this time, Sisters of Mercy explained the failure of their Whitefield, Maine, tuition boarding school for girls with an orphanage and free school attached: "Many parents hesitated about sending their daughters to a boarding school which was connected with a home for orphans."[33] Bishop John Timon's 1859 description of free schools explains middle- and upper-class attitudes, at least in part. "In the cities, and throughout the country, a very great number of children attend our Catholic schools. They are the schools for the poor; many of the poor scholars are literally in rags, and very generally during the last few years of distress, neither they nor their parents could help it."[34]

Benevolent appeals for schools for African Americans met resistance from Catholics in northern and western states as well as in the South. In 1860, for example, Presentation Sisters in San Francisco, already conducting a tuition school for white children, opened a free school for African Americans, using tuition revenues to subsidize it. The project soon failed as white parents threatened to remove their children from the tuition school unless the African American school were closed.[35]

Because Augustin Verot, bishop of Savannah, Georgia, could find no sisterhood in America to provide faculty for schools for African American children in Georgia and Florida in the immediate postbellum years, he appealed to Sisters of St. Joseph in his hometown, Le Puy, France, for assistance. "I have five or six hundred thousand Negroes without any education or religion . . . for whom I wish to do something," he told them.[36] Sixty French sisters volunteered to be among the first eight to take up the work. By 1870 this sisterhood was staffing five free African American schools, four in Florida and one in Savannah. Their boarding academy for white girls in St. Augustine provided the necessary funds. Not only did the sisters receive little support from whites, but they also initially met stiff opposition from African American ministers.[37]

Severely hampered by lack of financial support, free schools for African American children appeared only now and then in the 1880s. Catholic inactivity contrasted sharply with the benevolence of Protestants who at this time were funding many elementary schools and at least one hundred high schools for this population in the South. A Sister of Mercy reported in 1884 that while her community had schools for African American children connected with its southern convents, money was a continuing problem. "So far, I am sorry to say, Catholics have not done much for that despised race."[38]

In the postbellum years, southern public schools for African Americans were few in number, poorly equipped, and staffed by untrained teachers paid to teach only four months yearly. Since these conditions did not improve noticeably over succeeding decades, Katharine Drexel in 1915 determined to focus more of her financial and labor resources in this area. She began by establishing a high school for African Americans in New Orleans, incorporating in it a strong normal school program. Scholarships were offered to Xavier Normal School students who would agree to teach for two years after graduation, at a modest salary, in the small schools she planned to open throughout rural Louisiana. The principal of each school was to be a Sister of the Blessed Sacrament. Response to the proposal was excellent, and within fifteen years "Mother Katharine's girls" were staffing twenty-three elementary schools enrolling more than 2,300 children. Like all her schools, they were open to children of all religious faiths.[39]

Catholic colleges were still refusing in the 1930s to admit African American students, and the hierarchy remained silent on the matter. Katharine Drexel appealed unsuccessfully to the bishops on the Catholic University board of trustees to integrate that school,[40] and African American laymen also pressed the issue. Many, like Arthur Falls, saw racism in the trustees' inaction. Falls was particularly incensed when John Noll, bishop of Fort Wayne, Indiana, lauded the charity of Notre Dame University students for contributing used clothing to poor African Americans but made no mention of the fact that the university still refused to admit members of his race. The clothing collection, he advised Noll, "would not represent in the minds of the coloured population a significant interest in their basic needs. . . . Perhaps it would interest you to know that the bulk of the Negro population of the United States considers the Catholic Church as its bitter enemy."[41]

Given the temper of the times, Katharine Drexel took a revolutionary step when she founded Xavier University in New Orleans in 1932. Unlike most Catholic colleges of the era, it was coeducational, and its tuition was kept very low. When *Time* magazine stated that this first Catholic college for African Americans admitted only members of that church, Louise Drexel Morrell quickly corrected the report as "entirely wrong: the Institution is non-sectarian and no preference is shown to persons having any particular religious affiliations. Students are welcomed without regard to their religious beliefs."[42]

The propriety of financing free schools by conducting tuition schools was already a topic of controversy within sisterhoods in the 1840s. While bishops and pastors took it for granted that sisters would not only contribute their labor but also help to finance other school costs, young women joining sisterhoods wanted to spend their time teaching poor and working-class children. By relying on sisterhoods for cash as well as labor for parish schools, clergy and laity alike were asking them to undertake work that they did not define as charitable, namely, the education of middle- and upper-class girls.

The debate continued, with sisters on both sides of the issue. Some argued that tuition academies served an important social function in that they forged "a connecting link between all classes, elevating the social position of the Catholics of the town."[43] Sisters teaching in the tuition schools were vicariously serving the poor, since without the revenues they earned, many of the free schools staffed by the rest of the sisters would not survive. They agreed with bishops that academies were needed for the spiritual welfare of wealthy girls whose worldly parents would rather send them to public or Protestant schools than allow them to mingle with the children of the poor in parochial schools.[44]

Sisters on the other side of the debate considered the price of such "benefits" far too high. They contended that clergy and laity, not sisters, were responsible for raising operating revenues for parochial schools. By contributing a nearly free teaching force for the schools, sisters were already bearing a major responsibility for their support, and so the proposition that they subsidize them even further by undertaking work that ran counter to their corporate charitable mission was unjust. A Sister of Mercy warned sisters in her community in the 1850s that if they succumbed to these external pressures to shift their focus away from the poor, they would soon fall prey to the prevailing mentality that "every thing however unsuitable short of an act of heresy or downright sin is considered a

less evil than the loss of the money."[45] As bishops, pastors, and parents continued to press sisters to finance parochial schools, and as sisterhoods themselves
were forced, in time, to turn to academies for funds to cover the living expenses
of their own members, the debate died down for nearly a century.

The extent to which sisters subsidized free schools by gifts of money varied
by location, but it was significant everywhere. Many parish schools of the 1830s
depended so heavily on the cash contributions of the sisters, that when that
funding source disappeared, the schools closed. For example, Sisters of Charity
were conducting a free school and a tuition school in Norfolk, Virginia, in 1839.
When hard economic times caused the tuition school to fail, the free school also
had to close its doors.[46] A practice, common in many dioceses by the 1860s,
whereby sisterhoods were expected to borrow money to purchase land and construct parochial schools, demonstrates the extent of their subsidization. Once
the schools opened, their debts and sister-teachers' stipends alike were sup-
posed to be covered by tuition charges. But since most children in these schools
were too poor to pay even minimal tuition fees, the sisters had little choice but
to open "select schools" to support themselves as well as the schools. In 1875,
when a New Orleans sisterhood was unable to pay the debt on a new parish
school, the pastor advanced them the necessary funds at interest. However, as
a condition of the loan, he required them to train the church choir and supply
a church organist without charge for five years. He deducted from the debt his
estimate of the value of these services. Thus, with the approval of the local archbishop, Napoleon Perché, he and his parishioners successfully evaded all financial responsibility for their parish school.[47]

Brothers teaching in boys' parochial schools occasionally found themselves
in similar circumstances. For example, records of the lady managers of a Mobile,
Alabama, orphanage indicate that, until 1847, the brothers caring for the boys,
like the sisters caring for the girls, had been contributing academy tuition monies to support the institution. When a parish school opened on the orphanage
grounds in that year, the same financial expectation was simply extended to it.
Thus pastor and parishioners "had no worry as to the school expenses, neither
insurance nor repairs, nor regarding the education of the boys because the
Brothers took care of these." In 1870, the brothers purchased the school building
and land from the parish. Thirty-four years later, when the brothers decided to
withdraw from the school and offered to sell the property to the parish, the
bishop informed them they could not do that. According to his assessment, all
they had purchased in 1870 was "a right to the use of the property as long as
they maintained a school on the premises."[48]

About this time, Joseph Alemany, archbishop of San Francisco, described
for one of his pastors the policy that prevailed in many places in the late nine-

teenth century. Beyond providing a house for them, the pastor had little responsibility toward the sisters conducting his parish school. "Well to have some understanding between Sisters and Pastor—It can't be very precise, I suppose it will amount to this—that clergy must prepare place for them and give occasionally some encouragement, I dare say that in temporalities they'll manage to support themselves from school, charging a little to those that can pay and teaching them gratuitously altogether."[49] As parochial schools increased in number in the late nineteenth century, sisterhoods were, of course, less able to subsidize them financially. Academy and "select school" tuitions were now increasingly needed for the survival of the sisters themselves, since stipends paid by parishes or small tuition fees collected from parish school students remained very low, uncertain, or, not infrequently, nonexistent.

The hierarchy at the First Provincial Council in Baltimore in 1829 had called for the opening of parochial schools and, at the First and Second Plenary Councils, held in 1852 and 1866, repeated this message. But at the Third Baltimore Council in 1884, exhortation became mandate. Pastors in every diocese were instructed to build schools, and laity of every social class were enjoined to enroll their children in them.[50] This decree had an immediate impact on the traditional understanding of the education of poor and working-class children as religious philanthropy. Until this time, Catholic charitable enterprises had never formally restricted their services to church members, although, given their poverty and recurring religious friction, most of those served were, in fact, Catholic. The 1884 edict, however, generated a new and very heavy demand for admission to parochial schools that far exceeded their capacities. As a result, the ecumenical principle that underlay other charitable works of the church was permanently waived for these schools. In contrast, tuition academies continued, as in the past, to welcome children of all religious backgrounds.

The effect of the 1884 mandate on states with large Catholic populations was dramatic. In New England, a region that had been slower to construct schools than elsewhere before 1884, schools more than tripled in number between 1875 and 1903, from 100 to 352, and enrollments rose six-fold, from 20,000 to 142,000. Even in places where schools had been developing consistently, school expansion after 1884 was remarkable. In 1869, for example, the Philadelphia diocese had 42 parochial schools enrolling 15,232 students. By 1903, approximately twice as many children were attending its 113 schools. Total enrollment nationally at this time was over 1 million students, with elementary schools accounting for about 96 percent of the total. Since the Catholic population numbered 10.8 million in 1900, nearly half the children of elementary-school age were attending church schools. About 63 percent of the nation's parishes had schools at this time.[51]

Although the Third Plenary Council of Baltimore in 1884 had recommended education as the best way to address the needs of the African American
community, few free schools appeared for them, a situation church officials attributed to the increasing demand for teaching sisters in parochial schools.
Clergy working in African American communities rejected this explanation as
specious at best. A Josephite priest asked scathingly: "Why not let the rich suffer? The rich can hire lay teachers, the poor cannot."[52] Anthony Durier, bishop
of Natchitoches, Louisiana, reported his experience in 1885 in hiring teachers
for parochial schools in his diocese. He had no trouble, he said, finding sisterhoods to staff white schools, but not one community, either within or outside
the diocese, was willing to provide teachers for African American schools.[53] The
pastor of an African American parish in Mississippi told Katharine Drexel in
1909 how hard it was to explain the situation to his parishioners. "There was
not a school on the coast that I could point to as an example of Catholic effort.
All I could do was to formulate the Catholic teaching. Of course they are waiting
for me to carry out my principle into practice at my own church. They are
watching the efforts of the church to give them schools. The schools will redeem
the church's lost prestige among them."[54]

Progress was very slow, however. By 1918, thirty-eight African American
parishes staffed by Josephite priests each had its school, but only 122 priests,
more than half of them Josephites, were working among African Americans in
the entire country. Approximately 26,000 African American children attended
142 parochial and 19 institutional schools staffed by 798 sisters and 132 lay
teachers in the mid-1920s. Among the sisterhoods represented in these schools,
Katharine Drexel's community, the Sisters of the Blessed Sacrament, played a
leading role.[55]

African Americans in northern cities had sought since the 1890s, but without much success, to enroll their children in local parochial schools. Because
neighborhoods were segregated, so were the parish schools. African American
parishes rarely had the means to build and support parish schools. Nonetheless,
their leaders continued to give the education issue priority attention in three
national Colored Catholic Congresses held between 1889 and 1892. At the 1892
meeting in Philadelphia, delegates approved the formation of St. Peter Claver's
Benevolent and Loan Association to "establish a fund for benevolent purposes
and a fund out of which loans shall be made for the building of Catholic
churches and furnishing educational facilities among the colored people." The
keynote speaker, William E. Easton, proposed that other parish needs be made
secondary to education. "Although the importance and necessity of establishing
churches are apparent," he insisted, "the greatest need of Colored Catholics at
present is more schools and better educational facilities for their children, and

while these are being secured the building of churches could for a time be stopped, in order that the energies of the people could be devoted solely to the consummation of this great project."[56] Some speakers, like Lincoln Valle, took a conciliatory tone, pointing out the great potential for learning of African American children and assuring bishops and pastors that they would take full advantage of the benefits of Catholic schools. Others, like Charles Butler, representative to the 1893 Colored Catholic Congress, passionately insisted that admission of African American children to parochial schools was a matter of justice: "We ask it not alone for charity's sake, but as a right that has been dearly bought."[57]

Appeals by church officials for more young women to join teaching sisterhoods in the late 1880s came at a time of rising prestige for school teaching as a women's profession, and so these communities grew more quickly than those engaged in nursing and social service. Because the supply of teaching sisters never satisfied demand, bishops pressured communities like the Sisters of Mercy and the Sisters of Charity to divert sisters from orphanages, hospitals, and social welfare agencies to parochial schools. Within a few decades, the majority of American sisters were found in the parochial schools.[58]

The primary reason sisters were in such high demand was economic. They were willing to accept lower salaries than teaching brothers and, of course, lay teachers. The differential between salaries paid them and those paid brothers for the same work was significant. In 1876, for example, a St. Paul, Minnesota, parish offered Christian Brothers instructing boys in its school $450 for ten months. Twenty years later, sisters teaching in the same school were receiving $250.[59] The situation was the same across the nation. San Francisco sisters in one parish school had been paid nothing from 1878 until 1908, when they were offered an annual salary of $100. Brothers teaching boys in the same San Francisco parish school were already receiving a $400 salary in the 1890s, supplemented by a $350 annual grant to the community to help it meet its living expenses.[60] As a result of these disparities, and of the continuing scarcity of brothers, sisters soon monopolized parochial-school faculties. Representative was the diocese of Detroit, where in 1869 lay teachers comprised half of the total parochial-school faculty. Within two decades, sisters comprised 80 percent of the teachers.[61] Proportions were similar in other large dioceses. By 1910, for example, 88 percent of approximately 1,100 parochial-school teachers in the Boston archdiocese were sisters. And in Baltimore in the following decade, 87 percent of more than 1,500 teachers were sisters; brothers accounted for under 8 percent.[62] Pastors by the 1930s were in general agreement that brothers had become an expendable "luxury" to be replaced whenever possible with less expensive sisters.[63]

In the 1950s, the sisterhoods were heavily subsidizing the burgeoning schools. A 1953 National Catholic Educational Association survey reported that while the cost of living had risen by 93 percent between 1940 and 1953, the average salary paid a sister-teacher in a parochial school had increased by only 25 percent. The average annual salary in 1953 was $511.25, while the cost of living in a convent supplied by the parish was $489.50. The $21.75 difference was the sister's personal contribution to the central expenses of her community, including the costs of motherhouse and novitiate, the education of the sisters, the care of sick and aged members, and the payment of community debts. The survey concluded that it would take a sister thirty years to repay her community for one year's college education "without setting anything aside for her care in old age!"[64]

Pew rents and Sunday collections had served as the chief sources of parish support since the early nineteenth century. Once a church was constructed and pews rented, parishioners felt confident that they could finance the parish thereafter through regular and special collections. But after 1884, as the parochial school absorbed an increasing share of parish revenues, pastors began to reassess local benevolent activities. Some cut the traditional contribution from the parish to the St. Vincent de Paul Society for its work among the parish poor.[65] Others diverted the large holy day collections, formerly set aside for orphans, to the parish school. In 1888, for example, a Christmas collection covered 19 percent of the $3,200 annual cost of operating St. Mary's parish school in St. Paul, Minnesota. Its other income sources included a monthly twenty-five-cent tuition fee, covering 35 percent of annual costs; pew rents, covering 25 percent; and a ten-cent seat charge for adults attending the Sunday children's mass, covering 21 percent.[66] Monthly tuition fees by the early twentieth century ranged between fifty cents and one dollar per child. Although they were burdensome for many large families, they remained an important revenue source. In 1912, for instance, the average teaching sister's monthly salary of twenty-five dollars would be covered if she taught a class of fifty children, each of whom paid fifty cents per month in tuition.[67]

Even as larger numbers of Catholics advanced to the middle class in the early decades of the twentieth century, sisters continued to subsidize orphanage schools and even some parochial schools from tuitions earned in academies. Tuition income from a girls' academy was still accounting for one-third of the annual income of St. Ann's Orphanage in Belmont, North Carolina, in the mid-1920s.[68] This common situation not only obscured the fact that lay financial contributions were not supporting church charities to the extent generally assumed, but it also had the unfortunate effect of exaggerating lay perception of the scale of Catholic philanthropy relative to that of other denominations.

Despite growing pressure to focus their benevolence on the relief of material distress, nineteenth-century Catholics had taken the broad view that educating poor children was one of the works of charity. However, the 1884 mandate that children of all social classes should attend Catholic schools modified this perception significantly. The early free schools, like other church charities, originated in the parishes and were locally funded. But in contrast to other charitable institutions, the charity-organization reform movement of the early twentieth century took no steps to centralize the financing of parochial schools. Each school remained, as in the past, the financial responsibility of the parish in which it was located. Even with the contributed services of sisters, working-class parishioners by the early twentieth century were finding it very difficult to support their church and pastor, build and support a school, meet their parish quotas in the annual diocesan charity collection, and support the various national collections.

By mid-twentieth century, a substantial fraction of the middle-class Catholic population had migrated from city to suburban locations where they proceeded to build new parish schools. Because of the extremely decentralized character of school financing, this population shift placed many urban parish schools in a severe financial plight, resembling that faced by the parish orphanages a century before. The notable difference, however, was that the orphanages were eventually rescued, financially, by sharing in annual diocesan charity collections, while the city parish schools were not. In the 1970s, urban parishes were still struggling to finance their schools independently, relying on fairs, bingos, and special parish collections, methods charity reformers and bishops had rejected decades earlier as ineffective in the case of other charitable institutions.

A sharp decline in the number of women joining sisterhoods and a heavy exodus of current members, most of them relatively young, from communities during the 1960s immediately affected the nation's parochial schools. Because, by this decade, they no longer staffed many parochial schools, similar trends in brotherhoods had little impact. Between 1965 and 1980, the number of American sisters fell 30 percent, from 181,421 to 126,517.[69] Although the salaries paid lay teachers were low by public school norms, they were far higher than the stipends sisters traditionally received. The financial implications of this unexpected development were staggering for most dioceses. Illustrative was Bridgeport, Connecticut, where in the fourteen years following 1970 the parochial school faculty was transformed from being 85 percent sisters to being 85 percent lay.[70]

Between 1970 and 1991, the number of students nationwide attending parochial schools fell by 45.7 percent, from 4.6 million to 2.5 million. The number of schools declined by 24 percent in the same period, from 11,350 to 8,587. Urban schools make up nearly half of all Catholic schools, and of these, more than 1,000 are located in inner-city neighborhoods. Since many city parishes were barely covering the costs of their schools with sisters as faculty, they have felt the effects of the precipitous decline in voluntary labor most severely. Not surprisingly, inner-city schools figure disproportionately among more than 500 parochial schools that have closed across the country since 1986.[71]

A parallel development over the same period has been a rise in the proportion of minority students in the student bodies of inner-city parochial schools. For example, although overall enrollment in schools of the Brooklyn diocese declined 64 percent between 1970 and 1992, the percentage of minority students enrolled in them climbed from 16 percent to 50 percent. And while 29 percent of students in New York City schools within the New York archdiocese belonged to minority groups in 1970, by 1992 that figure was more than 63 percent. Two of every five schools reported minority enrollments of between 80 to 100 percent.[72]

The percentage of non-Catholic students in Catholic schools overall has risen steadily since the 1960s, reaching 13 percent in 1990. Since the movement of Catholics from city to suburban parishes freed seats in urban schools for neighborhood children of all faiths, urban schools report a much higher proportion of non-Catholic children than do suburban and rural schools. In Philadelphia elementary schools, for example, 15 percent of students are non-Catholic, while in Manhattan the proportion is 23 percent and, in the Bronx, 19 percent. Even including suburban-school enrollments, 16 percent of more than 147,000 students attending schools in the archdiocese of Chicago are non-Catholic. Of the 43,000 students attending its inner-city schools, however, the figure is nearly 40 percent, with some schools reporting a non-Catholic representation of 80 percent.[73] Other large cities report similar trends.

Most dioceses are currently providing some financial support to parochial schools in low-income parishes, but because subsidies are small, the schools cannot eliminate tuitions. Although inner-city schools in St. Louis have been receiving 14 percent of funds raised in the annual archdiocesan development appeal, tuitions there average $900 per child, plus $275 per family for fundraising needs. In most dioceses, subsidies come from central diocesan funds raised in annual diocesan appeals, now usually called the Bishop's Appeal or the Cardinal's Appeal. In a large archdiocese like Boston, for example, the central fund is regularly supporting the seminary, the chancery, and eighty-four archdiocesan agencies.

To the extent that parishioners respond generously in annual diocesan appeals, poor parish schools can continue to be subsidized from central funds. In 1991, however, the New York archdiocese, pleading insufficient funds, cut its annual contribution to a South Bronx parish school in half, leaving the school with a $106,000 deficit, or one-fifth of its operating budget. The school's only recourse was to raise tuition to $900 for students living within parish boundaries, $1,050 for others. Yet average family income in the neighborhood was only $7,600, and 60 percent of the children attending the school came from families receiving public assistance.[74] High schools in low-income neighborhoods face the same tuition dilemma as elementary schools. Detroit's East Catholic High School, for example, was charging a $1,475 tuition in 1991, even though most of its two hundred students qualified for the free-lunch program.[75] And when the New York archdiocese reduced by half an annual $1 million subsidy to Cardinal Hayes High School, tuition at the South Bronx boys' school rose in 1992 from $230 to $260 per month. Its student body, mainly African American and Hispanic, is poor, and two-thirds of its students come from single-parent homes. Yet because its tuition meets less than two-thirds of per-student cost, a school that currently sends 90 percent of its students on to college or further study faces an uncertain future. Twenty-one other schools in similar financial circumstances were closed by the archdiocese between 1987 and 1992.[76]

The Los Angeles archdiocese is attempting to address the tuition problem by distributing two-thirds of the annual income from its Educational Fund in the form of scholarships, earmarking the rest for school improvements.[77] Income from a recent large endowment gift and funds raised in an annual dinner to benefit inner-city schools allow the Catholic Schools Foundation of the Boston archdiocese to assist students in seventy-six schools, nearly half of them in inner-city parishes. Support for the new foundation has been strong. While the first benefit dinner, held in 1991, raised only $120,000, the second raised $850,000, funding scholarships averaging $440 for more than 2,000 inner-city students. Contributions to the Inner-City Scholarship Fund and to an endowment fund for Catholic schools totaled $1.9 million in 1994.

Church leaders give several reasons for the plight of schools in poor neighborhoods. First, they point out that the exodus of large numbers of parishioners from city parishes has caused school enrollments to decline, forcing some schools to close. Second, they note that middle-class suburban Catholics are indifferent to appeals for inner-city schools and that sisters are no longer available to subsidize them. Finally, they emphasize that diocesan subsidies for inner-city and other low-income schools are insufficient because Catholics are not contributing in accord with their means to the support of the church and its various programs.[78]

These reasons, however, raise some questions. The attribution of declining inner-city enrollments to the shift of Catholics from city to suburban parishes is particularly troublesome, since inner-city schools have not had a religion test for several decades, and demand for these schools by parents of various religious backgrounds is extremely high. Only rising tuitions prevent poor people from enrolling their children. As was the case in the parish schools of the early nineteenth century, the elimination of tuitions, or at least the imposition of fees commensurate with local family incomes, will produce soaring enrollments.

The decentralized structure of parochial-school financing plays the major role in explaining why low-income schools continue to close. Poor parishes cannot independently support schools with high labor and operating costs through parish collections and local fundraising projects. As long as diocesan subsidies remain insufficient and unpredictable, schools are forced to charge increasingly higher tuitions to cover rising costs. Annual tuitions approaching $1,000 for elementary school children are well beyond the means of the poor, and so enrollments fall, financial conditions deteriorate further, and the schools eventually close their doors.

In order that benevolent Catholics once again take collective responsibility for the education of poor children, they must view low-income parochial schools as charitable institutions, eligible in course for adequate funding from the annual diocesan appeals. Just as the diocesan charity collections of the past resolved financial crises in independent parish orphanages, so can they benefit beleaguered inner-city schools today. But in order for this to happen, this particular group of schools must be explicitly classified as diocesan charities, and this calls for a reassessment of the church's charitable priorities. Because it does not meet a primary condition for Catholic charity, namely, service to the poor, the middle-class, suburban parochial school ought not to be classified as a charitable enterprise eligible for support from diocesan central funds. Supported at personal sacrifice by parishioners, it nonetheless resembles the tuition academy more than a charitable institution. Tuitions paid by suburban parents are not philanthropic contributions, but rather payments for services rendered and benefits received.[79]

Unlike Catholic hospitals and social service agencies that receive significant government and community funding in addition to contributions from benevolent parishioners, low-income parochial schools receive little or no public financial support. No other Catholic benevolent work relies so entirely on private contributions. For this reason, the financial needs of low-income schools should take priority over other diocesan charitable institutions, agencies, and programs in the distribution of contributions made in the annual appeals. Catholic benevolent values have traditionally called for primary attention to those social needs relatively neglected by other benevolent groups, public and private. Inner-city and low-income parochial schools are effectively addressing one of the most critical social issues facing America today. A 1993 New York

State Education Department study reported that "the largest achievement advantage of New York State Catholic schools was observed when comparisons were made between Catholic and public schools with the highest level of minority student enrollment. . . . Catholic schools tend to expand their comparative achievement advantage to public schools as the percentage of minority students increases."[80] Despite their acknowledged success, however, the inner-city parochial schools continue to close.

Some recent developments, as well as historical precedent, justify a radical transformation in Catholic philanthropic perspectives. By already allocating a portion of central funds to the support of inner-city schools, dioceses are publicly acknowledging that these schools, unlike their middle-class, suburban counterparts, are indeed charitable institutions. In addition, dioceses in recent years have strongly encouraged each suburban parish to contribute resources to the support of a selected inner-city school. Parishioners involved in such projects unquestionably view their activities as charitable.

Neither independent lay initiative nor current diocesan subsidies will, however, permit a high quality system of schools in low-income neighborhoods to develop across the country. Under present organization, diocesan subsidies will remain inadequate, and fundraising projects sponsored by alumni and friends, while immensely beneficial to favored institutions, will leave the rest to deteriorate. Results of recent appeals to local businesses in major cities fluctuate with changing economic conditions. In 1981, for example, Philadelphia's business community united to raise an impressive $77 million to assist that city's Catholic schools. In contrast, response to the Partnership for Quality Education, a three-year, $100 million drive organized in 1991 by New York business leaders to benefit 140 inner-city Catholic schools has been disappointing.[81]

For a strong system of low-income schools to flourish, therefore, the entire Catholic community must perceive the education of poor children as a benevolent priority and fund it accordingly. Only when its philanthropy is large enough to allow these schools to abolish tuitions and, at the same time, provide excellent faculties, curricula, and facilities will more poor children be able to benefit from them. By generously endowing their inner-city schools, American Catholics in every diocese would advance the common good in unique and critical ways.[82]

"Free" schools in low-income neighborhoods manifestly meet the criteria of Catholic charity. Like other benevolent organizations, they welcome persons of all faiths and do not proselytize, although they profess and teach the Catholic faith. Most important, from a perspective of religious charity, they focus on today's outsiders: the poor, immigrants, members of racial and ethnic minorities. In keeping with traditional Catholic philanthropic priorities, these schools seek to aid children in need, many of them living in neighborhoods shattered by drugs and violence.

Catholics buttress their call for public support of parochial schools in the form of tax credits or tuition vouchers with the argument that, because the schools benefit the wider society, their support should not be borne solely by their users. However, an analogous case is rarely heard, namely, that all Catholics of the diocese should support its low-income and inner-city parochial schools because they enrich not just the students they enroll and the neighborhoods in which they are situated, but the entire church community. While most Catholics concur that the education of poor children is one of the greatest contributions private philanthropy can make to American society today, collectively they have not yet witnessed tangibly to these convictions by reforming the financial organization of their own inner-city and low-income parochial schools.[83]

Some insist that if low-income parochial schools are included prominently among charitable institutions supported by diocesan funds, contributions to the support of the church, declining since the 1960s, may fall even further. A mid-1960s study reported general apprehension that "revenue-reducing effects on voluntary contributions" would ensue should any changes be made in the traditional parish-based approach to school financing.[84] And it is certainly true that many middle-class Catholics continue to classify these schools as beyond the boundaries of their collective benevolence. Representative are suburban parishioners in the Youngstown, Ohio, diocese who show little interest in keeping that city's last two Catholic inner-city schools open. "Let's take care of our own Catholic kids" is their attitude.[85] On the other hand, the past thirty years have witnessed impressive voluntary initiatives by middle-class laity to help local inner-city schools. Although they remain uncoordinated, their vitality suggests that essential diocesan-level reforms in financing these schools may generate greater generosity rather than less.[86]

More than any single charitable venture, the low-income parochial school brings the philanthropic priorities of the contemporary church community into sharp, public focus. To close inner-city schools on efficiency grounds while encouraging resources to be used to open additional suburban schools reverses the traditional preference for the poor. "The church has the money," underlined one Boston priest, "It's a question of priorities."[87] Diocesan officials often counter that population, not finances, dictates the location of new schools. However, if they interpreted the term "population" to mean "poor children of all faiths," rather than "Catholic children of all income levels," their perspectives, and policy decisions following from them, would more faithfully honor the church's philanthropic tradition.

The historical experience of sisterhoods in parochial schools established unequivocally that, for voluntary service to continue to flourish, meaningful opportunities for direct contact with the poor must be present. Between 1809 and 1949, thousands of women conducted schools for children of poor and working-class families, most of them immigrants or first-generation Americans, social and religious outsiders. The nearly 8,000 elementary parochial schools, enrolling 2.1 million children in 1949,[88] would never have been possible without the sisters' contributed services. Although Catholics were moving to the middle class at a rapid pace by this time, they still assumed that sisters should and would subsidize the new schools they were constructing in suburban parishes. They acknowledged no differences between these new schools and the poor and working-class parish schools of the past. As a result, sisterhoods found themselves by mid-century subsidizing a rapidly expanding middle-class population.

By the mid-1960s, sisters were staffing most of the 13,400 parochial and diocesan schools nationwide. As demand for teachers in suburban schools continued to rise rapidly, sisters questioned more insistently why their labor was concentrated in these schools. They viewed their situation as similar to that which their predecessors faced a century earlier. While nineteenth-century sisters asked why they were conducting tuition academies when their chosen corporate mission was to teach the poor, sisters of the 1960s wanted to know why most of them were teaching middle-class suburban children rather than poor and working-class children living in low-income, urban neighborhoods. The public schools had posed no threat to the faith of Catholic children for many decades, and the sisterhoods had not been founded to subsidize the education of middle-class youth. Yet that is exactly what most of them were now doing. In the archdiocese of San Francisco in the 1960s, for example, parents in affluent and middle-class suburban parishes were paying the same low parochial-school tuition as parents in poor parishes, six dollars per month per family, "regardless of the number of school-age children in the family."[89]

A few sisterhoods had begun to address the problem as early as the 1940s. They asserted that it was not their mission to subsidize the education of Catholic children of all social classes, but rather to instruct poor and working-class children, regardless of their religious background. Therefore, they allocated fewer teachers to middle-class parishes that had the means to hire lay teachers for their schools in order to subsidize more inner-city and poor rural schools.[90] Not until the 1960s, however, did such changes become widespread. In 1968, through the Conference of Major Superiors of Religious Women, the American sisterhoods joined to inform the hierarchy of their dissatisfaction with their present role in Catholic education. "Religious women, as women, desire to listen to all and to serve all, but especially the weak," they said. "In the present Catholic educational structure, many women resent the fact that their service is frequently limited to the middle class. This resentment is underlined by an even narrower service to the Catholic middle class within a Catholic school structure, not to the entire People of God."[91]

Although this perspective astonished and often incensed the rest of the church, the sisters continued to challenge externally imposed definitions of their corporate benevolent works. A group of Los Angeles sisters explained their position in the late 1960s: "Women around the world, young and old, are playing decisive roles in public life, changing their world, developing new life styles.... Women who want to serve and who are capable of service have already given evidence that they can no longer uncritically accept the judgment of others as to where and how that service ought to be extended. American women religious want to be in the mainstream of this new, potentially fruitful and inevitable bid for self-determination by women."[92]

Explanations for the decline in the sisterhoods have centered on their strict lifestyle, the influence of the civil rights and feminist movements, and women's widening professional opportunities. While each of these factors certainly played a role, there is one critical agent that has been overlooked. It is the effect on sisters, most of whom were parochial-school teachers, of the rapid progress of American Catholics to middle-class status since the 1940s. If the progressive spirit that spurred nineteenth- and early-twentieth-century parishioners to fund free schools for poor and working-class children again flourishes, idealistic and generous young men and women, religious and lay, will again emerge to conduct and support them.[93] A radical diocesan commitment to sustain tuition-free schools in poor neighborhoods will strongly encourage gifts of voluntary service as well as money from every quarter of the American Catholic community.

Government social welfare programs, community agencies, and other private charities are today providing better material assistance and health care to citizens in need than they did in the past. At the same time, one of America's most acute social needs remains inadequately addressed by either government or the private sector, namely, the education of poor children, especially those living in the nation's cities. By generously financing excellent schools for children of all faiths, races, and ethnic backgrounds in low-income neighborhoods across the country, Catholics will testify again, not only to their traditional religious benevolence, but also to the formidable capacity of private initiative to address urgent social problems efficiently and effectively.

American Catholics today need to consider, as a community, which good works will take precedence in their collective philanthropy and then decide how to fund them properly. A century ago, their preference for the institutional approach to charity triggered harsh criticism. Today, however, few Americans dispute the social and educational merits of Catholic low-income and inner-city schools. Yet high tuitions and insufficient diocesan support are forcing these schools to close at an alarming rate.

The school question, then, is the most compelling challenge and opportunity facing modern Catholics. The provision of an extensive system of free, high-quality, private schools in inner cities and low-income neighborhoods across the country represents an enormous and distinctive contribution to the common good of society. By focusing on poor children in their neighborhoods, it affirms the commitment of Catholics to the pioneer benevolent work of their church in America. In short, more than any other good work, it promises to revitalize the liberal democratic spirit of their collective philanthropy.

8

Recent Trends in Catholic Giving

As the body without the spirit is dead, so faith without works is dead also.

—James 2: 26

U NLIKE MANY OTHER religious denominations, the Catholic Church does not exclude from membership those who contribute little or nothing to the support of its corporate good works. Yet it insists that, while religion encompasses more than these works, it is through them that members give public testimony to their faith. Thus charity critically defines the committed Catholic. Those who do not give in accord with their means, while not excluded from the church, are not full participants in its life.[1] In a narrow sense, individual giving might be thought to fulfill the philanthropic obligation. But the independent donor misses the spiritual benefits that result from joining with fellow believers in the works of charity. Since its charities are integral to the life of the church, Catholics enter that life to the degree that they join in these good works.

The American Catholic community until 1920 focused its philanthropy almost entirely on immediate relief of the materially poor. Overall representation of "big givers" remained small, although a substantial middle class and a small upper class had developed by the end of the nineteenth century. More than any single factor, the contributions of service by members of religious communities and lay benevolent societies permitted the development of a very large and comprehensive system of charities. Attitudes toward benevolent priorities and strategies shifted after 1920, as immigration and religious tensions abated and the socioeconomic status of the Catholic community advanced. Within the church itself, centralization of charitable institutions and agencies under diocesan bureaus seriously challenged traditional values and philanthropic styles. These historical changes, internal and external to the church, continue to affect the corporate altruism of Catholics today.

Whereas in 1945 American Catholics still ranked below both Protestants and Jews in social class, by the 1970s they had matched Protestants in economic status and nearly equaled them in educational background. White male heads of Catholic households were as likely as their counterparts in other denominations to hold professional and managerial positions. As members of the mainstream, Catholics examined with new eyes the schools, charitable institutions, and benevolent organizations they had developed and supported as an outsider community.[2] In important ways, social acceptance had already profoundly affected their collective benevolence. Professional standards in conducting the charities and in raising funds for them were in place, collaboration with mainstream charitable organizations and public agencies was taken for granted, and charitable trusts, endowments, and foundations were commonplace. The closing of parochial schools seemed to be following an earlier trend away from institutional child care, and government funds accounted for a high proportion of hospital and social agency revenues.

However, in 1980, practicing Roman Catholic households ranked lowest in annual contributions to the church among ten major religious groups. Nor was this a temporary aberration. Between 1963 and 1984, total contributions per full or confirmed church member declined by nearly 35 percent in constant 1982 dollars.[3] Although, collectively, Catholics gave $5.48 billion to the church in 1991, a national survey of randomly selected parishes found that the typical household contribution in regular parish collections that year was only $280.15, less than 1 percent of average household income. Of the 62 percent of households that gave under $200 annually in the Sunday collections, one-half gave nothing, and the rest, on average, donated $42. If the average annual income for households in this giving bracket equaled that of the aggregate Catholic population, then they were contributing only 0.10 percent of their income to the church.[4]

Although more affluent as a group than Protestants, America's 59 million Catholics today contribute, on average, only 1.1 percent of their per capita incomes to the church. This represents half their rate of giving in the 1960s, as well as half the current rate of Protestant giving.[5] This disparity between Protestants and Catholics, while apparent at every social class level, is particularly evident among the wealthy. While church-going Catholics earning over $40,000 gave, on average, 1.1 percent of their annual income to the church in 1984, Protestants in the same income bracket were contributing 4.4 percent. In contrast, giving by Catholics without a high school diploma earning under $15,000 nearly matched that of their Protestant counterparts.[6] There is no evidence that Catholics, as a group, are less generous to non-church philanthropic causes than members of other Christian denominations.[7]

In 1992, the episcopal authors of the first draft of a pastoral letter on stewardship attributed the decline in giving to problems internal to the church itself. They raised the possibility "that the message of generous stewardship has not been preached effectively, that people's real life needs may not be met, nor their voices heard within the church community."[8] Andrew Greeley and William McManus also ascribe the downturn in giving since the early 1960s to causes internal to the church. They maintain that because laity have little to say about how their financial contributions to the church are allocated, they are less inclined to give generously. In addition, appeals and collection procedures do not differentiate sufficiently between contributing to the support of the church, an obligation in justice, and giving to fulfill the charitable mandate, with adverse effects for both. However, they identify as the single most important explanatory factor "a selective alienation related to a decline in acceptance of the Church's authority and especially its authority on sexual matters."[9]

The most visible consequence of this severe slump in aggregate giving is that nearly one-third of American dioceses are in financial difficulty today. In 1992, for example, the archdiocese of New York reported its worst financial downturn in history. The archdiocese of Boston similarly recorded a deficit of nearly $2.4 million and projected a cumulative deficit of $45 million for the 1988–97 period, should giving and spending remain at current levels. Charitable contributions, when considered separately from contributions for church support, exhibit the same discouraging trends as the aggregate figures. Approximately one-third of yearly contributions benefit extra-parish causes, such as the twelve national collections and the support of diocesan programs, including Catholic charities. Yet 52 percent of respondents in a 1993 national Gallup poll of lay Catholics agreed that one can be a good Catholic without donating time or money to help the poor. This contrasts with 1987, when 44 percent of respondents agreed with that statement.[10] At the local level, support for church charities appears to lag well behind charitable giving by other religious groups. In 1991, for example, Boston's 1.8 million Catholics contributed approximately $11 million to support their archdiocesan charities, an average of $6 per capita. On the other hand, the local Jewish community, numbering only 225,000, donated more than $23 million to the Combined Jewish Philanthropies in that year, an average per capita gift of $102.[11]

A serious decline in contributions of voluntary service has accompanied the slump in monetary giving in recent decades. The ranks of the sisterhoods had been growing steadily during the twentieth century, and in the mid-1960s, they reported more than 180,000 members. Bishops, clergy, and laity alike took it for granted that this growth would continue and that parochial schools and charitable institutions would benefit, as in the past, from an army of lifetime volunteers. Thus, they were stunned when the number of sisters suddenly began to contract sharply. A downturn in the number of lay volunteers, as married women entered the labor force in increasing numbers, magnified the effects of this development. Labor costs in church charities and schools mounted swiftly, and it was clear that monetary contributions were not adequate to support the good works of the church at current levels.

For two hundred years, American Catholics cherished as a religious value the essential link between gifts of money and gifts of voluntary service. For them, benevolence had to meet two criteria, one more important than the other. Unless accompanied by some form of personal service, however modest, the financial contribution, however large, cannot fully satisfy the mandate of religious charity. John Ireland summarized the venerable doctrine at the turn of the century: "We do not fulfill our duty by paying a tax to the State or by sending to a committee an annual subscription, leaving to the State or the committee to stand proxy for us, and neglecting to come, ourselves, into contact with the poor. Charity is love for the victim of sorrow, and love demands personal attention."[12]

While this traditional message continues to be preached, opportunities for its meaningful expression have decreased considerably, with the serious result that the proportion of Catholics who volunteer personal service to any good work for any cause was only 39 percent in 1990, a figure well below the 47 percent and 46 percent reported for Protestants and Jews, respectively.[13] The church is clearly not attending to the lessons of its own philanthropic history or to the lessons of personal giving generally, since individuals who contribute voluntary service to a charitable work typically donate 60 percent more money to it than do non-volunteers.[14] Thus the explanation for the decline in monetary contributions to the church may lie, in large measure, in the secular decline in significant volunteer opportunities in its philanthropic sector.

As bureaucracy, clerical dominance, and reliance on government funding developed after 1920, lay voluntary initiative waned. Warnings of the impending danger could be heard from the outset of the centralization movement. In the 1920s, for example, Rev. Michael Scanlan had cautioned the hierarchy and diocesan charity directors that "the continuance of our charities will depend almost entirely upon the extent to which our people can be counted upon to devote their time and talents to works of supererogation. Too much coordination and too much supervision and too much efficiency may very easily lessen the warmth of our Catholic people's devotion to good works."[15] In the next decade, John O'Grady underscored Scanlan's message, reminding bishops that personal involvement is "far more important" than any other feature of church charity since it is "the only means of making the laity a part of the ministry of charity."[16] Members of the Catholic Worker Movement called for reform of the new system of charity organization in the 1930s and 1940s. "The ordinary work-a-day Catholic is not able to contribute as much as they [sic] could before the depression and they have no place on committees. Is it necessary that people of limited means and limited time shall be deprived of all opportunity to practice the Works of Mercy?"[17] Even the *Catholic Charities Review* was deploring the "discouragement of lay participation" that seemed to be the inevitable accompaniment of centralization. "By lay participation we do not mean professional workers," the editor emphasized in 1950. "They were in the picture and had a large share in the development of plans and programs. By lay workers we mean volunteers who were active not only as board members but as actual participants in our different lay groups."[18]

Nonetheless, by the 1960s, the organizational structure of diocesan charities made informal lay volunteer collaboration extremely difficult. The St. Paul and Minneapolis charitable bureau was representative of most. Its officers in this decade included the archbishop as corporation president, his vicar general as vice president, and the priest-director of the archdiocesan charities as secretary-treasurer. While its bylaws allowed up to twelve laymen to be appointed to the board, such appointments were largely token. In 1963, the board had not met in seventeen years, and according to a local bishop, "the list of members seems hard to obtain."[19]

Charity officials of the 1970s, for the most part, acknowledged fading grassroots support, but preferred to attribute it to lay provincialism and apathy. The director of the National Conference of Catholic Charities, for example, described modern parishioners as generally self-absorbed, pursuing money for personal pleasure and security, and viewing charity as "a work of supererogation over and above the call of duty, so to speak." His proposed remedy for the situation reflected the prevailing bureaucratic mentality: strengthen the National Conference of Catholic Charities.[20]

Most dioceses, especially the large ones, were routinely hiring professional fundraising firms to conduct their annual charity campaigns by the 1970s.[21] Since then, a number have taken centralized fundraising to new heights by adopting a single comprehensive annual drive for all diocesan needs and works. Although arguably more efficient and financially productive than two annual collections, one for central needs and the other for diocesan charities, the consolidated drive has at least two dangerous features. It minimizes the primary place of charity in the life of the church, and it consolidates further the already highly centralized process of church giving. Since diocesan charities are intended to witness to a collective honoring of the gospel call to give to the poor, appeals for them should not be merged with collections to cover administrative costs of a diocese. Parishioners do not necessarily respond to appeals for the support of the diocese in the same way that they respond to collections for charity.

Extra-church funding first assumed major importance in Catholic philanthropy in the 1930s as federal and state monies became more widely available

for the support of programs of private social welfare agencies. Diocesan charitable bureaus applied energetically for these funds, with the result that by the
1960s a significantly higher percentage of their agency budgets came from tax
monies than was the case for either Jewish or Protestant philanthropies.[22] Thereafter, annual diocesan charity appeals called on Catholics to give generously
because the level of their donations would determine the amount of government
and community agency funds that would be forthcoming. In 1976, for example,
San Franciscans were informed that their contributions in the annual charities
appeal had yielded an eight-fold return in external payments,[23] and the Chicago
bureau pledged to pursue aggressively what it considered its fair share of public
monies and community fund allotments.[24]

By the 1980s, government funds were accounting for the major proportion
of charity budgets in dioceses, large and small. In the Stockton, California, diocese, for example, contributions from parishioners in the 1984 annual appeal
covered less than 3 percent of the operating income of the diocesan charities.[25]
Representative of large archdioceses was Boston, where 75 percent of revenues
budgeted for its charities in 1988 came from government contracts, the United
Way, and program service fees.[26] Nationally, the picture was similar. A 1991 national survey of diocesan charities reported that the sources of 82 percent of
their collective income of over $1.8 billion were government funds, United Way
funds, and service fees. Government funds alone accounted for 63 percent of
the total, private donations for 11 percent.[27] Such heavy reliance on government
and community funds led many parishioners to conclude that their charitable
donations would mean more to other benevolent causes than to the charities of
their church.

Since long-term effects of extra-ecclesial funding on the benevolence of parishioners received little attention during decades of steadily rising appropriations, cutbacks in government and community agency funding in recent years
have had severe consequences in many dioceses. For example, Catholic Charities in Chicago, relying on the United Way for nearly two-thirds of its budget,
had to retrench its services significantly when that agency reduced its funding
for 1993 by $1.1 million.[28] And since federal funds were accounting for such a
high proportion of the income of Catholic Charities nationally, cuts in federal
appropriations for social programs in the 1980s were immediately reflected, not
only in their own agency budgets, but also in an increase in applications for
help from people whom other private agencies could no longer assist. Since state
appropriations to compensate for reductions in federal funding have not been
forthcoming, dioceses are now asking grassroots parishioners to make up the
shortfalls.[29]

Warnings of the dangers of reliance on government funds had been voiced in many quarters, but not sufficiently heeded. In the 1950s, concern that government funds were beginning to dominate diocesan charity budgets was raised. "When the voluntary groups depend on government for their entire support we have reached an age of impasse," declared one observer. "Such organizations for all practical purposes become government instrumentalities. . . . One may seriously raise the question as to how far it is compatible with the Christian and the democratic way of life."[30]

Over the next four decades, dependence on government and community funding affected Catholic giving in important, and not necessarily positive, ways. While, on the one hand, government and United Way funds permitted an enormous expansion in the scale, quality, and scope of services supplied by Catholic charities, on the other hand, they greatly reinforced the bureaucratic approach to giving and raised serious questions about the religious character of the charities themselves.[31] Dorothy Day cautioned in the 1960s that uncritical acceptance of government policies and goals by diocesan charities was weakening the foundations of Catholic philanthropy and urged that parishioners return to a standard of "true efficiency" that measured charity not by budget or agency size, but rather by the extent of personal exchange between local parishioners and the poor. "Would that every parish had some small house or store where this work could be begun!"[32] However, by this decade, the local parish, the traditional arena of lay benevolence, was functioning primarily as a diocesan-wide fundraising site.

Laity and religious of the 1970s were inquiring whether diocesan charitable bureaus, in their eagerness to qualify for designated government funds, were providing social services more congenial to civic and political agendas than to the benevolent priorities of church members. A study of the Boston archdiocesan charities in that decade, for example, detected "pressure to develop services only in response to public contracts."[33] At this time, government funds were accounting for nearly 70 percent of the charities budget. The question of how dependence on government and community agency funds affected the religious character of the charities became a matter of growing concern for those who managed and staffed the charitable institutions. Charity directors in New York City pointedly asked the National Conference of Catholic Charities in 1975: "How do you Christianize your services when your funding source (particularly government) is constantly trying to secularize the institutions?"[34]

Three years earlier, respondents in a national survey had similarly challenged the conference to provide them with "practical, pragmatic help, not theory" in dealing with this question.[35] A 1974 poll of Minnesota Catholic and Lutheran social service directors revealed significant confusion and distress. Nearly 75 percent of those responding could not identify any values distinguishing religious from secular social agencies. The Catholic respondents pleaded for a return to traditional Catholic benevolent values. They urged that the church reengage ordinary parishioners in voluntary service and take measures to ensure that charitable agencies and programs were, in fact, strictly honoring the church's preferential option for the poor.[36] Benevolent parishioners, in effect, were calling for a review of the definition of a Catholic charitable work as an activity, institution, or social agency approved by the church. If the charitable agencies of the church are indistinguishable from secular charity organizations, why should Catholics be expected to give them priority in benevolence?[37]

The systematic relegation of ordinary laity to the sidelines in the vast field of charity had a particularly devastating impact on women, since their only official roles in the church lay in that arena. Although Mary Gibbons had served as president of the National Conference of Catholic Charities in 1939, women remained virtually excluded from national and diocesan policy-making forums in the decades that followed. Her announcement that the laywoman "is not satisfied to make only a financial contribution for 'charity' even when she is able to do so; and when she cannot contribute money, the urge to give personal service is even greater"[38] was not taken seriously. Key national committees resembled, in gender composition, the 1970 Catholic Charities Appeal Committee of the National Conference of Catholic Charities. It included eleven priests, one religious brother, and one layman.[39] There was little improvement over the next two decades. For instance, a volunteer executive cabinet established by the National Conference in 1987 to initiate a national development program had a cardinal as its honorary chair, joined by two bishops, a priest, and nine men, all national leaders in business, politics, and the professions. The cabinet's lone female member was identified simply as a liaison from Catholic Charities USA. At the diocesan level, however, progress has occurred as women assume significant administrative posts in diocesan charity offices. By 1992 they were accounting for 30 percent of principal directors of diocesan charitable bureaus nationally, a significant change from 1960 when all directors were priests.[40]

The long-term cost of excluding women from decision-making roles in the philanthropic sphere is incalculable. By the 1970s, however, its effects on one group, the religious sisters, were evident. Their authority over charitable institutions had diminished considerably by this time, and they were not being offered leadership positions in diocesan charity offices. Their visibly subordinate status ran counter to the advances educated women generally were making in business and the professions and it had a deleterious effect on recruitment of new members for the communities.

There have been a few positive developments in recent years, nonetheless.

Independent lay benevolent initiatives have appeared in every diocese, most of them small, local, and focused on the poor. As such, they are thoroughly within the Catholic philanthropic tradition. Despite their shrinking numbers and limited financial resources, sisterhoods remain highly organized, their members well educated. This has allowed them to move vigorously and innovatively into "new" works. In 1971, for example, the largest American sisterhood, the Sisters of Mercy of the Union, established the Mercy Action Fund to benefit social welfare and reform projects. Sisters held all seats on its governing board, which controlled allocation of funds. By 1990, the fund had made 432 grants, totaling $2.5 million.

This project is by no means unique. An exemplary undertaking supported by sisterhoods is a chain of homes for female ex-prisoners and their infants, begun in 1979 in former convents and rectories in New York City. Nine Providence Houses shelter battered wives, homeless women, and former prisoners. Sisters, who live in each of the houses, contribute their salaries as social workers and school teachers to the work. The personal initiative, decentralized focus, and progressive spirit of traditional Catholic benevolence find renewed expression in such enterprises. According to one observer: "It is classic old-fashioned charity, barely noticed in the city and carried on without benefit of bureaucratic folderol. . . . There clearly is no religious theme in the houses, other than personal example."[41] As was the case a century ago, lay volunteers collaborate closely with sisters in the work.

When California state laws in the 1970s discouraged residential care for court referrals, Sisters of the Good Shepherd opened a home for San Francisco women in serious need, including prostitutes and women with marital and psychological problems. Although the archbishop in 1979 termed this "the *greatest* need in the city," the home was described the following year as "without an assured income."[42] The sisters' Los Angeles counterparts took up a work "undreamed of when the five foundresses arrived in the city 75 years ago," the care of battered women and their children. Within two years they had cared for over 800 in their shelter. "The sisters are once again poor with the poor women they are serving," wrote one sister, "and are dependent on the generosity of friends and other charitable groups for the food, clothing and daily necessities of the battered wives and the victimized children who come to them."[43] The independent, indeed competitive, spirit that marked sisterhoods before the 1960s has given way to mutual support and cooperative projects, like the Institute for Poverty and Social Reform established in the 1980s by four Michigan sisterhoods to address social problems and represent the interests of the poor.[44]

In order that the laity in large numbers become again full partners in the works of charity, dioceses must not only return some autonomy over the allocation of charitable contributions to the nation's more than 20,000 parishes, but also provide them with professional counsel and assistance through the diocesan charitable offices. While many dioceses actively encourage parish outreach programs, in which local parishioners offer service as well as funds to those in need,[45] few yet espouse the decentralized, democratic charity organization recommended more than twenty years ago by Rev. John Ahern, Assistant Director of Catholic Charities for the New York archdiocese. He called for movement "toward smallness, toward responsiveness, toward more accountability," and toward a parish-based charities structure. "It does not lie simply in doing our work on the parish premises. It does not lie simply in consulting with the parish on the content and in dividing the functions and the responsibilities of the parish. It does not lie solely in the use of non-professional staff or of professionals from other disciplines. I think it lies in our dismemberment of ourselves in the creation, on the community base, of new agencies."[46] This proposal, while firmly in the Catholic philanthropic tradition, still awaits comprehensive implementation.

That individuals of all social classes will give more generously in diocesan collections if they are personally involved in allocating contributions through their parishes was demonstrated in Detroit in 1982. Most money raised in the annual Archdiocesan Development Fund came from suburban parishes and was distributed by the central diocesan office to poor parishes. "After a decade of sluggish returns," the archdiocese changed course, renaming the collection the Catholic Services Appeal and promising to return to parishioners for local benevolent projects all funds contributed above parish quotas. Results were immediate and dramatic. Contributions of $8.2 million in 1982 exceeded the appeal target by 27 percent and the 1981 campaign by 200 percent.[47]

Smaller dioceses and parishes, wider social class and gender representation on diocesan and institutional charity boards, encouragement of individual initiative in addressing new social needs, and opportunity for all, not simply the rich, to designate beneficiaries of monetary contributions are reforms that do not jeopardize but rather enhance the benefits of coordination and efficiency that central charity organization provides.[48] While the extreme decentralization that marked Catholic charity organization of the last century certainly required substantial modification in the face of twentieth-century challenges, centralized bureaus were unable to accommodate popular participation satisfactorily. As a result, the sense of personal ownership of the charities of the church has declined. A paradox faces Catholic philanthropy. By adopting secular standards in organization and fundraising, and by relying heavily on extra-ecclesial funding, it has vastly expanded its capacity to assist the poor and to offer high-quality services. Yet in critical ways these strategies compete with primary religious values. The challenge facing Catholics today is how to retain the obvious benefits of central organization while at the same time widening significant personal involvement.

There are important lessons in the Catholic philanthropic experience for America's independent sector. More than any other major religious denomination, the Catholic Church, in its size and heterogeneous population, represents in microcosm the wider society. The history of its philanthropy reveals that poor and working-class citizens, no less than their middle- and upper-class counterparts, have immense potential for collective voluntary action in the public interest. That capacity will remain unfulfilled, however, as long as benevolent strategies, however "efficient," prevail that constrain popular involvement. By restoring and strengthening the democratic spirit of their collective charity, American Catholics will contribute critically to shaping the nation's social conscience. The time is ripe for a second organizational revolution in Catholic philanthropy.

Notes

Abbreviations Used in the Notes

AAB	Archives, Archdiocese of Baltimore, Maryland.
AABOS	Archives, Archdiocese of Boston, Massachusetts.
AAC	Archives, Archdiocese of Chicago, Illinois.
AALA	Archives, Archdiocese of Los Angeles, California.
AANO	Archives, Archdiocese of New Orleans, Louisiana.
AAPHIL	Archives, Archdiocese of Philadelphia, Pennsylvania.
AASF	Archives, Archdiocese of San Francisco, California.
AASL	Archives, Archdiocese of St. Louis, Missouri.
AASPM	Archives, Archdiocese of St. Paul and Minneapolis, Minnesota.
ACC-AAC	Associated Catholic Charities Collection, Archives, Archdiocese of Chicago.
ACUA	Archives, The Catholic University of America, Washington, D.C.
AJF	Archives, Josephite Fathers, Baltimore, Maryland.
AUND	Archives, University of Notre Dame, Notre Dame, Indiana.
BCIM	Bureau of Catholic Indian Missions Collection. Archives, Marquette University, Milwaukee, Wisconsin.
CC-USA	Archives, Catholic Charities USA, Alexandria, Virginia.
CCYB	*Catholic Charities and Social Welfare Activities of the Archdiocese of Philadelphia, Year Book [1924, 1926]*
CSJBOS	Archives, Sisters of St. Joseph, Brighton, Massachusetts.
CSJNY	Archives, Sisters of St. Joseph, Brentwood, New York.
CSJPHIL	Archives, Sisters of St. Joseph, Chestnut Hill, Pennsylvania.
CSJSL	Archives, Sisters of St. Joseph, St. Louis, Missouri.
CSJSP	Archives, Sisters of St. Joseph, St. Paul, Minnesota.
DCA	Archives, Daughters of Charity of St. Vincent de Paul, Albany, New York.
DCSL	Archives, Daughters of Charity of St. Vincent de Paul, St. Louis, Missouri.
DDCW	Dorothy Day-Catholic Worker Collection. Archives, Marquette University, Milwaukee, Wisconsin.
GCW-MHS	Guild of Catholic Women of St. Paul, Minnesota, Collection. Minnesota Historical Society, Minneapolis, Minnesota.
PAB-UND	Rev. Peter A. Baart Collection. Archives, University of Notre Dame, Notre Dame, Indiana.

PCCCSL	*Conference of Catholic Charities and Social Activities of the City of St. Louis, Proceedings*, 1912.
RSJOA	*Report of the Board of Managers of the St. John's Orphan Asylum for the Year [1838, 1846, 1850, 1852, 1854, 1855].*
SBS	Archives, Sisters of the Blessed Sacrament, Bensalem, Pennsylvania.
SCN	Archives, Sisters of Charity of Nazareth, Nazareth, Kentucky.
SMCA	Archives, Sisters of Mercy, Burlingame, California.
SMNC	Archives, Sisters of Mercy, Belmont, North Carolina.
SMNH	Archives, Sisters of Mercy, Windham, New Hampshire.
SMRI	Archives, Sisters of Mercy, Providence, Rhode Island.

1. American Society and Benevolent Enterprise

1. Thomas Hughes, *History of the Society of Jesus in North America*, 4 vols. (New York: Longmans, Green, 1907–1917), Documents, vol. 1, pt. 2: 743–44; Jay P. Dolan, *The American Catholic Experience: A History from Colonial Times to the Present* (Garden City, N.Y.: Doubleday, 1985), 86–91; James J. Hennesey, *American Catholics: A History of the Roman Catholic Community in the United States* (New York: Oxford University Press, 1981), 49–52; John Gilmary Shea, *History of the Catholic Church*, 4 vols. (New York: John G. Shea, 1886–1892), 1: 38–47; John Lancaster Spalding, *The Life of the Most Rev. M. J. Spalding* (New York: Catholic Publication Society, 1873), 141–42.

2. John Carroll, "Pastoral Letter, 28 May 1792," in Hugh J. Nolan, ed., *Pastoral Letters of the United States Catholic Bishops*, 5 vols. (Washington, D.C.: National Conference of Catholic Bishops, 1984), 1: 19; *Cathedral Records: From the Beginning of Catholicity in Baltimore to the Present Time* (Baltimore: Catholic Mirror Publishing, 1906), 5–6.

3. Thomas McAvoy, "The Catholic Minority in the United States, 1789–1821," *Historical Records and Studies* 39–40 (1952): 44–46.

4. "Resolutions, &c. Of The Roman Catholics In The City of New York. Extracted from a Pamphlet Lately Published," *The Reformer*, Philadelphia, 1 December 1824, 268–70; J. Carroll, 1: 23–24.

5. By the 1850s, the average pastor was earning a fair income. Stipends for masses for special intentions, weddings, funerals, and baptisms supplemented a $600 salary, plus room and board, permitting him to receive about $1000 annually. According to one New York priest, many in 1865 could "live luxuriantly." Diary of Rev. Richard L. Burtsell, 12 May 1865, quoted in Jay P. Dolan, *The Immigrant Church: New York's Irish and German Catholics, 1815–1865* (Baltimore: Johns Hopkins University Press, 1975), 65–66.

6. *U.S. Catholic Miscellany*, 6 June 1822; "The Diurnal of the Right Rev. John England," quoted in Peter Guilday, *The Life and Times of John England*, 2 vols. (New York: America Press, 1927), 1: 346–47. England's diary covered the period from 25 August 1820 to 5 December 1823.

7. An Account of the Receipts and Disbursements of St. James's and St. Paul's Churches, May 20–November 20, 1839, CSJNY; Dolan, 1975, 51.

8. Receipts and Expenditures, 1873, St. Vincent de Paul Parish, Brooklyn, New York, CSJNY; Dolan, 1975, 50–51, 58; Leslie Woodcock Tentler, *Seasons of Grace: A History of the Catholic Archdiocese of Detroit* (Detroit: Wayne State University Press, 1990), 75.

9. Michael N. Kremer, "Church Support in the United States" (D.C.L. diss., Catholic University of America, 1930), 89–93.

10. Michael Corrigan, "Pastoral Letter, on the Occasion of the Fifth Diocesan Synod, New York, November 17–18, 1886," quoted in Frederick J. Zwierlein, *Letters of Archbishop Corrigan to Bishop McQuaid and Allied Documents* (Rochester, N.Y.: Art Print Shop, 1946), 88–89.

11. Shea, 2: 600–601; *Cathedral Records,* 21, 26. Carroll's diocese at this time encompassed the thirteen original states.

12. Quoted in *Cathedral Records,* 21.

13. Stephen Badin to Bishop Carroll, 25 February 1801, Badin to Carroll, 26 March 1804, quoted in "The Church in Kentucky," *Records of the American Catholic Historical Society of Philadelphia* 23 (1912): 142, 150–51.

14. Raymond Corrigan, "Mission Aid Societies," *Thought* 10 (1935): 291, 296–97.

15. Quoted in A. J. Rezek, "The Leopoldine Society," *Acta et Dicta* 3 (July 1914): 318.

16. M. A. Pekari, "The German Catholics in the United States of America," *Records of the American Catholic Historical Society of Philadelphia* 36 (December 1925): 343–44; R. Corrigan, 197, 289; Mary Agnes McCann, "Archbishop Purcell and the Archdiocese of Cincinnati" (Ph.D. diss., Catholic University of America, 1918), 29; Samuel F. B. Morse, *Imminent Dangers to the Free Institutions of the United States, etc.* (1835). Morse's tract originally appeared as a series of articles in the *New York Journal of Commerce.* See Guilday, 2: 195–208.

17. R. Corrigan, 292.

18. Bishop Bruté to the Leopoldine Society, n.d. [c. 1835], quoted in *Souvenir of the Silver Jubilee in the Episcopacy of His Grace the Most Rev. Patrick Augustine Feehan, Archbishop of Chicago, November 1st. 1890* (1891), 6.

19. "Bishop Dubois on New York in 1836," *Historical Records and Studies* 10 (January 1917): 126; Guilday, 2: 391.

20. *The Jesuit* 1 (26 June 1830): 333–35.

21. Shea, 3: 503–504; M. Viatora Schuller, "A History of Catholic Orphan Homes in the United States, 1727 to 1884" (Ph.D. diss., Loyola University, 1954), 46.

22. Rose White's Journal, Philadelphia. St. Joseph's Orphan Asylum, 6 May 1814, handwritten account, 11-1, 1-7-1. 2a, DCA.

23. Rose White's Journal, 6 May 1814, 11-1, 1-7-1. 2a, DCA.

24. Martin I. J. Griffin, "St. Joseph's Orphan Asylum, Philadelphia," *American Catholic Historical Researches* 14 (1897): 12; Daniel Hannefin, *Daughters of the Church: A Popular History of the Daughters of Charity in the United States, 1809–1987* (New York: New City Press, 1989), 20–21. In the 1840s, sisters working in orphanages typically received room, board, and a fifty dollar annual salary. See Annals, 21 March 1849, CSJPHIL. Most Americans continued to address the Emmitsburg Sisters as "Sisters of Charity" after their 1850 affiliation with the French-based Daughters of Charity. See Hannefin, x.

25. John Connolly to Mrs. Seton, 14 July 1817, quoted in *Mother Rose White* (Emmitsburg, Md.: St. Joseph's Central House, 1936), 48.

26. Thomas Crimmins, comp., *The Diary of John D. Crimmins from 1878 to 1917* (New Rochelle: Knickerbocker Press, 1925), 1061–62.

27. *A Brief Historical Sketch of the Roman Catholic Orphan Asylum of Brooklyn, March 25, 1930* (New York: Roman Catholic Orphan Asylum Society, 1930), 20.

28. Quoted in *Souvenir of the Silver Jubilee,* 27.

29. *U.S. Catholic Miscellany* 9 (13 February 1830; 6 February 1830; 1 May 1830), cited in M. Gertrude McCray, "Evidences of Catholic Interest in Social Welfare in the United States, 1830–1850" (M.A. thesis, Notre Dame University, 1937), 45; Minute Book, Catholic Female Benevolent Society of Detroit, 1834–1836, cited in Tentler, 76–80.

30. Agnes Cecilia Miller, "A Study of the Convent of the Good Shepherd in New Orleans" (M.S.W. thesis, Tulane University, 1941), 16. No state provided public institutional child care before 1811.

31. Dominick Murphy, *Sketches of Irish Nunneries* (Dublin: James Duffy, 1865), 134. McAuley founded the Sisters of Mercy in 1831.

32. Dale Light, "The Reformation of Philadelphia Catholicism, 1830–1860," *Pennsylvania Magazine of History and Biography* 112 (July 1988): 377.

33. Daniel T. McColgan, *A Century of Charity: The First One Hundred Years of the Society of*

St. Vincent de Paul in the United States, 2 vols. (Milwaukee: Bruce, 1951), 1: 278; McCann, 22–23. It was the only such institution in the city at this time, and nearly a quarter of the children enrolled were Protestants.

34. William S. Pelletier, "Vincentian Tribute to the Late Archbishop Williams," *St. Vincent de Paul Quarterly* 13 (1908): 166; McColgan, 1: 224. The society's focus on education was not unique to Boston. In the 1850s, the Richmond, Virginia, society was conducting "a large school for boys in the basement of the Cathedral." Joseph Magri, *The Catholic Church in the City and Diocese of Richmond* (Richmond: Whittet & Shepperson, 1906), 83.

35. McCann, 17. At this time, free schools also commonly benefited from "charity sermons" and "anniversary orations." McCann, 27. See also George Paul Jacoby, *Catholic Child Care in Nineteenth Century New York* (1941; reprint, New York: Arno Press, 1974), 92, 102–103.

36. Guilday, 2: 160–63. Two-thirds of 125 Catholics who died in the 1838 epidemic were Irish immigrants. See also John K. Sharp, *History of the Diocese of Brooklyn, 1853–1953: The Catholic Church on Long Island*, 2 vols. (New York: Fordham University Press, 1954), 1: 78, 101.

37. Simon Bruté to S. Augustine, 21 September 1828, Box 11-STL, Correspondence Folder, DCSL.

38. Frances Xavier to Mother [Augustine], 21 November 1837, Box 11-STL, Correspondence Folder, DCSL.

39. Kilian Beirne, *From Sea to Shining Sea* (Valatie, N.Y.: Holy Cross Press, 1966), 138–39; Etienne Catta and Tony Catta, *Basil Anthony Mary Moreau*, 2 vols. (Milwaukee: Bruce, 1955), 1: 934.

40. Henry de Courcy and John Gilmary Shea, *History of the Catholic Church in the United States* (New York: J. G. Shea, 1879), 464.

41. Memo, deed of John Mullanphy to Joseph Rosati, 9 October 1828, Box 11-STL, History Folder, DCSL. This pioneer Catholic hospital in America served also as the city hospital until 1845.

42. Louise Callan, *The Society of the Sacred Heart in North America* (New York, 1937), 198–99; Alice Lida Cochran, *The Saga of an Irish Immigrant Family: The Descendants of John Mullanphy* (1958; reprint, New York: Arno, 1976), 66–67 n. 52.

43. G. W. Bioren to Anthony Frenaye, 5 August 1834, Mark Anthony Frenaye Papers Collection, AAPHIL.

44. RSJOA, 1838, 9–16.

45. James M. O'Toole, *Guide to the Archives of the Archdiocese of Boston* (New York: Garland, 1982), 76; *A Century of Service for the Sacred Heart in the United States by the Brothers of the Sacred Heart, 1847–1947* (New Orleans: Sacred Heart Brothers, 1946), 18.

46. Quoted in *Souvenir Sketch of St. Patrick's Church, Philadelphia, 1842–1892* (Philadelphia: Hardy & Mahony, 1892), 13, 64.

47. *The Constitution of St. John's Orphan Asylum, Chestnut-Street above Twelfth-Street* (Philadelphia: M. Fithian, 1834), preface. See also RSJOA, 1838, 14.

48. John Hughes, "St. John's Orphan Asylum," *Catholic Herald*, 23 January 1834, 10 April 1834. In this year, Hughes moved to New York as coadjutor bishop; he became New York's first archbishop in 1850.

49. John Hughes to John B. Purcell, 16 April 1834, quoted in John R. G. Hassard, *Life of the Most Reverend John Hughes, D.D.* (New York: D. Appleton, 1866), 148.

50. "Domestic. Archdiocese of Baltimore." *U.S. Catholic Magazine* 3 (June 1844): 402.

51. Motherhouse Annals, vol. 2, 1836, 15, SCN; Treasurer's Report, RSJOA, 1838, 8.

52. Nazareth Annals, vol. 1, 1812–1833, SCN.

53. Simon P. Lalumière to Angela Spink, 3 February 1832, Sisters of Charity of Nazareth Collection, AUND.

54. Motherhouse Annals, vol. 2, 1836, 15, SCN; Nazareth Annals, vol. 1, 1832, 82–83, SCN; Dolan, 1975, 127. An appeal to the bishop released the sisters from the supervision of the ladies' auxiliary.

55. Quoted in James Roosevelt Bayley, *A Brief Sketch of the History of the Catholic Church on the Island of New York* (New York: Dunigan, 1853), 72.

56. Edward Sorin, *The Chronicles of Notre Dame du Lac*, ed. James T. Connelly (Notre Dame: University of Notre Dame Press, 1992), 16.

57. *U.S. Catholic Magazine* 7 (1848): 151; A Friend of the House of the Angel Guardian, *The Life of Father Haskins* (Boston: Angel Guardian Press, 1899), 94–113. Not until 1874 were brothers found to manage the house.

58. M. Austin Carroll, "Education in New Orleans in Spanish Colonial Days," *American Catholic Quarterly Review* 12 (April 1887): 258–59. Today, the terms "nun" and "sister" are popularly used as synonyms. However, the nun is a strictly cloistered contemplative, whereas the sister may undertake educational and social welfare activities.

59. Maria Alma, "Foundations of Catholic Sisterhoods in the United States," *Records of the American Catholic Historical Society of Philadelphia* 52 (June 1941): 105, 108.

60. A Sister of Mercy, *Reminiscences of Seventy Years* (Chicago, 1916), 18.

61. Letter of Louis Florent Gillet, Savoy, France, 4 May 1891, quoted in Alma, 174.

62. M. Patricia to M. Gonzaga, 11 August 1913, SMNH.

63. Louis Baunard, *The Life of Mother Duchesne* (Roehampton, England: James Stanley, 1879), 218–25.

64. Annals of the Good Shepherd Convent, quoted in *The Good Shepherd of Angers: Province of St. Louis-U.S.A.* (St. Louis: Sisters of the Good Shepherd, 1980), 39.

65. M. Melania to P. A. Baart, 2 April 1887, PAB-UND; Schuller, 60–61, citing Archives, Daughters of Charity, Emmitsburg, Maryland.

66. Agnes Geraldine McGann, *Sisters of Charity of Nazareth in the Apostolate: Education, Health Care, Social Services, 1812–1976* (Nazareth, KY: Sisters of Charity of Nazareth, 1976), 22–23; de Courcy and Shea, 290.

67. John England to William Gaston, 25 February 1830, quoted in Guilday, 2: 135. Among bishops of the day, England was unique in his efforts to share aspects of church administration with the laity. See Gerald P. Fogarty, "The Parish and Community in American History," *U.S. Catholic Historian* 4, no. 3–4 (1985): 234–36.

68. John DuBois to the Rev. Mr. Hurley, Vice President & the Gentlemen Trustees of the Orphan Asylum of St. Joseph's in Philadelphia, n.d. [c. 1820], 11-1, 1-7-1, 4, DCA.

2. Resource Mobilization in a Working-Class Church

1. "Pastoral Letter of the Fifth Provincial Council of Baltimore, Fifth Sunday after Easter, 1843," in Nolan, 1: 147; "An Old-Time Talk to a St. Vincent de Paul Conference by J. V. Huntington," *St. Vincent de Paul Quarterly* 10 (May 1905): 127–28. The talk was given in the mid-1850s.

2. Quoted in Thomas T. McAvoy, "The Catholic Minority in Early Pittsburgh: The First Bishop: Michael O'Connor," *Records of the American Catholic Historical Society of Philadelphia* 72 (December 1961): 73.

3. Dolan, 1985, 277. By 1850, sisters numbered 1,344, priests 1,109.

4. Calculated from data in Record Book of Sisters from 1860 to June, 1912, SMNH. French and German communities reported similar demographic trends.

5. M. Anne Francis Campbell, "Bishop England's Sisterhood, 1829–1929" (Ph.D. diss., St. Louis University, 1968), 233–34; Copies of Records, Sisters of Mercy, Belmont, N. C., 1915–1946, 35–36, SMNC.

6. Columba Carroll to Mary Ann [1865], in Agnes Geraldine McGann, *Mother Columba Carroll, Sister of Charity of Nazareth, 1810–1878* (Nazareth, Ky.: Sisters of Charity of Nazareth, 1973), 5. Sisters of Charity were amused by one young Protestant's insistence that she wanted to be "a Sister and a Catholic, if necessary." Columba Carroll to Honora Young, 20 January 1877, Letter Book, 1877, SCN.

7. Sorin, 212, an 1858 entry. See also John Talbot Smith, *The Catholic Church in New York,* 2 vols. (New York: Hall & Locke, 1905), 2: 354.

8. John R. G. Hassard, "Private Charities and Public Money," *Catholic World* 29 (1879): 264; A Religious of the Congregation, *Fifty Years in Retrospect: Which Related the Progress Made by the Dominican Congregation of Our Lady of the Rosary Whose Motherhouse Is at Sparkill, New York* (1927), 57.

9. "Report of the Cumminsville Orphan Asylum for the Year Ending Dec. 31st, 1883" [Cincinnati] *Catholic Telegraph,* news clipping, n.d. [c. January 1884]; Lou Baldwin, "St. Francis in Eddington, 1888–1988," in *St. Francis in Eddington: A History of the Transition of an Institution, 1888–1988* (n.p., n.d.); Big Book of Accounts, 170–71, 255, Archives, Sisters of the Holy Cross, Notre Dame, Indiana.

10. Augustine Hewit, "Duties of the Rich in Christian Society," 6 parts, *Catholic World* 14, 15 (1872): 4: 147.

11. Circular for Hospital Appeal, in Annals of This Convent of the Religious Called Sisters of Mercy of Divine Providence, San Francisco, California, 4 July 1856 entry, SMCA.

12. Sarah Peter to M., 18 June 1857, in Margaret R. King, *Memoirs of the Life of Mrs. Sarah Peter,* 2 vols. (Cincinnati: Robert Clarke, 1889), 2: 369. Peter (1800–1877) joined the Catholic Church in 1854. For another example of this popular division of labor, see Shea's account of the philanthropy of Ann Biddle of St. Louis in the 1840s. (Shea, 4: 219.) The discussion of laywomen's benevolence in this chapter draws on Mary J. Oates, "The Role of Laywomen in American Catholic Philanthropy, 1820–1920," *U.S. Catholic Historian* 9 (Summer 1990): 249–60.

13. John Timon, Pastoral Letter, Given from St. Joseph's Cathedral on the Feast of the Ascension, 1859, Box 27-C, CSJPHIL.

14. Sisters of St. Joseph, Brief History of the Catholic Home for Destitute Children, June 1899, typescript, Box 7, Folder: Sisters of St. Joseph, Catholic Home, Martin I. J. Griffin Papers Collection, AAPHIL.

15. Mrs. J. V. Bouvier, "New York Foundling Hospital," *St. Vincent de Paul Quarterly* 1 (1895–96): 169.

16. "The Charities of New York," *Catholic World* 8 (November 1868): 284–85.

17. Eugene J. Crawford, *The Daughters of Dominic on Long Island: The Brooklyn Sisters of St. Dominic* (New York: Benziger, 1938), 251–54. After a lay auxiliary was formed in 1878, the sisters were able to devote themselves entirely to nursing.

18. Peter Salmon to Anthony Blanc, 31 January 1854, AANO.

19. "Obituary," *New York Times,* 18 August 1893; *Annual Report for 1901, New York Foundling Hospital,* 17–18; Isaac T. Hecker, "The Catholic Charities of New York," *Catholic World* 43 (August 1886): 688; Marie de Lourdes Walsh, *The Sisters of Charity of New York, 1809–1859,* 3 vols. (New York: Fordham University Press, 1960), 3: 70–71.

20. Hecker, 691–92.

21. Minute Book, St. Vincent's Infant Asylum, Baltimore, Archives, Associated Catholic Charities, Baltimore, Maryland.

22. Handwritten account, n.d., DCA.

23. *A Short Sketch of the New York Catholic Protectory from Its Origin to the Present, 1863–1885* (West Chester, N.Y.: New York Catholic Protectory, 1895), 20–21.

24. "Who Shall Take Care of the Poor?" 2 parts, *Catholic World* (February, March 1869): 2: 734–35.

25. Edward A. Carrell, S. J., to Archbishop John Purcell, 28 February 1853, AUND.

26. "Who Shall Take Care of Our Sick?" *Catholic World* 8 (October 1868): 48.

27. J. R. Bayley to M. A. Frenaye, 11 February 1848, Mark Anthony Frenaye Papers Collection, AAPHIL; William Forbes Adams, *Ireland and Irish Emigration to the New World from 1815 to the Famine* (New Haven: Yale University Press, 1932), 358–59; Dolan, 1985, 323.

28. CCYB, 1924, 15. For a discussion of early Irish fraternal societies, see Michael F. Funchion, ed., *Irish-American Voluntary Organizations* (Westport, Conn.: Greenwood Press, 1983).

29. William P. Preston, *Eulogy of "Good Father Dolan," The Apostle of the Point* (Baltimore: Kelly, Piet, 1879), 26–32.

30. James Dolan, "Address in St. Patrick's Church, Baltimore, 14 July 1850," quoted in Preston, 32–33. Dolan's single most generous financial supporter in this crisis was Hugh Jenkins, a Protestant.

31. Annals of This Convent, 21 April 1867 entry, SMCA; A Friend of the House of the Angel Guardian, 81.

32. "A Worthy Boston Charity," *The Pilot*, 6 April 1889.

33. St. Mary Asylum to John Fitzpatrick, 26 June 1848, Bishop John Fitzpatrick Papers, AABOS.

34. CCYB, 1924, 149. The pioneer American conference of this international society was formed by Bryan Mullanphy, son of philanthropist John Mullanphy, in St. Louis.

35. Mark K. Gannon, *Ten Decades of Charity, 1845–1945*, St. Louis, 1945 [pamphlet], DCSL.

36. Joan Marie Donohoe, "The Irish Catholic Benevolent Union" (Ph.D. diss., Catholic University of America, 1953), 170 n. 52; M. Adele Francis Gorman, "Evolution of Catholic Lay Leadership, 1820–1920," *Historical Records and Studies* 50 (1942): 130–34.

37. Richard Gilmour, Address at Meeting of 8th Annual Convention of the Irish Catholic Benevolent Union, Cleveland, Ohio, 20 September 1876, handwritten transcript, ERG 69, Irish Catholic Benevolent Union Records, AAPHIL; Minutes of the Board of Directors, Catholic Aid Association, St. Paul, Minnesota, 16 April 1878 and 15 October 1878, cited in Vincent A. Yzermans, *With Courage and Hope: The Catholic Aid Association* (St. Paul: Catholic Aid Association, 1978), 19.

38. Henry Spaunhorst to [Michael] Glennon, St. Louis, 26 February 1874, quoted in Donohoe, 91.

39. John O'Grady, *Catholic Charities in the United States* (Washington, D.C.: National Conference of Catholic Charities, 1930), 318–19.

40. M. Irene to Anthony Blanc, 14 November 1850, AUND. In her charitable work, the Irish-born Haughery (1813–1882) collaborated closely with the Sisters of Charity. She bequeathed her $500,000 estate to New Orleans charities. Private Records, St. Elizabeth's Home, New Orleans, cited by Schuller, 28.

41. Thomas F. Ring, "Children as a Special Work," *St. Vincent de Paul Quarterly* 1 (1895–96): 50.

42. Dr. Raborg, "The Homeless Poor of New York City," *Catholic World* 16 (November 1872): 211.

43. *The Fifty-Fourth Annual Report of the Board of Managers of the Roman Catholic Orphan Asylum Society of Brooklyn, for the Year Ending March 25, 1884*, 1.

44. S. Margaret to M. Catherine Spalding, 26 August 1849, SCN.

45. RSJOA, 1850, 6.

46. *Souvenir Book of the One Hundredth Anniversary, Saint Joseph's Home and School* (Washington, D.C.: Ladies Board, 1955), 7.

47. RSJOA, 1852, 19; 1855, 26; Schuller, 152–53, citing Archives, School Sisters of Notre Dame, Eastern Province, Baltimore, Maryland.

48. Jules Brady, "St Ann's Foundling Asylum," PCCCSL, 19–20.

49. History of the Sisters of Mercy; St. Johnsbury [Vermont] Foundation, 1872–1874, typescript [c. 1958], File E, Folder: California 1871, SMNH.

50. Sisters of Charity to P. A. Baart, 15 April 1885, Box 1, PAB-UND.

51. R. Laurence Moore, "Religion, Secularization, and the Shaping of the Culture Industry in Antebellum America," *American Quarterly* 41 (June 1989): 235.

52. RSJOA, 1846, 5; Cash Account, Treasurer's Report, June 1, 1853–June 1, 1854, RSJOA, 1854, 23.

53. James Fitton, *Sketches of the Establishment of the Church in New England* (Boston: Patrick Donahoe, 1872), 138; Annals of This Convent, 4 July 1856 entry, SMCA.

54. "Father Burke Pleading for the Orphans," *The Pilot*, 20 July 1878; McCray, 35–36.

55. M. Margaret to Archbishop [Anthony Blanc], 9 October 1856, AUND.

56. *Annual Report of the Roman Catholic Society of St. Joseph for Educating and Maintaining Poor Orphan Children, for the years 1855-'56-'57-'58* (Philadelphia: McLaughlin Brothers, 1859), 7, 11–1, 1–9–1, 2, DCA.

57. "A Powerful Charity Sermon," *The Pilot*, 15 January 1876.

58. Founded by the St. Vincent de Paul Society, the home was enlarged and renamed the Mission of the Immaculate Virgin by Father Drumgoole. About 1,600 boys lived there in 1888. James E. Dougherty, "John Christopher Drumgoole," *Charities Review* 8 (September 1898): 324–26.

59. Thomas de Cantillon Church, "Father Drumgoole's Work," 2 parts, *Donahoe's Magazine* (September, November 1879): 2: 430. Although publishing a magazine required initial resources lacking to most small institutions, the practice had a long tradition. In 1837, for example, the German St. Aloysius Orphan Society in Cincinnati funded an orphanage through the *Wahrheitsfreund*, edited by Rev. John Henni, the first such magazine published by Germans in this country. It continued until its sale by the 600-member society in 1843. Schuller, 107–108. In the 1890s, an African American orphanage, with few financial resources, was publishing an annual, the *St. Benedict's Home Journal*, which was sent to members of its benevolent society. Thomas M. O'Keefe, "St. Benedict's Home, Rye N.Y.," *The Rosary* (March 1894): 840.

60. John Rothensteiner, "Historical Sketch of the German St. Vincent's Orphan Association," in *Remembrance of the Diamond Jubilee, 1850–1925* (St. Louis: German St. Vincent's Orphan Society of St. Louis, Mo., 21 June 1925), 11; Frederick J. Zwierlein, *The Life and Letters of Bishop McQuaid*, 3 vols. (Rochester, N.Y.: Art Print Shop, 1925), 1: 232.

61. Lawrence Miller, "A Study of Angel Guardian Orphanage" (M.A. thesis, University of Chicago, 1943), 21, 29, 32–33.

62. M. Joseph to P. A. Baart, 13 April 1885, Box 1, PAB-UND; CCYB, 1924, 49.

63. J. A. Connolly, "St. Mary's and St. Joseph's Orphan Asylums," PCCCSL, 31–32; *Charter Constitution and By-Laws of the German St. Vincent Orphan Association, Organized June 13, 1850; Incorporated March 1, 1851*, AASL.

64. Sharp, 1: 142.

65. Schuller, 72–73, quoting from Archives, Daughters of Charity, Emmitsburg, Maryland. The orphanage benefited from a thriving benevolent society of 1,000 Albanians.

66. RSJOA, 1855, 8–10; RSJOA, 1853, 8.

67. *Metropolitan Magazine* 1 (June 1853): 238.

68. Martin J. Spalding to Reverend Pastors of Baltimore and Washington City, 17 September 1864, quoted in Louis G. Weitzman, "One Hundred Years of Catholic Charities in the District of Columbia" (Ph.D. diss., Catholic University of America, 1931), 6.

69. Eugenia Logan, *The History of the Sisters of Providence of Saint Mary-of-the-Woods, Indiana* (Terre Haute: Moore-Langen, 1978), 155. Similarly, although the House of the Good Shepherd in New Orleans was receiving some city funds for care of delinquent girls and women in this period, it got little help from other quarters. Twenty-five sisters supported the house by "taking in sewing and washing." *Report of Committee on Charitable Institutions to the Legislature of the State of Louisiana, Session—January, 1867* (New Orleans: J. O. Nixon, 1867), 3.

70. Claire Lynch, *St. Joseph's Home for Children 1877–1960* (St. Paul: North Central Publishing, 1982), 15–16.

71. "St. Joseph's Notes Centennial," in *Catholic Charities of the Archdiocese of St. Paul-Minneapolis* (Spring 1976), 3.

72. Weitzman, 404.

73. Peter A. Baart, *Orphans and Orphan Asylums* (Buffalo: Catholic Publication, 1885), 221; M. Cecilia to P. A. Baart, 28 February 1885, Box 1, PAB-UND. Exempt from the tax were country parishes that sent few children to the institution. They were asked instead to hold an annual collection for the orphanage.

74. Michael J. Hynes, *History of the Diocese of Cleveland: Origin and Growth (1847–1952)*

(Cleveland: World Publishing, 1953), 221; Brother Gontrau to P. A. Baart, 23 February 1885, Box 1, PAB-UND.

75. Baart, 177–78.

76. Archives, Daughters of Charity, Emmitsburg, Maryland, cited by Schuller, 195–96.

77. Peter L. Johnson, *Daughters of Charity in Milwaukee, 1846–1946* (Milwaukee: Daughters of Charity, 1946), 151–52.

78. William Quarter, "Pastoral to Clergy," 4 December 1846, quoted in *Souvenir of the Silver Jubilee*, 41.

79. Diary of Bishop William Quarter, Chicago, 14 April 1845, quoted in *Souvenir of the Silver Jubilee*, 74. Quarter wrote his diary in the third person. Southern bishops, like John Chanche of Natchez, Mississippi, and his successor, James Van de Velde, made frequent tours of northern and eastern dioceses in search of funds in the 1840s and 1850s. James J. Pillar, *The Catholic Church in Mississippi, 1837–65* (New Orleans: Hauser Press, 1964), 6–7.

80. James Gibbons to Mother Augustine, 24 April 1871, "Letters 1869-ff., James Cardinal Gibbons," letter 17, SMNC; John Tracy Ellis, *The Life of James Cardinal Gibbons, Archbishop of Baltimore, 1834–1921*, 2 vols. (Milwaukee, 1952), 1: 104–106.

81. *Memorial History of St. Mary's Industrial School for Boys to Commemorate Its Participation in the Sesqui-Centennial Celebration, October 11th, 1880* (Baltimore: St. Mary's Industrial School, 1880), 4–5, CCFX 111 1869—St. Mary's Home for Boys, Md., Annual Reports, AUND; O'Grady, 1930, 119.

82. John Luers, Bishop of Fort Wayne, "Circular," 6 November 1867, *Ave Maria* 3 (23 November 1867): 744. See also his "Pastoral Letter, Feast of the Ascension, 1865," *Ave Maria* 1 (3 June 1865): 49–52. The conviction that unmarried wage earners accounted for a major proportion of delinquents persisted in the twentieth century. Some clergy argued that they were simply not being asked properly. John F. Noll, "The Practical Way of Supporting Religion," *Ecclesiastical Review* 62 (1920): 273.

83. Humphrey Moynihan, "Archbishop Ireland's Colonies," *Acta et Dicta* 6 (October 1934): 217, 230.

84. John Lancaster Spalding, *The Religious Mission of the Irish People* (New York: Catholic Publication Society, 1880), 195.

85. M. Jerome to Halifax [motherhouse], 23 June 1856, quoted in Bernadette McCauley, " 'Who Shall Take Care of Our Sick?' Roman Catholic Sisterhoods and Their Hospitals, New York City, 1850–1930" (Ph.D. diss., Columbia University, 1992), 145–46.

86. *Catholic Herald*, 23 June 1849, quoted in Gail Farr Casterline, "St. Joseph's and St. Mary's: The Origins of Catholic Hospitals in Philadelphia," *Pennsylvania Magazine of History and Biography* 108 (July 1984): 301.

87. "The Thirteenth Annual Report of the Mount Hope Institution," *The Metropolitan* 4 (March 1856): 127–28; "Mount Hope," *U.S. Catholic Magazine* 6 (September 1847): 492; Hannefin, 75–76, 261. By 1862, similar hospitals had been established in St. Louis, Buffalo, and New Orleans.

88. Casterline, 291.

89. William McCloskey to Frances [Gardiner], 1 July 1869, SCN.

90. J. Trobec to Mother Seraphine, 22 September 1891, CSJSP.

91. Evelyn Campbell Beven, *City Subsidies to Private Charitable Agencies in New Orleans: The History and Present Status, 1824–1933* (New Orleans: Tulane University, 1934), 33. Public support for African American orphans was certainly less than the provision for white children in the Female Orphan Asylum of the Immaculate Conception, which in the same year was under 80 cents per month per child. Beven, 34.

92. High costs discouraged most parishes from opening their own hospitals. When a New York City German parish opened one in 1865, it was with the understanding that Germans of all parishes in the city would patronize and support it. See "Who Shall Take Care of Our Sick?" 45–46; McCauley, 150.

93. "Collection for Hospitals," 16 October 1875, Chancery Circulars, Box 1, Folder 8,

AABOS; *Annual Report of the Carney Hospital for the Year 1897* (Boston: Washington Press, 1898), 13, 11–35, 1–1–2, 5, DCA.

94. Bernice M. Mooney, *Salt of the Earth: The History of the Catholic Diocese of Salt Lake City, 1776–1987* (Salt Lake City: Catholic Diocese of Salt Lake City, 1987), 58. Although the hospital was caring for an average of fifty patients daily in 1880, the decline in silver mining led to its closing seven years later.

95. *St. Cloud Times,* 30 May 1888, quoted in Grace McDonald, "The Benedictine Sisters and the St. Cloud Hospital," *Minnesota History* 33 (Autumn 1953): 294; Ignatius Loyola Cox, "Notes on the Early History of the Sisters of St. Joseph in Minnesota," *Acta et Dicta* 3 (July 1914): 266; Mary John Crumlish and Celestine McCarthy, *Daughters of Charity: 1809–1959* (Emmitsburg, MD: St. Joseph's Central House, 1959), 107, 109.

96. Account of St. Louis Mullanphy Hospital by S. Anacaria, typescript, May 1901, 26–27, Box 11-STL, Correspondence Folder, DCSL. Her apprehensions were warranted. A Cincinnati financial crisis in this decade was the result of a similar scheme. Since the 1830s, Rev. Edward Purcell, brother of Archbishop John Purcell, had been receiving private deposits and paying interest on them in the name of the archdiocese. During the depression of 1878–79 the "bank" failed, occasioning severe distress for depositors and embarrassment for the church. See McCann, 101–103.

97. Francis J. Bath, *St. Joseph's Hospital* (Omaha, 1930), 10, cited in Mary Edmund Croghan, "Sisters of Mercy of Nebraska, 1864–1910" (Ph.D. diss., Catholic University of America, 1942), 49.

98. Mary Alphonsa Lathrop, "For Poor Cancer Patients in New York," *The Pilot,* 23 June 1900. Lathrop, a convert to Catholicism, was Nathaniel Hawthorne's daughter Rose.

99. "Cancer Homes," *Catholic Charities Review* 1 (October 1917): 256.

100. Richard H. Clarke, "Catholic Protectories and Reformatories," *American Catholic Quarterly Review* 20 (July 1895): 610.

101. M. Charles Curtin, Annals, Sacred Heart Convent, 1841–1892, typescript, n.d., 18, Archives, SMNC.

102. Erastus Brooks, "Speech at the New York Constitutional Convention, 1867–68," quoted in Hassard, 1879, 257.

103. George William Curtis, quoted in Hassard, 1879, 257.

104. *Carney Hospital, Boston: One Hundredth Anniversary, 1863–1963* (1963), 11–35, 1–2, 6, DCA.

105. *Memorial History of St. Mary's Industrial School for Boys,* 9–10. In 1907, 676 boys were attending this school.

106. *Annual Reports of the Board of Trustees of St. Mary's Industrial School for Boys, of the City of Baltimore* (Baltimore: St. Mary's Industrial School, 1873, 1877, 1878), CCFX 111 1869—St. Mary's Home for Boys, Md., Annual Reports, AUND.

107. "The Charities of New York," *Catholic World* 8 (November 1868): 279.

108. "Our Roman Catholic Brethren," *Atlantic Monthly* 21 (April 1868): 445.

109. Thomas F. Ring, "Catholic Child-Helping Agencies in the United States," in *Proceedings of the National Conference of Charities and Correction,* June 1896 (Boston: Geo. H. Ellis, 1896), 339–40.

110. Levi Silliman Ives, "Appeal for the New York Catholic Protectory, 1863," quoted in Clarke, 618. Ives was the former Episcopal Bishop of North Carolina. See McColgan, 1: 245–47.

3. Social Needs and Mainstream Challenges

1. "Historical Sketch of the Mission of Goshenhoppen, Now Churchville, PA," *Woodstock Letters* 5 (1876): 203–13; *Cathedral Records,* 16.

2. Hassard, 1866, 129.

3. M. Lilliana Owens, *The St. Louis Hospital, 1828* (St. Louis: St. Louis Medical Society,

1965), 11–12; Regina Smith to Most Rev. & Dear Bishop [Joseph Rosati], 18 September 1830, Rosati Papers, AASL.

4. Resolutions, Minutes, Board of Guardians, 20 May 1833, in The Cholera in Philadelphia, handwritten account, 11–1, 1–3–2, 1, DCA. The sisters declined the invitation.

5. William Steuart to A. J. Elder, 3 November 1833, in "The Sisters of Charity and the Cholera in Baltimore and Philadelphia, 1832," *American Catholic Historical Researches* 14 (1897): 113–14.

6. *U.S. Catholic Miscellany*, 16 November 1839.

7. Sharp, 1954, 1: 77.

8. Catherine Spalding to M. Josephine, 30 October 1857, quoted in Berenice Greenwell, "Nazareth's Contribution to Education, 1812–1933" (Ph.D. diss., Fordham University, 1933), 435–36. Although the American Party stirred strong anti-foreign and anti-Catholic sentiments after its formation in 1854, its influence was short-lived, as slavery became the overriding political issue of the late 1850s. It was dubbed the "Know-Nothing" Party because the secret society from which it developed, the Order of the Star Spangled Banner, founded in New York in 1849, required members to answer queries about its activities with the words: "I know nothing." For more on this movement, see Ray Allen Billington, *The Protestant Crusade, 1800–1860* (New York: Macmillan, 1938); and Tyler Anbinder, *Nativism and Slavery: The Northern Know Nothings and the Politics of the 1850's* (New York: Oxford University Press, 1992).

9. Quoted in M. Eleanore, *On the King's Highway: A History of the Sisters of the Holy Cross of St. Mary of the Immaculate Conception, Notre Dame, Indiana* (New York: Appleton, 1931), 252.

10. Annals of Saint Vincent Academy, Union County, Kentucky, 125–26, in Betty Ann Perkins, "The Work of the Catholic Sister-Nurses in the Civil War" (M.A. thesis, University of Dayton, 1967), 35–36; Benjamin J. Blied, *Catholics and the Civil War: Essays* (Milwaukee, 1945), 118.

11. Thaddeus J. Butler, *The Catholic Church in America* (Chicago, 1869), 37.

12. *Galveston Daily News*, 16 April 1867; *Daily Galveston Bulletin*, 26 May 1867.

13. "Bishop McQuaid in Canada. 'Catholic Works of Charity,' " *The Pilot*, 13 May 1876.

14. Digby, "True and False Charity," *The Metropolitan* 1 (1853): 30–31.

15. M. Bernard, *The Story of the Sisters of Mercy in Mississippi, 1860–1930* (New York: P. J. Kenedy, 1931), 84–85.

16. Bernard, 88–89. Six young sisters died at their posts during this crisis. The community managed the hospital for twenty-seven years, leaving when it was incorporated as a state hospital.

17. *Chicago Daily Democrat*, 24 October 1846.

18. Kathryn Prindiville, "The Catholic Life of Chicago," *Catholic World* 67 (July 1898): 481. They were still managing this hospital in 1898.

19. Annals of This Convent, 16 October 1855, SMCA.

20. "Associated Charities," *The Pilot*, 29 March 1879.

21. "What Is Charity?" *The Pilot*, 27 November 1880.

22. J. W. Helmes, "Thomas M. Mulry: A Volunteer's Contribution to Social Work" (Ph.D. diss., Catholic University of America, 1938), 69.

23. Ibid., 75. Mulry (1855–1916), a New York banker and insurance executive, served as director of many Catholic charitable organizations and, in 1907, as president of the National Conference of Charities and Corrections.

24. Thomas M. Mulry, "Catholic Co-Operation in Charity," *Charities Review* 8 (October 1898): 383; Helmes, 70–71, 75–76.

25. Thomas M. Mulry, "Catholics and Charity Conferences—A Plea and a Protest," *St. Vincent de Paul Quarterly* 6 (August 1901): 176.

26. "The Society: The Louisville Convention, October 20, 21, and 22, 1897," *St. Vincent de Paul Quarterly* 2 (1897): 311. Farley became archbishop of New York in 1902.

27. Thomas M. Mulry, "Co-Operation and Religion in Charity Work," *St. Vincent de Paul Quarterly* 6 (1901): 19.

28. Baart, 136, 245–46.

29. Dexter A. Hawkins, *Archbishop Purcell Outdone! The Roman Catholic Church in New York City and Public Land and Public Money* (New York: Phillips and Hunt, 1880), 1, 19.

30. "Charitable Frauds," *The Pilot*, 28 February 1874, quoting a *New York Herald* probe of public charities. See also "The Relative Cost of Catholic and Other Charities," *The Pilot*, 9 March 1878; and "Catholic Charities of Boston: Comparative Cost of Catholic and Non-Catholic Charity," *The Pilot*, 7 April 1883.

31. "The Attack on Catholic Charities in New York," *Catholic World* 59 (August 1894): 702; "Catholics to Pay Sisters in Future, Group Declares," news clipping, n.d. [c. 1912], Scrapbook, ScB 8, St. Joseph's Home, Flushing, 1919–1924, CSJNY.

32. "Catholic Charities Under the Microscope," *Catholic World* 60 (October 1894): 118. Although church officials dismissed criticisms in the committee's report as relatively minor, the State Charities Aid Association's 1898 report that Catholics were three times more likely than Protestants to accept public wards in large institutions and to keep them there longer than necessary kept the controversy alive. State Charities Aid Association, *Twenty-Sixth Annual Report* (New York, 1898), 7; State Charities Aid Association, *Public Appropriations to Private Charities in New York City* (New York, 1899), 11.

33. Peter Romanofsky, "Saving the Lives of the City's Foundlings: The Joint Committee and New York Child Care Methods, 1860–1907," *New York Historical Society Quarterly* 61 (1977): 55–56.

34. William J. Kerby, The Demand for Social Service, Address at First Annual Convention, National Council of Catholic Women, Washington, D.C., 13 October 1921, 4, NCCW History Drawer, ACUA. Until that date, there was only one national publication in the field, the *St. Vincent de Paul Quarterly*, which had commenced in 1888.

35. James E. Roohan, "American Catholics and the Social Question," *Historical Records and Studies* 43 (1954): 9.

36. *Freeman's Journal*, 24 January 1874, quoted in Roohan, 8.

37. Robert E. Curran, "The McGlynn Affair and the Shaping of the New Conservatism in American Catholicism, 1886–1894," *Catholic Historical Review* 66 (1980): 188; Roohan, 20.

38. Sylvester L. Malone, ed., *Dr. Edward McGlynn* (New York: Dr. McGlynn Monument Association, 1918), 95.

39. Michael Corrigan to Bernard McQuaid, 12 December 1892, quoted in R. E. Curran, 192 n. 28. Five years after his censure and excommunication by Corrigan in 1887, McGlynn was reinstated by Rome.

40. Peter Foy, "The New Social Order," in William H. Hughes, ed., *Official Report of the Proceedings of the Catholic Congress* (Detroit: Wm. H. Hughes, 1889), 47–68.

41. Peter C. Yorke, "Sermon, 1922," quoted in D. J. Kavanagh, *The Holy Family Sisters of San Francisco* (San Francisco: Gilmartin, 1922), 301.

42. John Ireland, "The Charity of Christ," *St. Vincent de Paul Quarterly* 12 (August 1907): 230–32; Robert D. Cross, *The Emergence of Liberal Catholicism in America* (Cambridge: Harvard University Press, 1958), 218–19.

43. John A. Ryan, "The Church and the Workingman," *Catholic World* 89 (September 1909): 781. Because it lacked grassroots support, the bishops' 1919 pastoral letter, based on *Rerum Novarum* and incorporating Ryan's socially progressive ideas, had little substantive impact. See Hennesey, 243–45.

44. Dorothy A. Mohler, "The Advocate Role of the St. Vincent de Paul Society," *Records of the American Catholic Historical Society of Philadelphia* 86 (1975): 80–81, 83; Donald P. Gavin, *The National Conference of Catholic Charities, 1910–1960* (Milwaukee: Bruce, 1962), 157.

45. Mulry, 1898, 386; Roohan, 3–4.

46. M. Irene to P. A. Baart [c. 1885], Box 1, PAB-UND; Helmes, 43.

47. Crimmins, 23 May 1916 entry, 930.

48. Josephine Shaw Lowell, *Report Upon the Care of Dependent Children in the City of New York and Elsewhere* (Albany, 1890), 5.

49. Society of St. Vincent de Paul, "Special Works and Gleanings from Conferences," *Report of the Upper and Particular Council of St. Louis, Mo. to the General Council in Paris November 1, 1896 to November 1, 1897* (St. Louis, 1898), 14.

50. William J. Kerby, "Social Work of the Catholic Church in America," *Annals of the American Academy of Political and Social Science* 30 (1907): 476.

51. Grace O'Brien, "Catholic Settlement Work in Brooklyn," *The Survey* 24 (7 May 1910): 204. See also "The White Memorial Settlement," *Catholic Charities Review* 2 (1918): 216–17.

52. Philip Gleason, *The Conservative Reformers: German-American Catholics and the Social Order* (Notre Dame, Ind.: Notre Dame University Press, 1968), 12. This book gives the history of the Central-Verein. By the 1930s, as Germans moved into mainstream society, its membership and influence had declined considerably.

53. Ibid., 204–20; Dolan, 1985, 311–12. The Americanist controversy is discussed in Thomas T. McAvoy, *The Great Crisis in American Catholic History, 1895–1900* (Chicago: Henry Regnery, 1957).

54. William J. White, "The First National Conference of Catholic Charities," *The Survey* 25 (8 October 1910): 93–94.

55. Dorothy Day, "Fall 1968 Appeal," W-1 Box 1, Folder: Appeals, 1933–1976, DDCW.

56. The African American Catholic experience is explored in Cyprian Davis, *The History of Black Catholics in the United States* (New York: Crossroad Publishing, 1991).

57. Thomas S. Byrne, quoted in Mary Elizabeth Herbert, "The Missionary Spirit of Cardinal Vaughan," *Ave Maria* 60 (27 May 1905): 643.

58. *Annales* 10 (1838): 498; Guilday, 2: 274–76.

59. Michael F. Rouse, *A Study of the Development of Negro Education Under Catholic Auspices in Maryland and the District of Columbia* (Baltimore: Johns Hopkins University Press, 1935), 42.

60. Oblate Sisters, typescript, n.d., 4, AAB; *150th Anniversary—Oblate Sisters of Providence* (Baltimore: Oblate Sisters of Providence, [c. 1979]), AAB.

61. Joseph B. Code, "A Colored Catholic Educator before the Civil War," *Catholic World* 146 (1938): 441. In 1842, Harriet Delisle and Juliet Gaudin, New Orleans "free women of color," formed the second African American sisterhood, the Sisters of the Holy Family.

62. Hennesey, 161.

63. Cyprian Davis, "The Catholic Church and the Question of Black Ministry: An Historical Perspective," *NBCCC [National Black Catholic Clergy Caucus], The Newsletter* (October 1984): 3.

64. Stephen J. Ochs, *Desegregating the Altar: The Josephites and the Struggle for Black Priests, 1871–1960* (Baton Rouge: Louisiana State University Press, 1990), 41; B. Chocarne to John M. Odin [c. 1866], AANO; and Hortensia Trevigne to Odin, 15 December 1866, AANO. Since Odin's request "seem[ed] like treason," the priest refused to honor it.

65. Minutes of the Annual Meeting of the Archbishops of the United States, Catholic University of America, Washington, D.C., 26 April 1905, Folder: Anciaux, Rev. Jos., AJF; Katharine Mary Drexel to James O'Connor, 28 October 1889, SBS Writings no. 73, 156, SBS; and M. M. K. [Mother Mary Katharine] to Thomas M. O'Keefe, 25 January 1906, 10, Box 43, no. 14, SBS.

66. Spalding, 1873, 338–39. Spalding made the point that the pastor is severely handicapped in teaching religion if the congregation is illiterate.

67. "The Negroes and the Indians," *Catholic World* 48 (March 1889): 728.

68. John Slattery to Herbert Vaughan, 1 October 1877, Box DX4, Folder: MHT9, Mill Hill Archives, Transcripts 1860, AJF; J. Noonan to Herbert Vaughan, 21 September 1874, Box DX4, Folder: 5MHT33, Mill Hill Archives, Transcripts 1860, AJF.

69. Herbert Vaughan to Mary Elizabeth Herbert, 8 December 1871, quoted in Herbert, 641–42. St. Joseph's Society of the Sacred Heart for Foreign Missions was founded in 1866 in Mill Hill, near London. Vaughan became Bishop of Salford in 1872, Archbishop of Westminster in 1892, and was named cardinal in 1893. See John G. Snead-Cox, *The Life of Cardinal Vaughan,* 2 vols. (London: Burns and Oates, 1910).

70. Diary entry, 25 January 1872, quoted in Snead-Cox, 1: 171.

71. Napoleon J. Perché to Herbert Vaughan, 16 February 1872, Box DX4, Folder: 3MHT7, Mill Hill Archives, Transcripts 1860, AJF.

72. Thomas Layton, Treasurer, Catholic Relief Association, New Orleans, to Thomas M. Price, Yellow Fever Sufferers Committee, Philadelphia, 9 October 1878, Box 7, Griffin Collection, AAPHIL.

73. T. Edgar Lyon, "Religious Activities and Development in Utah, 1847–1910," *Utah Historical Quarterly* 35 (Fall 1967): 294.

74. H. Schieffelin Sayers, "Rome in New York," in *Catholic Charities and the Constitutional Convention of 1894 of the State of New York. Report of the Committee on Catholic Interests of the Catholic Club* (New York: O'Brien & Son, 1894), 9. Sayers's observations originally appeared in a series of five weekly articles in the *New York Observer* that began on 20 April 1893.

75. "William Cardinal O'Connell to All the Clergy and Faithful of the Archdiocese, 21 September 1927," *The Pilot,* 24 September 1927.

76. *Mission Work among the Negroes and Indians, 1889* [Annual Report of the Commission for Catholic Missions among the Colored People and the Indians], 1; *St. Joseph's Advocate* 2 (October 1891): 508; 3 (April 1894): 530–40.

77. Congregatio Pro Causis Sanctorum P.N. 1113, Philadelphien, *Canonizationis Servae Dei Catharinae Mariae Drexel, Fundatricis Congregationis Sororum a SS. Sacramento pro India et Colorata Gente (1858–1955), Positio Super Virtutibus, vol. 1, Expositio Historica et Documenta* (Roma: Tipografia Guerra, 1986), 18–19, SBS.

78. James Gibbons, Patrick J. Ryan, and John J. Kain, "An Appeal," *Mission Work among the Negroes and the Indians* (January 1903): 2.

79. *Mission Work among the Negroes and the Indians* (January 1914). Nearly a century later, in 1992, the $6.7 million mission collection represented a per capita gift of 13 cents.

80. *Mission Work among the Negroes and the Indians* (January 1922): 3–4. The archbishops reported that the average contribution was one cent per Catholic, the same record as in 1893. (*Mission Work among the Negroes and the Indians* (January 1923): 3–5.)

81. A. Van de Vyver to Joseph Anciaux, 21 September 1901, 17-A-38, AJF; "The Pope Creates Mrs. Ryan a Countess," *St. Vincent de Paul Quarterly* 12 (1907): 390–91. In 1901, the Ryans gave the Richmond diocese funds to construct its "long-wished-for Cathedral." (Magri, 9–10.)

82. "Report of the Superior General," *The Colored Harvest* 26 (April–May 1938): 5.

83. Rouse, 73.

84. Jos. Anciaux, *De Miserabili Conditione Catholicorum Nigrorum in America,* Brussels, 19 August 1903, 1, 4–5, AJF.

85. John E. Burke, "Parochialism and the Missions," *Our Colored Missions* 10 (January 1924): 3. Bishops could request financial support from the American Board for Catholic Missions, funded from the African American share of Society for the Propagation of the Faith receipts. John T. Gillard, *The Catholic Church and the American Negro* (Baltimore: St. Joseph's Society Press, 1929), 218.

86. George K. Hunton, *All of Which I Saw, Part of Which I Was: The Autobiography of George K. Hunton, Crusader for Racial Justice, as Told to Gary MacEoin* (Garden City, N.Y.: Doubleday, 1967), 50–51. The property reverted to the Baltimore archdiocese in 1933. Hunton, a white New York lawyer, joined the governing board of the National Association for the Advancement of Colored People in 1954.

87. "The Oblate Sisters of Providence, Normandy, MO," PCCCSL, 27. In the 1940s, or-

phanage directors were calling on restrictive clauses in their institutional charters to justify exclusion of African American children. See Rules for the Orphanage; Angel Guardian Orphanage, Articles of Incorporation of Ketteler School, 1912, Angel Guardian Orphanage Record Series, Box 37, AAC; and L. Miller, 62.

88. M. Louisa Noel to P. A. Baart, 27 February 1885, Box 1, PAB-UND. See also M. Reginald Gerdes, "To Educate and Evangelize: Black Catholic Schools of the Oblate Sisters of Providence (1828–1880)," *U.S. Catholic Historian* 7 (1988): 183–99.

89. L. A. Dutto, "The Negroes in Mississippi," *Catholic World* 46 (February 1881): 583.

90. William Audley Osborne, "The Race Problem in the Catholic Church in the United States: Between the Time of the Second Plenary Council (1866) and the Founding of the Catholic Interracial Council of New York (1934)" (Ph.D. diss., Columbia University, 1954), 135 n. 3.

91. M. Dorothea to Thomas E. Molloy, 6 November 1933, quoted in McCauley, 258; Hunton, 140.

92. McCauley, 251.

93. McColgan, 1: 136, 139–40; Christopher Kauffman, *Faith and Fraternalism: The History of the Knights of Columbus* (1982; revised, New York: Simon & Schuster, 1992), 412–13, 416. A parallel African American society, the Knights of St. Peter Claver, had been established in 1909.

94. Community Journal, 19 July 1890, in Mission Helpers of the Sacred Heart, The Early History of Our Congregation, vol. 1, book 1, 8 December 1978, 37 [typescript], Box: Religious Communities—Women, AAB; *Golden Jubilee, St. Elizabeth's Home, Maryland, 1931*, pamphlet (n.p., n.d.).

95. Diary of Sister Demetrias, 1 June 1896, in Mission Helpers of the Sacred Heart, The Early History, 105–107, AAB.

96. As of 1883, Drexel's estate was the largest that had ever been reported in Philadelphia. Lou Baldwin, *A Call to Sanctity* (Philadelphia: The Catholic Standard and Times, 1988), 28–29; Boniface Hanley, *A Philadelphia Story* (Paterson, N.J.: St. Anthony Guild, 1984), 9. Another pair of sisters, Adele Parmentier Bayer (1814–1892) and Rosine Parmentier (1829–1908) of Brooklyn, also gave generously to Indian and African American work. Two-thirds of the latter's residual estate went to these causes. Will of Rosine M. Parmentier, 27 March 1907, typescript copy, CSJNY.

97. Consuela M. Duffy, "Mrs. Louise Drexel Morrell," *Records of the American Catholic Historical Society of Philadelphia* 56 (December 1945): 333; Annals, Sisters of the Blessed Sacrament, vol. 25, 1929, 192–93, SBS.

98. James O'Connor to Katharine M. Drexel, 16 February 1889, SBS. O'Connor was a pastor in Holmesburg, Pennsylvania, from 1872 until 1876, when he became vicar apostolic of Nebraska.

99. "Catholics and the Negro Question," *America* 21 (19 July 1919): 380.

100. Osborne, 146–47.

101. Pedro Arrupe, "To the Members of the Society of Jesus in the United States," *Catholic Mind* 66 (January 1968): 20.

102. "Our Negro Problem," *America* 26 (8 April 1922): 590.

103. James M. King, *Sectarian Indian Schools* (New York: Office of the National League for the Protection of American Institutions, 1890), 8.

104. M. M. Katharine to J. A. Stephan, 23 June 1897, Box 35, Folder 26, BCIM.

105. Archbishop [Patrick] Ryan to My Dear Child [K. Drexel], 30 July 1890; M. M. Katharine, Conversation held in Most Reverend Archbishop's parlor July 31, 1893. Fathers Stephan, Hylebos, and M. M. Katharine being present, M. M. K.-10, Box: Ryan, Archbishop Patrick, 1889–1910, Folder: July 30, '90–July 31, 1893, SBS; William A. Ketcham, "Editorial," *The Indian Sentinel* (1904–1905): 31. Government contracts to Catholic schools between 1874 and 1897 totaled $4.5 million. Over the same period, Mother Katharine gave $1 million to these schools. J. F. Stephan, Report on Funds for Indians, 19 July 1898, Box 16, Folder 30, BCIM.

106. M. M. Katharine to Reverend and dear Father, 17 February 1894, Box 33, Folder 9; M. M. Katharine to J. A. Stephan, 1 August 1898, Box 36, Folder 31; J. A. Stephan to M. M. Katharine, 20 June 1899, Box 38, Folder 1, BCIM.

107. James O'Connor to My dear Child [K. Drexel], 26 July 1889, Sisters of the Blessed Sacrament Annals, vol. 2, 242–44, SBS.

108. J. A. Stephan to Miss K. M. Drexel, 23 February 1886, Sisters of the Blessed Sacrament, Annals, vol. 2, 198–202, SBS. Stephan directed the Bureau from 1884 until his death in 1901.

109. Peter J. Rahill, *The Catholic Indian Missions and Grant's Peace Policy, 1870–1884* (Washington, D.C.: Catholic University of America Press, 1953), 155. Rahill's source is the *Manual of Catholic Indian Missionary Associations*, an 1876 Bureau pamphlet.

110. Henry G. Ganss, "How Have We Dealt with the Indians?" *St. Vincent de Paul Quarterly* 10 (August 1905): 242.

111. T. B. Minihan et al. to All the Societies Affiliated with The American Federation of Catholic Societies, 18 January 1903, Griffin Collection, Box 7, AAPHIL.

112. James A. Burns, *The Growth and Development of the Catholic School System in the United States* (1912; reprint, New York: Arno Press, 1969), 341. For more on Katharine Drexel's philanthropy, see Annals, vol. 25, 1928, 198–99, SBS.

113. As long as they sustained the 90 percent figure, their charitable contributions would not be taxed. "Rich Nun's Fortune Exempted from Tax," *New York Times*, 28 May 1924.

114. *Philadelphia Bulletin*, 29 May 1924; "Income Tax Exemption for Mother Katharine Drexel," *The Indian Sentinel* 4 (July 1924): 102; Joseph F. Lowry, "The Nun Who Was a Millionaire," *Philadelphia Sunday Bulletin Magazine*, 31 July 1966. The 1924 amendment soon became a prime tax loophole for the very rich, and in 1969 Congress finally closed it. Richard A. Stewart, "Kennedy Cites 'Nun' Provision as Tax Escape," *Boston Globe*, 9 December 1969.

4. The Charity Consolidation Movement

1. James A. McFaul, "The American Federation of Catholic Societies," *Donahoe's Magazine* 52 (July 1904): 87–88; CCYB, 1926, 13.

2. James Sullivan, "Care of Dependent Children," *Proceedings of the First National Conference of Catholic Charities* (1910): 286.

3. "Calls Orphan Asylums 'Pauper Factories,' " *Brooklyn Daily Eagle*, 9 December 1903.

4. V. T., "The New York Charities Controversy," *Catholic Charities Review* 1 (January 1917): 16–23. Catholic enterprises were not the only ones under attack by mainstream charity organization societies at this time. The Salvation Army's relief work, for example, was castigated as unscientific, inefficient, and more harmful than beneficial. See Karen Tice, "The Battle for Benevolence: Scientific Disciplinary Control vs. 'Indiscriminate Relief': Lexington Associated Charities and the Salvation Army, 1900–1918," *Journal of Sociology and Social Work* 19 (June 1992): 59–77.

5. Humphrey J. Desmond, *Chats within the Fold: A Series of Little Sermons from a Lay Standpoint* (Baltimore, 1901), 116–17.

6. John J. O'Shea, "Little People and Great Ideas," *Catholic World* 61 (April 1895), 83–84.

7. D. I. McDermott, "Sermon at Cornerstone-laying of Gonzaga Memorial Asylum, Philadelphia, October 1, 1898," typescript, DCA.

8. Robert Biggs, "The Problem of Dependency," *Proceedings of the First National Conference of Catholic Charities* (1910): 95.

9. Minutes of Meeting of the Executive Committee and New Charities Committee, Conference of Catholic Charities, St. Louis, 13 May 1914, Archives, Catholic Charities, St. Louis.

10. Maureen Fitzgerald, "The Perils of 'Passion and Poverty': Women Religious and the Care of Single Women in New York City, 1845–1890," *U.S. Catholic Historian* 10 (1991): 49–50.

11. "Catholic Deaf Mutes," *Ave Maria* 42 (18 April 1893): 437.

12. Mrs. O. R. Lake, "Deaf-Mute Institute," PCCCSL, 1912, 41, 44.

13. McDermott, "Sermon," DCA.

14. Sayers, 10.

15. Austin Dowling, Address at National Conference of Catholic Charities Meeting, Des Moines, Iowa, 11 September 1924, RG-74, Austin Dowling (1868–1930) Papers, Box 3, Folder 9, AASPM.

16. "Improving Catholic Charities in St. Louis," *Catholic Charities Review* 1 (1917): 50; John J. Glennon, "Preface," *Eleventh Annual Report of Catholic Charities of the City of St. Louis, 1922* (St. Louis: Central Bureau of Catholic Charities and Kindred Activities of St. Louis, 1922).

17. CCYB, 1926, 11.

18. John O'Grady, Notes Prepared for His Excellency Archbishop Cushing, n.d., 1, 4, Catholic Charitable Bureau Files, Box 6, Folder 7, AABOS.

19. Edward J. Galbally, "A View of Co-operation," *St. Vincent de Paul Quarterly* 20 (May 1915): 107.

20. "Modern Charities," *The Pilot*, 16 September 1916.

21. Agnes Regan, Report of Executive Secretary, National Council of Catholic Women [1926 Convention], 1–2, National Council of Catholic Women History Drawer, Folder: NCCW-Executive Secretary Reports, 1925–1927; Address at Meeting of Council of Catholic Women, Newark, New Jersey, n.d., National Catholic School of Social Service Collection, Box 16, Folder: NCCW Addresses and Reports, Regan, Miss Agnes G., ACUA.

22. Henry Somerville, "National Conference of Catholic Charities," *Catholic World* 105 (August 1917): 593–94.

23. William J. Kerby, "New and Old in Catholic Charity," *Catholic Charities Review* 3 (January 1919): 11–12.

24. William J. Kerby, The National Catholic Service School: Is It a Duty or an Opportunity? [typescript of address given at convention of the National Council of Catholic Women, Washington, D.C., 22 November 1922], ACUA.

25. John M. Mulroy, "The Relationship between the Diocesan Catholic Charities and Auxiliary Organizations," *Proceedings of the 23d Annual Meeting of the National Conference of Catholic Charities* (1937): 136–37. A number of early priest-directors of diocesan charity bureaus shared the sisters' apprehensions about introducing professional social workers into Catholic charitable work. See Roger J. Coughlin and Cathryn A. Riplinger, *The Story of Charitable Care in the Archdiocese of Chicago, 1844–1959* (Chicago: Catholic Charities of Chicago, 1981), 214.

26. John O'Grady, "Monsignor Kerby—In Memoriam," *Catholic Charities Review* 30 (September 1936): 226; William Kerby, *The Social Mission of Charity: A Study of Points of View in Catholic Charities* (New York, 1921), 172.

27. The Cholera in Philadelphia [c. 1890], 11-1, 1-3-2, 1, DCA.

28. John P. Leahy, "The Institutional Care of Older Children," news clipping, 10 October 1908, 11–11, DCA.

29. Rothensteiner, 26.

30. M. Luella Sauer, "St. Joseph's Orphanage, Pittsburgh, Closes Its Doors," *Catholic Charities Review* 23 (January 1939): 9–10.

31. Chronicle of the Mission St. Mary and St. Aloysius, Quincy, Adams Co., Ill., 17 December 1944 entry, Archives, School Sisters of Notre Dame, St. Louis, Missouri.

32. Chronicle of the Mission, 16 March 1945 entry, Archives, School Sisters of Notre Dame, St. Louis.

33. Homer Folks, quoted in *St. Vincent de Paul Quarterly* 5 (1900): 55.

34. "Vincentian Tribute to the Late Archbishop Williams," *St. Vincent de Paul Quarterly* 13 (1908): 162; McColgan, 2: 288; "Annual Meeting of the Society in Philadelphia," *St. Vincent de Paul Quarterly* 14 (1909): 214.

35. Thomas Dwight, "The Trials and Needs of the Society of St. Vincent de Paul," *St. Vincent de Paul Quarterly* 7 (1902): 100–104.

36. Thomas M. Mulry, "The Society of St. Vincent de Paul," *St. Vincent de Paul Quarterly*

4 (May 1899): 105. The society in America was always heavily urban. See McColgan, 2: 534, appendix 2.

37. Thomas Dwight, "The Work of the Society," *St. Vincent de Paul Quarterly* 11 (1906): 323, 325–26.

38. Thomas Dwight, "The Condition and Needs of the Society of Saint Vincent de Paul," *St. Vincent de Paul Quarterly* 5 (1900): 305–306.

39. "The National Conference of the Society of St. Vincent de Paul," *St. Vincent de Paul Quarterly* 16 (August 1911): 216.

40. Executive Committee to Mr. Kelly, 16 July 1923, Box 2, ACC-AAC.

41. "The Voice of the Laity," *Catholic Charities Review* 5 (December 1921): 339.

42. John M. Petermann to "Jack," 29 May 1936, Box 3203, Folder 9, St. Vincent de Paul Collection, AAC; McColgan, 1: 510; 2: 65. The Metropolitan Central Council territory included Chicago, Springfield, Rockford, and East St. Louis.

43. O'Grady, 1930, 446.

44. "Cites Need of Volunteers in Social Work," *The Pilot*, 6 August 1938.

45. Richard J. Condon, "Contribution of the Volunteer to the Diocesan Bureau of Catholic Charities," *Catholic Charities Review* 32 (February 1948): 50–51.

46. "The Society's Failure to Attract Young Members," *Catholic Charities Review* 34 (September 1950): 188.

47. "Need of Organization by Catholic Women," *The Pilot*, 25 May 1918.

48. *The New World* [Chicago], 18 December 1931.

49. "Great Future for Columbus Knights," *The Pilot*, 15 March 1919.

50. "K. of C. Hold Night School Convention," *The Pilot*, 10 July 1920. For a history of this fraternal association, see Kauffman.

51. John O'Grady, *The Catholic Church and the Destitute* (New York: Macmillan, 1929), 90–91; O'Grady, 1930, 336.

52. Kate M. Reilly to Brother Delegates, 12 March 1892, RG 69, Irish Catholic Benevolent Union Records, AAPHIL.

53. Kate M. Reilly, Organize Women's Branches of the ICBU n.d. [c. 1892]; K. M. Reilly, Appeal to Catholic Women to Organize, n.d. [c. 1892], RG 69, Irish Catholic Benevolent Union Records, AAPHIL.

54. See, for example, McColgan, 1: 278. As charitable institutions demanding their services expanded after 1850, most sisterhoods, too, had to withdraw from this work.

55. Mary Agnes Amberg, *Madonna Center: Pioneer Catholic Social Settlement* (Chicago: Loyola University Press, 1976), 194; Aaron I. Abell, *American Catholicism and Social Action: A Search for Social Justice, 1865–1950* (Notre Dame, Ind.: University of Notre Dame Press, 1963), 121–23.

56. Robert Biggs, "What We Are Doing in Settlement Work," *St. Vincent de Paul Quarterly* 19 (November 1914): 242. A few new sisterhoods specializing in settlement work had appeared by 1915, but their memberships were small. See Abell, 155, 165.

57. Amberg, 42.

58. Biggs, 1914, 237.

59. A History of the Guild of Catholic Women, 1906–1943, n.d., 8–9, Box 1 23.M.4.8F, Folder: Historical Background, Articles of Incorporation, By-laws, 1912–1974, GCW-MHS.

60. "Charity Work Highly Lauded," *The Pilot*, 10 May 1924.

61. Minutes of the Guild of Catholic Women, Recording Secretary's Book, 6 December 1909–4 May 1914, vol. 1, 6 February 1911 entry, GCW-MHS.

62. Minutes, Recording Secretary, 1916–6 May 1918, 3 February 1917 entry, vol. 2; Minutes, Recording Secretary, June 1920–3 April 1922, 6 February 1922 entry, GCW-MHS.

63. Minutes, Recording Secretary, June 1920–3 April 1922, 20 January 1922 entry, GCW-MHS.

64. Minutes of General, Board and Special Meetings, Recording Secretary, 1927–1928, 7 March 1927 entry; Minutes, Volume of Recording Secretary, 1965–1973, 6 April 1970 entry, GCW-MHS.

65. Minutes, Volume of Recording Secretary, 1965–1973, Board Meeting, 10 May 1972; 21 June 1973 entry, GCW-MHS.

66. James M. Reardon, *The Catholic Church in the Diocese of St. Paul* (St. Paul: North Central Publishing, 1952), 661, 663.

67. Tentler, 226–27, 432. By 1935, association membership had declined significantly.

68. John D. Mahoney to Garret W. McEnerney, 30 June 1922, Folder 1: Catholic Ladies Aid Society, AASF.

69. Annie E. Ward to Pietro Fumasoni-Biondi, Apostolic Delegate, May 1927, Folder 1: Catholic Ladies Aid Society; Ward to [Edward] Hanna, 28 November 1927; Ward to John A. Lally, 19 December 1927, Folder 2: Catholic Ladies Aid Society, AASF.

70. Mary A. Barr, "Work of the Ladies' Catholic Club Association of Boston," *Proceedings, Third National Conference of Catholic Charities* (1914): 231–33; Robert Barry to Jeremiah Minihan, 8 October 1935, Catholic Charitable Bureau Files, Box 4, Folder 17, AABOS.

71. Quoted in Margaret M. McGuinness, "A Puzzle with Missing Pieces: Catholic Women and the Social Settlement Movement, 1897–1915," *Cushwa Center Working Paper* [Notre Dame University], series 22, no. 2 (Spring 1990): 3, 11, 22.

72. John O'Grady, "The Catholic Settlement Movement," *Catholic Charities Review* 15 (May 1931): 137–38. This is a good survey of the early Catholic settlements. In 1915, they represented under 10 percent of settlements nationwide.

73. Sayers, 6–7.

74. M. Austin to M. Gonzaga, 31 December 1885, SMNH.

75. J. T. Smith, 2: 502.

76. M. Austin to M. Gonzaga, 26 January 1886, File A, Folder: Original Letters of Sister M. Austin Carroll to Sister M. Gonzaga O'Brien, 1880–1895, SMNH; Annals of the Community of the Sisters of Mercy in the Diocese of Fall River [Mass.], St. Mary's Convent, 68–70, SMRI.

77. "Cardinal Outlines History of Charitable Institutions," *The Pilot*, 17 April 1926.

78. Minutes of a Special Meeting of the Directors who are also the only members of "The Managers of the Roman Catholic Orphans' Asylums of St. Louis," 29 May 1952; Minutes of the Meeting of Managers of the Roman Catholic Orphan Asylums of St. Louis, 25 October 1951, Archives, Catholic Charities, St. Louis.

79. McCauley, 271.

80. M. Vincentia to the Sisters of Charity, 30 September 1955, quoted in McCauley, 275–76.

81. William H. O'Connell to Reverend dear Father, 21 September 1909, Chancery Circulars, Box 2, Folder 18, AABOS; "Bureau of Charities for Philadelphia," *The Pilot*, 1 January 1910. The board in each diocese was entirely male, with a priest as president.

82. "In Your Charity," *The Pilot*, 24 September 1938. O'Connell was by no means unusual in his perception of his role and responsibility. George Mundelein, who arrived in Chicago in 1916, described himself similarly. See Coughlin and Riplinger, 195.

83. Richard Haberlin to Michael J. Scanlan, 28 November 1916, Catholic Charitable Bureau Files, Box 1, Folder 8, AABOS.

84. McColgan, 2: 348–49; Minutes of the Meeting of the Clergy and Laity of St. Louis, 13 December 1916; Harmon J. Bliss to President of the St. Vincent de Paul Society, 8 January 1918, incorporated in Minutes of the Second Meeting of the Associated Conference of Catholic Charities, St. Louis, 17 January 1917; Minutes of Special Committee Meeting of the Associated Conference of Catholic Charities, St. Louis, 31 January 1917; Minutes of General Meeting of the Associated Conference of Catholic Charities of St. Louis, 14 February 1917, Archives, Catholic Charities, St. Louis. The new structure replaced the more informal Annual Conference of Catholic Charities of St. Louis.

85. McColgan, 1: 496–99.

86. McColgan, 2: 223.

87. Teresa Teh-Ying Loh, "A Study of the Organization of Catholic Charities" (M.S.W. thesis, Catholic University of America, 1947), 10–11.

88. O'Grady, 1929, 132; Michael J. Scanlan to Richard J. Haberlin, 23 September 1918, Catholic Charitable Bureau Files, Box 1, Folder 12, AABOS; Gavin, 93.

89. M. D. Imhoff, "Personal Service in Relief Work," *Proceedings, Fourth Biennial Meeting of the National Conference of Catholic Charities* (1916): 146.

90. "Modern Charity," *The Pilot*, 28 May 1921; "What Social Service Means," *The Pilot*, 20 October 1928.

91. John O'Grady, "Lay Participation in Catholic Charity," *Catholic Charities Review* 9 (December 1925): 379–80. Tensions between "institutional and anti-institutional people" remained strong in the 1930s. John O'Grady, "Child-Caring Institutions—The Challenge for 1936," *Catholic Charities Review* 20 (May 1936): 135.

92. "Women's Convention an Event of Nation-wide Importance," *National Catholic Welfare Council Bulletin* 3 (November 1921): 2; *The National Catholic School of Social Service* (Baltimore: Belvedere Press, 1927), 27. Schools of social service had been established earlier at Loyola University, Chicago (1913) and Fordham University, New York (1917). By 1941, there were seven. John O'Grady, "Catholic Charities in 1941," *Catholic Charities Review* 25 (February 1941): 42.

93. Annual Report, Bureau of Catholic Charities, Diocese of Monterey and Los Angeles, 1 January 1921–1 January 1922, AALA; Gavin, 96.

94. Minutes of Annual Meeting, Baltimore, 9 February 1908, Minute Book, St. Vincent's Male Orphan Asylum, Archives, Associated Catholic Charities, Baltimore. Boards of female auxiliaries attached to various institutions were similarly enlarged.

95. *Second Annual Report, January 1, 1920–January 1, 1921, of the Affiliated Catholic Charities of the Archdiocese of San Francisco*, 3–4, AASF.

96. William J. Kerby, "The Catholic Charities of a City," *Ecclesiastical Review* 48 (June 1913): 683, 695.

97. Chronicle of Sacred Heart Hospital, Aviston, Illinois, Day Book, 1891–1955, 24, CHJCO39/14, Folder: Aviston, Illinois, Sacred Heart Hospital and Home for the Aged-Chronicles 1891–1955, AUND.

98. O'Grady, 1930, 278.

99. Articles of Association, Article 6th, St. Vincent's Infant Asylum, Minute Book—St. Vincent's Infant Asylum, Baltimore, Maryland, AAB.

100. Minutes, Regular Meeting of Board of Directors, St. Vincent's Infant Asylum, Baltimore, Maryland, 24 October 1949; Minutes, Special Meeting, 23 May 1938, Minute Book, Archives, Associated Catholic Charities, Baltimore.

101. Minutes of Meeting of Board of Directors, Catholic Charities of St. Louis, 12 January 1938, 28 February 1938, Archives, Catholic Charities, St. Louis.

102. Department of Children, Catholic Charities, Minute Book, 1 October 1929–1 January 1930, Archives, Catholic Charities, St. Louis; Alice R. May, Historical Synopsis of Associated Catholic Charities, March 1968, 2–3, typescript, AAB.

103. *Centennial Anniversary of German Saint Vincent Orphan Association of St. Louis, Missouri, 1850–1950*, AASL.

104. Joseph Ritter to Edgar J. Freivogel, 28 August 1963, AASL.

105. "Isolationism among Catholic Agencies," *Catholic Charities Review* 40 (April 1956): 2–3.

106. Austin Dowling, Address at the National Conference of Catholic Charities Meeting, 11 September 1924, AASPM.

107. "Modern Charities," *The Pilot*, 4 November 1916; Peter Fumasoni-Biondi, "Address to the Charities Conference, Washington, D.C.," *The Pilot*, 19 September 1925; "Charity," *The Pilot*, 7 October 1911.

108. "Charity, Organized and Private," *Ave Maria* 78 (11 April 1914): 467.

109. Biggs, 1910, 90–92.

110. William J. Kerby, "Impressions of the National Conference of Catholic Charities," *St. Vincent de Paul Quarterly* 21 (November 1916): 307; T. D. Hurley, "Our Relations with Other Societies," *St. Vincent de Paul Quarterly* 3 (1898): 92–93.

111. "Charity Sunday," *The Pilot*, 23 September 1933.

112. "The Coming National Conference of Catholic Charities," *St. Vincent de Paul Quarterly* 15 (August 1910): 238, 241. For more on the National Conference, see Patrick B. Lavey, "William J. Kerby, John A. Ryan, and the Awakening of the Twentieth Century American Catholic Social Conscience, 1899–1919" (Ph.D. diss., University of Illinois, 1986); and Gavin, 1962. It met biannually until 1920 and annually thereafter. Shahan headed the conference for nineteen years; Kerby served as its secretary until 1920; and O'Grady succeeded Kerby as secretary.

113. John J. Burke, "Special Catholic Activities in War Service," *Annals of the American Academy of Political and Social Science* 89 (1918): 220. For a history of this organization, see Earl Boyea, "The National Catholic Welfare Conference: An Experience in Episcopal Leadership, 1935–1945" (Ph.D. diss., Catholic University of America, 1987). Its name was changed from "Council" to "Conference" in 1923. After 1965 its functions were assumed by the new National Conference of Catholic Bishops and United States Catholic Conference.

114. William J. Engelen, S. J., to Frederick P. Kenkel, 27 December 1918, Frederick P. Kenkel Papers, AUND.

115. Agnes G. Regan, "Financing a National Organization," *National Catholic Welfare Conference Bulletin* 5 (December 1923): 26.

116. Memorandum, William Montavon to Michael Ready, 11 October 1938, quoted in Thomas W. Tifft, "Toward a More Humane Social Policy: The Work and Influence of Monsignor John O'Grady" (Ph.D. diss., Catholic University of America, 1979), 281.

117. Gavin, 160; "Work of St. Vincent de Paul Society in America Reviewed," *The Pilot*, 27 May 1933; "Religion in Social Work," *The Pilot*, 5 October 1935.

118. Ignatius A. O'Shaughnessy to M. Francis, 25 October 1955, Box 4. 26.D.7.7B, I. A. O'Shaughnessy Collection, Minnesota Historical Society, Minneapolis.

119. "In Your Charity," *The Pilot*, 24 September 1938.

120. Gavin, 73.

121. William J. Kerby, " 'Who Is My Neighbor?' " 4 parts, *Catholic World* 87, 88 (1908–1909): 4: 615.

122. "The Enthusiasm of Yesteryears," *Catholic Charities Review* 21 (September 1937): 197.

5. New Strategies in Fundraising

1. Tentler, 76. About this time, the average annual family contribution to the parish in the Baltimore archdiocese was twenty-five dollars, excluding contributions for special national and diocesan collections. Pew rentals averaged fifty dollars per year. James Gibbons, "Wealth and Its Obligations," *North American Quarterly* 152 (April 1891): 389.

2. M. Bonaventure, Appeal Letter of 1905, St. John's Orphan Asylum, Philadelphia, CSJPHIL.

3. CCYB, 1924, 43.

4. Jacoby, 94, 102; Lelia Hardin Bugg, *The People of Our Parish* (Boston: Marlier, Callanan, 1900), 136.

5. John Ireland to the Clergy of the Diocese, St. Paul, 5 January 1891, Roll 4: 1882–1982, John Ireland Papers, AASPM.

6. Minutes of Quarterly Meeting, 21 April 1901; Minutes of Meeting, 9 February 1908; Minutes of Annual Meeting of Board of Directors, 2 February 1913, Minute Book, St. Vincent's Male Orphan Asylum, Baltimore, Archives, Associated Catholic Charities, Baltimore.

7. Minutes of Meeting of Board of Directors, 15 January 1909, Minute Book, St. John's Male Orphan Asylum, Baltimore, Archives, Associated Catholic Charities, Baltimore.

8. "Editorial Notes," *Our Lady's Orphan Boy* 3 (September 1905): 2–3.

9. Quoted in Charles E. Nolan, *Mother Clare Coady: Her Life, Her Times, and Her Sisters* (New Orleans: Academy Enterprises, 1983), 117–18.

10. Hynes, 278–79; Letter from Cardinal George Mundelein, Pentecost Sunday, 28 May

1939, The Catholic Charities of the Archdiocese of Chicago, Box 14, Folder 17, Mundelein Collection, AAC.

11. D. F. Kelly to Chairmen of Parish Drives, Minutes of the Meeting of the Executive Committee of the Associated Catholic Charities of Chicago, 9 December 1918, Box 1, ACC-AAC. The Associated Catholic Charities, known after 1924 as Catholic Charities, conducted annual campaigns for funds; the Central Charity Bureau supervised charitable institutions. Chicago's per capita contributions in the early 1920s were similar to those recorded in other dioceses. For instance, in 1925 the per capita contribution in the Syracuse, New York, diocesan charities collection was $8.50. John O'Grady, "A Bishop's House of Charity Built on a Firm Foundation," *Catholic Charities Review* 9 (January 1925): 22.

12. Minutes of Executive Committee Meeting, Associated Catholic Charities, 16 July 1926, Box 2, ACC-AAC; Statement of the Number of Contributors and Amounts Donated in Respective Divisions Last Year [1920], Box 1, ACC-AAC; John O'Grady, "The Associated Catholic Charities of Chicago," *Catholic Charities Review* 7 (February 1923): 42.

13. Minutes of Executive Committee Meeting, Associated Catholic Charities, 12 July 1920; Executive Committee Matter, 6 June 1921; Minutes of Executive Committee Meeting, 10 July 1921, Box 1, ACC-AAC.

14. The Associated Catholic Charities' Executive Committee Matter, 1 June 1920; Minutes of Meeting of Executive Committee of Associated Catholic Charities, 1 June 1920; Suggestions for Meeting of the Associated Catholic Charities, 15 April 1920, Box 1, ACC-AAC.

15. Minutes of Executive Committee Meeting, Associated Catholic Charities, 16 July 1926, Box 2, ACC-AAC.

16. Minutes of Annual Meeting of the Members of the Associated Catholic Charities of the Archdiocese of Chicago, 16 April 1923, Box 2; List of Directors of Associated Catholic Charities of Chicago, 10 May 1920, Box 1; Minutes of Executive Committee Meeting, 18 October 1920, Box 1, ACC-AAC.

17. [Edward Hoban] to Mr. Kelly, 3 January 1921; Minutes of Meeting of the Associated Catholic Charities of the Archdiocese of Chicago, 12 June 1922, Box 2; Unsigned letter to Mr. Kelly, 21 February 1921, Box 1, ACC-AAC. At this time, it was thought that only about 50 percent of American Catholics contributed to the support of the church. Noll, 273. The picture was worse in some places. In 1927, for example, John Mitty, bishop of Salt Lake City, claimed that only 5 percent of his parishioners contributed to the diocesan collections. Mooney, 179.

18. Minutes of Meeting of Executive Committee of Associated Catholic Charities, 8 October 1923, Box 2, ACC-AAC. When 1930 returns fell far short of the campaign goal, Mundelein ordered pastors to meet their quotas and remit returns directly to his office. Coughlin and Riplinger, 225.

19. M. Alexis to P. A. Baart, 26 March 1885; M. LeMasson to P. A. Baart, 13 April 1885; E. W. Herman to P. A. Baart, 13 March 1884, Box 1, PAB-UND.

20. Article 308: Code of the Diocese of Des Moines, quoted in *The Tithe* (Des Moines: St. Ambrose Cathedral, n.d.), RG-74, Dowling Papers, I, Iowa Papers, Box 1, Folder 1: Des Moines, Iowa, Papers (25 April 1912–20 December 1916), AASPM.

21. Kremer, 37, 64.

22. Ibid., 37.

23. George Gallup, Jr., and Jim Castelli, *The American Catholic People: Their Beliefs, Practices, and Values* (Garden City, N.Y.: Doubleday, 1987), 39.

24. Robert F. Keegan, "Surveys of Catholic Charities," *Proceedings, Sixth National Conference of Catholic Charities* (1920), 34.

25. "The Capacity for Giving," *Catholic Charities Review* 2 (May 1918): 131–32.

26. Patrick J. Hayes, "The Unification of Catholic Charities," *Catholic World* 117 (May 1923): 149. In 1923, contributions averaging $4.10 from 241,000 donors raised nearly $1 million.

27. Hayes, 149–50, 153; John O'Grady, "The Cardinal of Charities Who Builded Wisely and Well Passes On," *Catholic Charities Review* 22 (September 1938): 199.

28. "The Charity Problem," *The Pilot*, 23 August 1913.

29. Keegan, 454; Unsigned letter to Mr. Kelly, 12 February 1923; and Minutes of the Executive Committee Meeting, 9 January 1922, Box 2, ACC-AAC.

30. Minutes of Executive Committee Meeting, 12 July 1920; and Minutes of Executive Committee Matter, 8 November 1920, Box 1, ACC-AAC.

31. Executive Committee Matter, 6 June 1921, Box 1, ACC-AAC.

32. Executive Committee Business, 5 January 1922, Box 1; and Minutes of Executive Committee Meeting, 11 July 1923, Box 2, ACC-AAC.

33. Frank Tucker, "The Finances of Private Charities," *St. Vincent de Paul Quarterly* 5 (1900): 211–12. Tucker was General Agent of the Association for Improving the Condition of the Poor.

34. Hayes, 151; Minutes of the Meeting of the Executive Committee of the Associated Catholic Charities of the Archdiocese of Chicago, 8 January 1923, Box 2, ACC-AAC.

35. Robert M. Sweitzer to [donor], 18 July 1918; "Catholics Show Your Colors: Join The Associated Catholic Charities," in *[Holy Family, Chicago] Church Calendar and Sodality Bulletin* 31 (June 1918): 27, Box 1, ACC-AAC.

36. Executive Committee Matter (Mr. Watts to Mr. [D. F.] Kelly), 8 October 1923, Box 2, ACC-AAC.

37. Minutes of the Executive Committee Meeting, 16 July 1926, Box 2, ACC-AAC; George Mundelein, The Catholic Charities of the Archdiocese of Chicago, 28 May 1939, Box 14, Folder 17, Mundelein Collection, AAC.

38. "Archbishop's Fund Links Its Donors to Charities," *The Tidings*, 14 April 1961.

39. "Charity Expansion Plan Inaugurated," *The Tidings*, 11 January 1952; Martin McNicholas to Rev. dear Father, 29 December 1955, AALA.

40. Folders: The Archbishop's Fund, Direct Contributions, 1961, 1963, 1965, 1967, 1968; and Raymond J. O'Flaherty to Reverend and Dear Father, n.d., AALA.

41. M. F. Smith to the Archbishop's Fund, 16 January 1967, Folder: The Archbishop's Fund, Direct Contributions, 1967, AALA.

42. James McIntyre, to William J. Barry, 4 April 1967, AALA.

43. John J. Glennon, "Preface," *Fourteenth Annual Report of Catholic Charities of the City of St. Louis, 1925* (St. Louis: Central Bureau of Catholic Charities and Kindred Activities of St. Louis, 1925).

44. A Plan of Fund Raising for the Archdiocese of St. Paul-Minneapolis, A Confidential Report prepared by the Community Counselling Service, N.Y., n.d. [c. 1968], 11–12; 18; 24–27, RG-4, Box 8, Folder 31, AASPM. The belief that ordinary Catholics will emulate the generosity of the very wealthy explains, in part, the perennial imbalance in sex and class representation on boards of directors of Catholic charities.

45. In 1930, publication of names and donations for parish support was approved as an incentive to those who otherwise would not meet their obligation. Kremer, 85–87.

46. "Charity," *The Pilot*, 2 October 1920.

47. See Dean R. Hoge and Douglas L. Griffin, *Research on Factors Influencing Giving to Religious Bodies* (Indianapolis: Ecumenical Center for Stewardship Studies, 1992), 47. Reactions to pledging, of course, varied with the cause. Bishop James Van de Velde of Natchez, Mississippi, sought pledges in June 1854 to retire the cathedral debt, a cause that evoked little enthusiasm. He asked that, by October 15, half the funds subscribed be remitted, the rest three months later. By mid-January 1855, he had not yet received $2 of the $4,200 pledged. Pillar, 56–57.

48. Richard J. Cushing to Dearly Beloved in Christ, 7 November 1969, ANB Files, AA.B, AABOS.

49. *Overview: A Continuing Survey of Catholic Trends and Opinions*, [Newsletter of the Thomas More Association], 15 April 1968, 6.

50. Thomas J. Holbrook to Dear Friend of Catholic Charities, 5 May 1975, with accompanying flyer, Box: NCCC Projects, Folder: Catholic Charities Campaign Material, CC-USA.

51. Walter P. Kellenberg to Dear Friend of Catholic Charities, in flyer for 1976 Catholic Charities Appeal, Box: Diocese of Rockville Centre, NCCC, Folder: Catholic Charities Campaign Material, CC-USA.

52. "Reviewpoint," *Catholic Review*, 8 April 1949.

53. *The Edwardian* 9 (April 1949), Archives, Associated Catholic Charities, Baltimore.

54. "Reviewpoint," *Catholic Review*, 8 April 1949; *Baltimore Sun*, 4 June 1949. The *Sun* observed that "many non-Catholics, Jews, besides numerous Catholics who never before contributed to a Catholic cause, sent donations to the appeal."

55. "Editorial," *Baltimore Sun*, 10 May 1949; *Baltimore Sun*, 14 May 1949.

56. *Baltimore Evening Sun*, 17 May 1949; *Baltimore Sun*, 4 June 1949.

57. O'Neill Ryan to Thomas C. Hennings, 11 May 1922, in Minutes of Meeting of the Board of Directors of the Central Bureau, 10 May 1922, Minute Book, Archives, Catholic Charities, St. Louis.

58. Gavin, 162.

59. John J. Butler, "Preface," *Catholic Charities of St. Louis, Twenty-Sixth Annual Report, 1936* (St. Louis: Catholic Charities of St. Louis, 1936).

60. Centennial Anniversary of German Saint Vincent Orphan Association of St. Louis, Missouri, 1850–1950, commemorative booklet, AASL; Hynes, 344–45, 394; Agenda of Annual Meeting of Board of Directors of Catholic Charitable Bureau, 10 January 1949, Catholic Charitable Bureau Files, Box 6, Folder 9, AABOS; *Twenty-fifth Anniversary, Associated Catholic Charities of New Orleans, 1924–1949* (October 1949), 41–42, AANO.

61. "A Quarter of a Century of Chest Leadership," *Catholic Charities Review* 32 (October 1948): 198–99.

62. Karl Alter, Reply to "Memorandum on Community Chests" or "General Campaigns" in vogue in some parts of the U.S., typescript, n.d., Box 2: NCSSS, Alter, K. J., Addresses and Reports, ACUA.

63. Elisabeth Allhoff, "History and Development of St. Elizabeth Settlement and Day Nursery" (B.S. in Ed. thesis, St. Louis University, 1941), 25; Hynes, 278–79.

64. Second Annual Report, 1 January 1920–1 January 1921, of the Affiliated Catholic Charities of the Archdiocese of San Francisco; Report of the Affiliated Catholic Charities of the Archdiocese of San Francisco, 1 January 1923–1 January 1924, AASF.

65. Bernard J. Sheil, Public and Private Charity, typescript, n.d., 5, Box 2, Folder 81: Bernard J. Sheil Papers, AAC.

66. "Catholic Point of View on National Health Bill," *Catholic Charities Review* 23 (June 1939): 168; David J. O'Brien, "Social Teaching, Social Action, Social Gospel," *U.S. Catholic Historian* 5, no. 2 (1986): 199.

67. Thomas J. O'Dwyer, "New Opportunities for Private Charitable Agencies," *Catholic Charities Review* 21 (May 1937): 136.

68. *The Catholic Charities of the Archdiocese of Chicago*, Pentecost Sunday, 29 May 1939, flyer, Box 14, Folder 17: Catholic Charities: Pentecost Sunday Appeal, 1939, Mundelein Collection, AAC.

69. "Catholic Point of View," 175; "Advantages of the Community Fund," *The Pilot*, 13 January 1940; "Cites Glorious History of Charity in Appeal for Boston Fund," *The Pilot*, 27 January 1940.

70. "Statement of the Archbishops and Bishops of the Administrative Board, N.C.W.C., on the Church and Social Order, 7 February 1940," in Raphael M. Huber, ed., *Our Bishops Speak, 1919–1951* (Milwaukee: Bruce Publishing, 1952), 340; "Like the Early Christians," *Catholic Charities Review* 36 (February 1952): 26–27. For a discussion of political issues related to Catholic Charities involvement in government welfare programs, see Gene D. L. Jones, "The Chicago Catholic Charities, the Great Depression, and Public Monies," *Illinois Historical Journal* 83 (Spring 1990): 13–30.

71. Richard J. Cushing, "The Survival of Our Private Charities," *Catholic Charities Review* 34 (April 1950): 88.

72. William A. O'Connor, "Do Americans Support Their Charities?" *Catholic Charities Review* 33 (May 1949): 114.

73. John O'Grady, "Are We Serving the Poor?" *Catholic Charities Review* 35 (January 1951): 1.

74. Dorothy Day, *The Long Loneliness* (1952; reprint, New York: Harper and Row, 1981), 150. For a biography of Day, see William D. Miller, *Dorothy Day: A Biography* (San Francisco: Harper and Row, 1982). In 1938, the Russian exile Catherine de Hueck opened in Harlem the nation's first Friendship House where lay volunteers promoted racial equality while living among and assisting the poor. For a history of this movement, see Elizabeth L. Sharum, "A Strange Fire Burning: A History of the Friendship House Movement" (Ph.D. diss., Texas Tech University, 1977); and Albert Schorsch, " 'Uncommon Women and Others': Memoirs and Lessons from Radical Catholics at Friendship House," *U.S. Catholic Historian* 9 (Fall 1990): 371–86.

75. Neil Betten, "The Great Depression and the Activities of the Catholic Worker Movement," *Labor History* 12 (Spring 1971): 249–52. Bishops strongly supported Catholic Worker efforts on behalf of the poor and unemployed, but interest faded considerably when the movement embraced an active pacifist stance in the 1940s.

76. Dorothy Day, *Loaves and Fishes* (New York: Harper and Row, 1963), 87. The first issue of *The Catholic Worker*, the group's monthly tabloid, appeared in May 1933.

77. Day, 1981, 150–51. A few members today see in the acceptance of any external financial support a threat to the radical character of the movement. "Reliance on donations, and the cultivation and appeasement of benefactors, lies at the heart of our subtle co-option into the structures of oppression." Ciaron O'Reilly, "A Critique of the Catholic Worker Movement in the United States," *The Little Way* (Winter 1990).

78. "A Religious Order's View of Renewal," *Catholic Mind* 66 (January 1968): 9.

79. Receipts and Expenditures, 1873, St. Vincent de Paul Parish, Brooklyn, New York, CSJNY.

80. James Gibbons to Thomas D. Beaven, 25 September 1915, Bishop Thomas J. Shahan Papers Collection, RG-19, Box 1, AAPHIL. The Peter's Pence and the Indian and Negro Missions collections were introduced by the Second Plenary Council of Baltimore, 1866, and the Third Plenary Council of Baltimore, 1884, respectively. By 1930, the latter was combined with the foreign mission collection and called the Home and Foreign Missions Collection. The Good Friday collection for the church in the Holy Land was initiated by Pope Leo XIII in 1887.

81. Ferdinand Kittell to Thomas Shahan, 12 December 1915, Shahan Collection, RG-19, Box 1, AAPHIL.

82. "Co-ordinate Work of Catholic Missions," *The Pilot*, 18 December 1920.

83. "Resolution of the Hierarchy of the United States Regarding Home and Foreign Missions, September 15, 1927," in Huber, 189–90.

84. "Report of the Superior General," *The Colored Harvest* 70 (May 1958): 4.

85. Edward E. Swanstrom, "War Relief Services," *Catholic Charities Review* 28 (February 1944): 53–56; Eileen Egan, "Relief to the War Stricken," *Catholic Charities Review* 30 (March 1946): 60–63.

86. CRS, *Catholic Relief Services, United States Catholic Conference, Annual Report 1992* (Baltimore: Catholic Relief Services-USCC, 1993), 22–23. For a brief history of this agency, see Robert McCloskey, *A CRS Chronicle, Fiftieth Anniversary* (Baltimore: Catholic Relief Services-USCC, 1993).

87. National Conference of Catholic Bishops, "Resolution on the Campaign for Human Development, November 1970," in Nolan, 273–74; *Chronicle of Philanthropy*, 10 August 1993. Over its first sixteen years, contributions in real dollars actually declined 25 percent, leading the hierarchy to revise the guidelines used to conduct the campaign. William E. McManus, "Stewardship and Almsgiving in the Roman Catholic Tradition," in Robert Wuthnow and Virginia

A. Hodgkinson, eds., *Faith and Philanthropy in America* (San Francisco: Jossey-Bass, 1990), 130. See also D. J. O'Brien, 213–14.

88. Eugene R. Gillis to Joseph Berg, 5 June 1984, Box: NCCC Projects, CC-USA.

89. "Inquiring Reporter. The Question: What Is Your Chief Problem This Year?" [Chicago] *Catholic Charities* 1 (Spring 1946): 6.

90. Harold W. Henry to Monsignor Gilligan, 10 December 1975, RG-10.6, Folder 5, Society for the Propagation of the Faith Records, AASPM.

6. Social Class and Ways of Giving

1. RSJOA, 1846, 12.

2. Baart, 112–13; "A Layman" to Napoleon J. Perché, 8 May 1874, AUND.

3. Johnson, 182, 184; "Catholic Boys' Home Began in a Hotel," *Minneapolis Star*, 12 May 1953.

4. "The Orphan's Fair," news clipping [c. December 1858], Box 11–11, 1-2-1, 5, DCA. In addition to fairs, benefit lectures, concerts, May festivals, and picnics also raised "handsome sums" in the 1850s. Sharp, 1: 235.

5. Weitzman, 33–34.

6. "The Little Sisters of the Poor. A Sketch of the History and Mission of This Remarkable Order," *Chicago Sunday Times*, 6 October 1878.

7. Weitzman, 80.

8. "Pastoral Letter, Second Plenary Council of Baltimore, 21 October 1866," in Nolan, 1: 202.

9. Mary Charles Curtin, Annals, Sacred Heart Convent, 1841–1892, typescript, n.d., 6, SMNC. A half-century later, bishops still frowned on dances, "no matter how decorous," for the purpose of parish fundraising. Austin Dowling to the Clergy and Laity of the Archdiocese, 24 February 1927, Austin Dowling (1868–1930) Papers, RG-74, Box 1, Folder 7: Official Diocesan Directives (1924–9 December 1929), AASPM.

10. Kerby, 1908–1909, 1: 354–55.

11. "Charity With a Hook," *Ave Maria* 56 (9 May 1903): 596. The writer quotes approvingly a mainstream verse decrying "the sociable":

Give their quarters! Why, of course not!
Do you think them foolish quite?
It's amusement for their money
That has brought them out to-night.

See also an unsigned, handwritten statement, Catholic Philopatrian Literary Institute, Philadelphia, 10 February 1899, Box 7, Griffin Collection, AAPHIL.

12. John I. Rogers, President, to Members, 5 November 1892, Catholic Club of Philadelphia Collection (1871–1923), Box 1, AAPHIL.

13. Charles Phillips to Charles Devenny, Esq., Librarian of the [De Sales] Institute, 28 March 1876, Box 1, Catholic Club of Philadelphia Collection, 1871–1923, AAPHIL.

14. "Catholic Philopatrian Literary Institute," *Catholic Standard*, 11 April 1886; Edward Robins, President, The Catholic Club of Philadelphia, Confidential Circular, 16 September 1881, Box 1, Catholic Club of Philadelphia Collection, AAPHIL. The Institute evolved from the Aerina Association, an organization that had held annual balls since 1857. Not until 1879 did the event become a Charity Ball, however.

15. Prindiville, 488–89.

16. Minutes of the Executive Committee Meeting, Associated Catholic Charities, 27 April 1920, Box 1, ACC-AAC.

17. L. J. Lindon, "Out-Door Relief as Administered by Church Societies," *St. Vincent de Paul Society* 4 (1899): 25. Very rich members, including the founder of the first American con-

ference, Bryan Mullanphy of St. Louis, gave money, but rarely undertook the main work of the society, personal visitation of the poor. McColgan, 2: 442.

18. "Our Roman Catholic Brethren," 434.

19. Canon Peter L. Benoit, Diary of a Trip to America, 6 January 1875 to 8 June 1875, 3 vols., Mill Hill Fathers Archives, transcribed by Peter E. Hogan, 1965, 23 January 1875 entry, 30, Canon Peter L. Benoit Collection, AUND.

20. Benoit, Diary, 21 February 1875 entry, 77–78; 1 March 1875 entry, 85, Benoit Collection, AUND.

21. Benoit, Diary, 28 February 1975 entry, 80, Benoit Collection, AUND.

22. Patricia K. Good, "Irish Adjustment to American Society: Integration or Separation?" *Records of the American Catholic Historical Society of Philadelphia* 86 (1975): 22 n. 15. See also Hennesey, 176.

23. Hewit, 1: 577–78.

24. Quoted in "Our Roman Catholic Brethren," 446.

25. H. L., *Irish Faith in America: Recollection of a Missionary* (New York: Benziger, 1881), 96–97.

26. Benoit, Diary, 5 February 1875 entry, 51, Benoit Collection, AUND.

27. Ireland, 1903, 343, 337–38.

28. William Caldwell to Columba Carroll, February 1873, quoted in McGann, 1973, 13–14. Caldwell, a gas industrialist, also endowed the hospital, contributing $50,000 in railroad stock yielding, at the time, 7 percent annually. He supported charities in other dioceses as well. See Magri, 111–12.

29. Katharine Drexel, "Oral Memoir, 29 November 1935," SBS.

30. Annals, no. 1, 34–35, SBS; Journal of Emma Bouvier Drexel, 29 July 1877 entry, Record Book, LBDM-55, SBS.

31. Crimmins, 25 December 1888 entry, 43; 25 December 1904 entry, 364. Crimmins followed this routine on virtually every holiday.

32. Luers, 1865, 49–52.

33. Quoted in Zwierlein, 1925, 3: 407.

34. Church, 1: 203.

35. Jeremiah J. O'Connell, *Catholicity in the Carolinas and Georgia: Leaves of Its History* (New York: Sadlier, 1879), 298; Annals of This Convent, 2 January 1892 entry, SMCA. Since bequests, even from those who had never given in life, would help Catholic charities, most bishops preferred a milder stand. For example, Rochester's Bernard McQuaid praised bequests, but argued that gifts by the living were more spiritually meritorious. In addition, they "run no risk of being disputed and diverted from the intention of the deceased giver by unscrupulous relatives." Quoted in Zwierlein, 1925, 3: 407.

36. Patrick J. Riordan to Thomas J. Shahan, 28 October 1912, RG-19, Box 1, Shahan Collection, AAPHIL.

37. J. P. Carrigan to Thomas Shahan, 12 December 1915, RG-19, Box 1, Shahan Collection, AAPHIL.

38. Ferdinand Kittell to Thomas Shahan, 12 December 1915, RG-19, Box 1, Shahan Collection, AAPHIL.

39. CCYB, 1924, 61; Joseph L. J. Kirlin, *Catholicity in Philadelphia* (Philadelphia: John Jos. McVey, 1909), 445; *Souvenir Sketch of St. Patrick's Church, Philadelphia*, 46–48.

40. Hewit, 4: 147.

41. Hewit, 3: 41.

42. Matthew O'Doherty, "Charity versus Philanthropy—An Appeal to Young Men," *St. Vincent de Paul Quarterly* 10 (1905): 176–78.

43. James O'Connor to My dear Child [K. M. Drexel], 26 July 1889, Annals, vol. 2, 242–44, SBS.

44. John J. Glennon, "An Apology for Charity," *St. Vincent de Paul Quarterly* 11 (1906): 191, 194–95. Prominent benevolent laity were posing the same question at this time. See, for exam-

ple, William Onahan, "Address before the Students and Professors of the Northwestern University Medical College, Octo. 6, 1903," William Onahan Collection, Folder: Chicago Topics, AAC.

45. "Most Generous Aid Comes from the Poor," *The Pilot*, 10 December 1910.

46. Noll, 273.

47. "Charity Sunday," *The Pilot*, 28 September 1918; "Most Generous Aid Comes from the Poor," *The Pilot*, 10 December 1910.

48. For typical early-twentieth-century articles in the secular and church press on the bestowal of papal honors on wealthy donors, see "Miss Annie Leary a Countess," *New York Times*, 5 January 1902; and "The Pope Creates Mrs. Ryan a Countess," *St. Vincent de Paul Quarterly* 12 (1907): 390–91. Penny Lernoux, *People of God: The Struggle for World Catholicism* (New York: Viking Penguin, 1989), chap. 10, provides a brief account of the contemporary structure and activities of the Knights of Malta.

49. "True Charity," *The Pilot*, 28 February 1920.

50. James Donahoe, *The Scope of Charity* (St. Paul, Minn.: Webb, 1914), 23–25.

51. "Miss Eliza Andrews Leaves $1,206,000," news clipping, 1914, *Scrapbook*, Archives, Associated Catholic Charities, Baltimore.

52. George W. Mundelein, "Address to the Knights of Columbus—The Care of Delinquent Boys, February 22nd, 1916," in George W. Mundelein, *Two Crowded Years* (Chicago: Extension Press, 1918), 185–86.

53. William O'Connell, Wealthier Catholics to Increase Support, 26 October 1916, Chancery Circulars, Box 3, Folder 6, AABOS.

54. "Cardinal Makes Plea for Genuine Charity," *The Pilot*, 23 December 1916.

55. "Help Our Charitable Institutions," *The Pilot*, 6 October 1923; "William Cardinal O'Connell to All the Clergy and Faithful of the Archdiocese, 23 September 1929," *The Pilot*, 28 September 1929.

56. "Report of the Cumminsville Orphan Asylum for the Year Ending Dec. 31st, 1883," [Cincinnati] *Catholic Telegraph*, news clipping, n.d. [c. January 1884]; RSJOA, 1855, 7–8; Kremer, 69.

57. Annual Report of the Roman Catholic Society of St. Joseph for Educating and Maintaining Poor Orphan Children, for the years 1855–'56–'57–'58 (Philadelphia: McLaughlin Brothers, 1859), 6, Box 11–1, 2–9–1, 2, DCA. For a consideration of the effects of economic forces on giving strategies, see Mary J. Oates, "Economic Change and the Character of Catholic Philanthropy, 1790–1940," in Conrad Cherry and Rowland Sherrill, eds., *Religion, the Independent Sector, and American Culture* (Atlanta: Scholars Press, 1992), 31–49.

58. *Annual Report of the Roman Catholic Society of St. Joseph*, 8, Box 11–1, 2–9–1, 2, DCA. Between 1807 and 1858, the orphanage received only 56 legacies, totaling nearly $27,000.

59. House of the Good Shepherd to John M. Odin, 1 June 1863, AUND.

60. "Catholic Protectory," *Catholic Review* 37 (28 June 1890): 412.

61. Yorke, "Sermon, 1922," quoted in Kavanagh, 305.

62. "Charity Sunday," *The Pilot*, 30 September 1916.

63. M. Georgiana Rockwell, comp., History of Community Rules, typescript, 2 April 1985, 25–26, SBS. She removed the restriction a year later.

64. Free Beds, n.d. [c. 1889], Box 11–35, 4, DCA. Response to the appeal was poor; nearly a decade later the 200-bed hospital had only a few endowed beds.

65. McCauley, 155–56. By 1907 it had forty-one perpetually endowed beds. In addition to perpetually endowed beds, this hospital also solicited $2,500 beds, endowed for the donor's lifetime, beds funded for a single year, and beds collectively funded by clubs and benevolent societies.

66. "For the Sick and Afflicted," *The Monitor*, 23 January 1904.

67. *Report of the St. Vincent's Orphan Asylum for the Year Ending December 31, 1911*, 4–5, Box 11–11, 1–1, 3, DCA.

68. Rules of the Society of Saint Vincent de Paul, 1943, 1, Box 5, Folder 7: Catholic Charitable Bureau Files, AABOS. The rules permitted the investment of some funds so that resources would be available at times of civic disaster.

69. Minutes of the Charitable Bureau Meeting, 6 December 1944, Box 5, Folder 12: Catholic Charitable Bureau Files, AABOS.

70. "The Little Sisters of the Poor," *Catholic World* 8 (October 1868): 115–16. This sisterhood's rule forbade it to accept any charitable gift that would provide a regular income, a requirement incomprehensible to Americans.

71. Beirne, 189.

72. Kremer, 94–97. In the more informal days of the early nineteenth century, priests begged on occasion. For example, in 1835, Rev. Timothy O'Brien of Richmond, Virginia, traveled to Lynchburg to collect for a church building fund among Irish laborers working on a canal there. James H. Bailey, *A History of the Diocese of Richmond: The Formative Years* (Richmond: Diocese of Richmond, 1956), 73.

73. Peter Beckman, "The Catholic Church on the Kansas Frontier, 1850–1877" (Ph.D. diss., Catholic University of America, 1943), 118.

74. R. P. Brennan to M. Bridget Russell, 13 January 1875, Annals of This Convent, SMCA. Those working in diocesan institutions were allowed to continue to beg locally. For sisters at a Lafayette, Indiana, orphanage, this was still a regular weekly duty in the 1890s: "It was the custom for two Sisters to go [to] town once a week to collect money, then another half day to collect meat and groceries, and once a month they made a general collection calling on all the stores, shops, etc." St. Mary's, Notre Dame, 1834–1878, vol. 1, 352, Box: Indiana, Notre Dame. Saint Mary's Convent, 1834–Oct. 1891, Archives, Sisters of the Holy Cross, Notre Dame, Indiana. See also McCauley, 248.

75. Pia Backes, *Her Days Unfolded*, trans. Bernardina Michel (St. Benedict, Oreg.: Benedictine Press, 1953), 10 June 1881 entry.

76. Kremer, 61–62; "Help the Diocesan Charities," *The Pilot*, 1 October 1921; *The Pilot*, 30 September 1922. Grassroots objections to endowments did not simply reflect financial conservatism. The charitable gift annuity, introduced in the 1920s by the Catholic Church Extension Society, caught on quickly. See Harry C. Koenig, ed., *Caritas Christi Urget Nos. A History of the Offices, Agencies and Institutions of the Archdiocese of Chicago*, 2 vols. (Chicago: Archdiocese of Chicago, 1981), 1: 23.

77. Martin J. Spalding and James F. Wood, The American College in Rome. Appeal to the More Wealthy among the Catholics of the United States (21 November 1868), Chancery Circulars, Box 1, Folder 4, AABOS.

78. "Story of the Seminary," [San Francisco] *The Monitor*, 23 January 1904.

79. "A Beneficent Catholic Multi-Millionaire," *The Pilot*, 16 February 1907; M. P. Dowling, "Creighton University," *The Catholic Encyclopedia*, 15 vols. (New York: Robert Appleton, 1908), 4: 480–81.

80. "A Munificent Charity," *The Pilot*, 7 June 1884; "Obituary of Joseph Banigan, 1839–1898," news clipping, 28 July 1898, Scrapbook 1891–1906, SMRI.

81. Although higher education was not generally a popular cause in the nineteenth century, each college had always had its corps of loyal supporters, and a few had endowments. In contrast, in the 1980s and 1990s, colleges and universities have been the beneficiaries of the largest individual gifts to Catholic causes. For example, in 1986, Liliore Green Rains gave $40 million to Loyola Marymount University, and in 1989, Notre Dame University received $33 million from Edward De Bartolo.

82. Mary Gwendoline Caldwell (1863–1909), daughter of philanthropist William Shakespeare Caldwell, left the Catholic Church in 1904.

83. Bernard J. McQuaid to Richard Gilmour, 31 January 1887, quoted in John Tracy Ellis, *The Formative Years of the Catholic University of America* (Washington, D.C.: American Catholic

Historical Association, 1946), 220. The 5 December 1887 appeal was written by John Ireland of St. Paul, John Keane of Richmond, and John Lancaster Spalding of Peoria.

84. For an account of the establishment of the 1904 and 1914 chairs, see Kauffman, 157–65. In 1989, the Knights committed $2 million to establish the Bicentennial of the United States Hierarchy Fund for the Benefit of the Pontifical Catholic University of America.

85. George L. Duval to Thomas Shahan, 23 November 1915, RG-19, Box 1, Shahan Collection, AAPHIL.

86. Mary J. Hill to Thomas Shahan, 29 November [c. 1915]; M. R. Brown to Thomas Shahan, 13 December 1915, RG-19, Box 1, Shahan Collection, AAPHIL.

87. Joseph P. Donovan, "Catholic Clannishness," *Commonweal* 11 (30 April 1930): 736; H. Edward Cain, "The National Center of Catholic Education," *Sign* 11 (1931): 173.

88. Shahan solicited an additional $250,000 from Mullen two years later to complete the library. See John K. Mullen to Thomas Shahan, 17 July 1925, and Thomas Shahan to Edith, 8 November 1927, RG-19, Box 1, Shahan Collection, AAPHIL.

89. Gertrude C. Mathews to Albert B. Brevard, Jr., 19 May 1964, Box 3, 26.D.7.5B; I. A. O'Shaughnessy to Margaret Barat, 8 June 1960, Box 1, 26.D.7.4F, O'Shaughnessy Collection, Minnesota Historical Society. Except for local St. Catherine's College, O'Shaughnessy refused to support women's colleges.

90. Francis J. Butler, "Catholic Foundations and Sharing the Faith: An Inside Look at Participation," *The Fund Raising Forum* (February 1988). Two new foundations appeared in the 1980s: the Vicarius Christi Foundation, established by the Knights of Columbus in 1983 to support papal charities, and the U.S. Papal Foundation, founded five years later by eight cardinals and two archbishops to supplement the annual Peter's Pence collection. See also Kauffman, 454; Proceedings of a Consultation with FADICA by Archbishop Theodore E. McCarrick on the Financial Condition of the Holy See, South Bend, Indiana, 19 June 1987, FADICA Archives; and *FADICA Directions* 9 (July–August 1989): 4.

91. For more on this controversial case, see Anne Lowrey Bailey, "The Strange Case of Harry John," *Chronicle of Philanthropy*, 4 May 1993, 6–7, 12–14; Paul Wilkes, "Harry John Was Not Your Average American Catholic," *National Catholic Reporter*, 17 September 1993, 13–20; "Court Removes Founder and Director of De Rancé Foundation," *Philanthropy Monthly* (July–August 1986): 5–12; and Dave Hendrickson, "Bittersweet Charity," *Wisconsin* (10 June 1990): 10–19. *"If You Love Me You Will Do My Will"* (New York: Norton, 1990), by Stephen G. Michaud and Hugh Aynesworth, recounts the extended legal controversy surrounding another large Catholic foundation, the Texas-based Sarita Kenedy East Foundation.

92. In 1988, for example, it earmarked $1 million for matching grants and loans to assist twelve dioceses establish planned-giving offices and build diocesan endowments. *FADICA Directions* 5 (November 1988): 2.

93. Articles of Incorporation, Official Minutes of FADICA, vol. 1, FADICA Archives, Washington, D.C.

94. In 1948, the St. Paul, Minnesota, archdiocese, like many others, was still paying an average salary of only $15 per month to sisters working in diocesan institutions. The monthly salary rose to $30 in 1949. Lynch, 38.

95. Annual Meeting of Members, 28 May 1985; Board of Directors Meeting, 22 September 1982, 28 September 1984, 13 February 1985, Official Minutes of FADICA, vol. 2, FADICA Archives.

96. Board of Directors Meeting, 19 September 1986, Official Minutes of FADICA, vol. 3, FADICA Archives. A *Wall Street Journal* article of 19 May 1986 brought the issue to national attention. The FADICA organization was called Save Our Aging Religious [SOAR].

97. FADICA, *Annual Report, 1988* (Washington, D.C.: FADICA, 1988).

98. FADICA, *Annual Report, 1986* (Washington, D.C.: FADICA, 1986).

99. Kremer, 117, 122–23. George Mundelein, buoyed by an especially generous response

in the 1924 Chicago charities collection, established a $250,000 archdiocesan trust fund, using surplus funds in the 1924 collection and a large gift from philanthropist Frank Lewis. But the project was unsuccessful since later charity collections yielded no surpluses. Coughlin and Riplinger, 208–209.

100. See, for example, the *1988 Annual Report, The Catholic Foundation of the Archdiocese of New Orleans*, AANO. Boston's Third Century Campaign, inaugurated in 1990 to raise $30 million for archdiocesan needs, including an endowment, targets the wealthy, who are defined as those able to contribute at least $25,000. *Boston Herald*, 1 February 1990.

101. *Chronicle of Philanthropy*, 19 September 1989. The importance of lay volunteers is being increasingly recognized, however. See *The Pilot*, 22 March 1993.

7. Parochial Schools and the Social Conscience

1. "A Colonial Catholic Family," *Freeman's Journal*, 7 January 1911.

2. John T. Reily, *Conewago: A Collection of Catholic Local History* (Martinsburg, W. Va.: Herald Print, 1885), 89–90. Irish-born real estate entrepreneur and merchant Dominick Lynch (1754–1825) was another important early supporter of Georgetown College.

3. Agenda from the Archives of the Academy of the Sacred Heart, Grand Coteau, 1822 etc., Series IV: St. Louis Province, E. Grand Coteau, Archives, Religious of the Sacred Heart, St. Louis, Missouri; *Centenary, Convent of the Visitation, Frederick, Maryland, 1846–1946* (privately printed, 1946), 39, 42.

4. Dolan, 1975, 113.

5. Bishop John England, "Address to Delegates of Seventh South Carolina Convention," 23 November 1829, quoted in Guilday, 2: 134. See Dolan, 1985, chapter 10, on the development of parochial schools in America.

6. Lawrence F. Flick, ed., "Minute Book of St. Mary's Church, Philadelphia, Pa. 1782 to 1811," 30 April 1804 Meeting, *Records of the American Catholic Historical Society of Philadelphia* 4 (1893): 330–31, 354. By 1810, although a few donations had been received to endow the school, economic circumstances precluded progress toward that goal. Given that St. Mary's was "the largest and richest" parish in the country in 1800, the financial situation of other parish schools was certainly more precarious. James A. Burns, *The Catholic School System in the United States: Its Principles, Origin, and Establishment* (New York: Benziger, 1908), 141.

7. "Petition of the Catholic People of Color in Philadelphia, 1817," *American Catholic Historical Researches* 7 (1890): 186. There is no record that the trustees ever acted on the request.

8. Burns, 1969, 275–76; Dolan, 1975, 107–109. St. Peter's parish school in New York City opened in 1800, the first Catholic school in the state. In 1820, quarterly fees in two New York pay schools ranged between $1.50 and $2.50, according to the course of study followed. Fees in the 1850s were much the same, varying between $.25 and $.50 per month.

9. The Catholic Boy's [*sic*] Home, typescript, n.d., 41, Box 200.3.1–6, 8–10, Folder: M-S3, Catholic Boys' Home, CSJSP. When, occasionally, a diocese sponsored a free school, tuitions were lower. In 1848, for example, a boys' school in Wheeling, West Virginia, established by the local bishop, charged only $1.00 to $2.00 in quarterly tuitions, depending on family means. Poor boys paid no tuition, and no child was denied admission because of inability to pay. J. Bailey, 98.

10. Tentler, 237.

11. Burns, 1908, 142–43; M. Rosalita, *Education in Detroit Prior to 1850* (Lansing: Michigan Historical Commission, 1928), 81. The French-born Richard (1767–1832) championed education at all levels and was a founder of the University of Michigan. See Burns, 1908, 180–98, for a summary of his remarkable career.

12. *Cathedral Records*, 99.

13. Burns, 1908, 274–75; Reardon, 1952, 655.

14. Quoted in M. Lilliana Owens, "The Pioneer Days of the Lorettines in Missouri, 1823–1841," *Records of the American Catholic Historical Society of Philadelphia* 70 (1959): 70–71, 77–78; Benedict J. Webb, *The Centenary of Catholicity in Kentucky* (Louisville: Charles A. Rogers, 1884), 152, 247.

15. Felicité de Duras, Comtesse de la Rochejaquelin, to Monseigneur Rosati, 4 January 1836, CSJSL.

16. J. Bailey, 97–98.

17. Quoted in George Paré, *The Catholic Church in Detroit, 1701–1888* (1951; reprint, Detroit: Wayne State University Press, 1983), 462.

18. There were a few instances when states supported Catholic schools, but the aid was transitory. For example, an 1851 act passed by the California state legislature allowed tax money, about $40,000 annually, to fund free "Ward Schools" for Catholic children. Protestant opposition ended these grants in 1855. W. Gleeson, *History of the Catholic Church in California*, 2 vols. (San Francisco: A. L. Bancroft, 1872), 2: 273–74.

19. Council Minutes, Sisters of Charity of Our Lady of Mercy, 12 May 1848, quoted in Campbell, 64–65; Peter E. Hogan, Robert E. McCall, and Peter J. Kenney, *The Josephites: A Century of Evangelization in the African American Community* (Baltimore: The Josephites, 1993), 10.

20. Thomas Boese, *Public Education in the City of New York; Its History, Condition, and Statistics* (New York: Harper & Bros., 1869), 100–102, 107–10; Francis J. Donohue, "Financial Support for Early Catholic Schools," *Catholic Educational Review* 40 (April 1942): 214–15; Tentler, 84, 87–89.

21. Geo. W. Webb, "Domestic. Archdiocese of Baltimore, May 5, 1844," *U.S. Catholic Magazine* 3 (June 1844): 402–403.

22. C. de la Croix to E. Rousselon, 25 September 1858; E. N. Montardier to Monseigneur l'Archeveque de la Nouvelle Orleans, 18 August 1852, AUND.

23. Burns, 1908, 71. Evening and Sunday catechism classes were offered for African American women and children.

24. Ibid., 204.

25. For Seton's biography, see Annabelle Melville, *Elizabeth Bayley Seton, 1774–1821* (New York: Scribner's, 1951); and Joseph I. Dirvin, *Mrs. Seton: Foundress of the American Sisters of Charity* (New York: Farrar, Straus, and Cudahy, 1962).

26. M. Eulalia Herron, "Work of the Sisters of Mercy in the United States, Diocese of Chicago, 1846 to 1921," *Records of the American Catholic Historical Society of Philadelphia* 32 (1921): 316, 320.

27. Ignatius Loyola Cox, "The Mission in Long Prairie," *Acta et Dicta* 3 (July 1914): 276–82. Sisters of Loretto and Sacred Heart Sisters opened schools for Potawatomie and Osage children in 1850. For a description of some postbellum Indian schools, see S. Carol Berg, "The Economic Foundations of a Mission: The Benedictines at White Earth Reservation," *Midwest Review* 9 (Spring 1987): 22–29; and Susan C. Peterson, "Doing 'Women's Work': The Grey Nuns at Fort Totten Indian Reservation, 1874–1900," *North Dakota History* 52 (Spring 1985): 18–25.

28. Mathias Loras, 6 January 1849, Annals of the Faith, 348, quoted in John F. Kempker, *History of the Catholic Church in Iowa* (Iowa City: Republican Publishing, 1887), 33.

29. *Minnesota Democrat*, 14 February 1855; John M. Culligan and Harold J. Prendergast, "St. Joseph's Hospital in St. Paul," *Acta et Dicta* 6 (October 1934): 197–98.

30. *Souvenir Sketch of St. Patrick's Church, Philadelphia, 1842–1892*, 10, 16, 20, 23, 35.

31. Council Minutes, Sisters of Charity of Our Lady of Mercy, 7 November 1848, quoted in Campbell, 64–65. See also Schuller, 366.

32. M. Charles Curtin, Annals, Sacred Heart Convent, 1841–1892, typescript, n.d., 20, SMNC. Of thirty-six students in the first class, ten were Protestants; the first Jewish students enrolled in the 1880s.

33. Whitefield, Maine, typescript, n.d., File E, Folder: Omaha—1864, SMNH.

34. John Timon, "Pastoral Letter, Given from St. Joseph's Cathedral on the Feast of the Ascension, 1859," CSJPHIL. Timon opposed tuition schools, even when they helped fund free schools. He tolerated them only because he feared that if he did not, sisterhoods would withdraw from the free schools. "I desire to suppress Select Schools—they oppose it—yield to keep both," he wrote in his diary on 5 September 1857. Quoted in Zwierlein, 1925, 1: 136.

35. Annals of Presentation Order in California from 1854 to 1909, Archives, Presentation Sisters, San Francisco, California. See also Catherine A. Curry, "Financial Sponsorship of Social and Religious Works by Sisters in San Francisco," paper presented at the Conference on the History of Women Religious, Tarrytown, New York, June 1992, 4. Strict racial segregation also marked both pay and free schools for Anglo and Mexican American children in the Southwest at this time. See Maria Luisa Valez, "The Pilgrimage of Hispanics in the Sisters of Charity of the Incarnate Word," *U.S. Catholic Historian* 9 (Winter–Spring 1990): 185.

36. Quoted in Michael V. Gannon, *The Cross in the Sand: The Early Catholic Church in Florida, 1513–1870* (Gainesville: University Presses of Florida, 1989), 183; Annals of the Georgia Community from 1867 to 1921, Record Book, entry for the Sharon Foundation, June 1896, CSJSL.

37. Annals of the Georgia Community from 1867 to 1921, Record Book, entries for 1867, January 1868, November 1875, and May 1877, CSJSL; M. V. Gannon, 184. In 1913, when Florida prohibited white teachers from instructing African American children, St. Augustine sisters were arrested for refusing to comply. The ordinance was overturned three years later. See Jane Quinn, "Nuns in Ybor City: The Sisters of St. Joseph and the Immigrant Community," *Tampa Bay History* 5 (1983): 38.

38. M. Austin to M. Gonzaga, 9 June 1884, File A, Folder: Original letters of Sister M. Austin Carroll to Sister M. Gonzaga O'Brien, 1880–1895, SMNH; "The Negroes and the Indians," 730. Carroll noted that great prudence had to be exerted "so as not to offend the whites."

39. M. Agatha, "Xavier University," *Interracial Review* 9 (1936): 167; Hogan, McCall, and Kenney, 40. Drexel had followed the same strategy in the 1890s in establishing Indian schools. She gave as the objects of her new sisterhood "the education, training and instruction directly or through the agency of others of the American Indian and Colored Races, the education of said races throughout the State of Pennsylvania and beyond its borders, the training of teachers for this purpose and especially the training of the youth of these races without religious distinction to become self-sustaining men and women." Catharine M. Drexel, Indenture, 6 January 1894, SBS; M. M. Katharine to Reverend and dear Father, 17 February 1894, Box 33, Folder 9, BCIM.

40. Minutes of the Meeting of the Board of Trustees, Catholic University of America, Washington, D.C., 1 May 1935, cited in Boyea, 341.

41. Arthur G. Falls to John Noll, 28 December 1934, Correspondence Files, Incoming, 1933–, DDCW. Episcopal inaction certainly contributed to discriminatory admission policies in Catholic colleges. For a specific example see Marilyn W. Nickels, "Showered with Stones: The Acceptance of Blacks to St. Louis University," *U.S. Catholic Historian* 3 (Spring 1984): 255 n. 1.

42. "For the Tenth Man," *Time*, 24 October 1932; Louise Drexel Morrell, "Letter to Editor," *Time*, 7 November 1932.

43. Curtin, Annals, Sacred Heart Convent, 1841–1892, 12, SMNC.

44. H. P. Gallagher to Mother Bridgman, 9 August 1854, Annals of This Convent, SMCA.

45. M. Francis Bridgman to M. Baptist, 29 February [1856], Annals of This Convent, SMCA. The Emmitsburg Sisters of Charity closed most of their academies in the 1850s in order to focus entirely on the poor.

46. J. Bailey, 76–77.

47. Roger Baudier, *Annunciation Parish: A Century of Parish Activities, 1844–1944* [c. 1944], 67, 70. The practice continued until the 1890s when the parish finally began to contribute to the school.

48. *A Century of Service*, 94–95, 97–99. A brother's comments at this time reflect the com-

munity's indignation: "After a stay of sixty-seven years in Mobile we own no property in the city excepting a lot in the Catholic cemetery where twenty of our men lie buried." p.99. The brothers finally left the parish school in 1919.

49. Joseph Alemany to [John?] Prendergast, 9 December 1865, Journal of Correspondence of Archbishop Alemany, AASF.

50. Bernard J. Meiring, *Educational Aspects of the Legislation of the Councils of Baltimore, 1829–1884* (1963; reprint, New York: Arno Press, 1978), 137.

51. Morgan M. Sheedy, "The Catholic Parochial Schools of the United States," in *Report of the Commissioner of Education for the Year 1903, Vol. 1* (Washington: Government Printing Office, 1905), 1088–89; Peter H. and Alice S. Rossi, "Background and Consequences of Parochial School Education," *Harvard Educational Review* 27 (Summer 1957): 175. Variation among dioceses, always considerable, continued. For example, nearly four of every five parishes in the Newark diocese already had schools in 1879. M. Laurina Kaiser, "The Development of the Concept and Function of the Catholic Elementary School in the American Parish" (Ph.D. diss., Catholic University of America, 1955), 57.

52. "Report of the Superior General," *The Colored Harvest* 5 (June 1909): 194–97.

53. M. Generosa Callahan, *The History of the Sisters of Divine Providence, San Antonio, Texas* (Milwaukee: Bruce, 1955), 172.

54. Samuel J. Kelly to M. M. Katharine, 15 March 1909, Box: Sister Georgiana Rockwell, SBS—Materials, Folder: Chapter of Renewal—Reel 32—Side I & II, AJF.

55. Hogan, McCall, and Kenney, 30; Edward C. Cramer, "What the Church Is Doing for the Negro Race," in *The Negro and the Catholic Church* (Huntington, Indiana: Our Sunday Visitor Press, [c. 1925]), 6; A. C. Monahan, "The Church and the Negro," *Catholic Charities Review* 8 (March 1924): 97.

56. "Proceedings of the Third Colored Catholic Congress, Held in Philadelphia, Penn., Jan. 5, 6, and 7, 1892," in *Three Afro-American Congresses* (New York: Arno Press, 1978), 145, 146–47.

57. *Progress of the Catholic Church in America and the Great Columbian Catholic Congress of 1893*, 4th ed. (Chicago, 1897), 121–25; Lincoln Valle, "Address at the Silver Jubilee Celebration, October 20, 1890," in *Souvenir of the Silver Jubilee*, 320–21.

58. For a discussion of social and economic factors affecting the expansion of teaching sisterhoods after 1870, see Mary J. Oates, "Organized Voluntarism: The Catholic Sisters in Massachusetts, 1870–1940," in Janet Wilson James, ed., *Women in American Religion* (Philadelphia: University of Pennsylvania Press, 1980), 147–49.

59. James M. Reardon, "The Church of St. Mary of St. Paul," *Acta et Dicta* 6 (October 1934): 247, 250. Neither group received parish-funded housing.

60. Archives, Christian Brothers, Mont LaSalle, California, cited in Curry, 7.

61. Tentler, 86, 91, 444. By 1900, 63 percent of Detroit parishes had opened schools, a figure that did not change appreciably over the next sixty years. Although lay teachers nationally accounted for only 7–10 percent of parochial school teachers in 1912, they represented a much higher proportion in some urban archdioceses, like New York and Chicago. Lay salaries remained very low. See Burns, 1969, 279–80.

62. George A. Lyons to William O'Connell, 17 January 1911, RG III. D.11, Department of Education Files, 1907–15, AABOS; Owen B. Corrigan, *The Catholic Schools of the Archdiocese of Baltimore: A Study in Diocesan History* (Baltimore: St. Mary's Industrial School Press, 1924), 201–202. The 1922 Baltimore data include all types and levels of schools.

63. Typically, the dismissal in 1940 of brothers who had taught parochial-school boys in a Long Island, New York, parish since 1909 was justified on this ground. See *A Century of Service*, 315.

64. Survey on Cost of Living and Education, National Catholic Educational Association, Section on Teacher Education, 21 February, 1953, Box 20.15, S. B. Poupore, CSJSP. Survey data came from a sample of teaching sisterhoods in parochial schools in all parts of the country.

65. "Special Works and Gleanings from Conferences," *Report of the Upper and Particular*

Council of St. Louis, Mo. to the General Council in Paris, November 1, 1896 to November 1, 1897 (St. Louis, 1898), 15, St. Genevieve Parish Records, AASL. Opposition to parochial schools was relatively stronger among middle- and upper-class parishioners, who believed public schools would offer their children better opportunities for useful social contacts. See David F. Reilly, *The School Controversy (1890–1893)* (Washington, D.C., 1943), 265.

66. Reardon, 1934, 249–50. By 1896, the tuition fee had been eliminated.

67. Burns, 1969, 276. Any deficiencies would be paid from general parish funds.

68. Yearly Statement of St. Ann's Orphanage, Belmont, N. C., Year Ending 31 December 1926, Box A-2, Folder: St. Ann's Orphanage—Belmont, N. C., SMNC.

69. Hennesey, 329. The number of brothers declined by nearly 32 percent, from 12,539 to 8,563 over the same period.

70. Dolan, 1985, 442.

71. James S. Coleman, "Community Key to School Success: Catholic Education's Broad Triumph," *Wall Street Journal*, 18 May 1989; *U.S. Catholic Elementary Schools and Their Finances* (Washington, D.C.: National Catholic Educational Association, 1989); Susan Chira, "Where Children Learn How to Learn: Inner-City Pupils in Catholic Schools," *New York Times*, 20 November 1991; *Roman Catholic Schools in New York State: A Comprehensive Report* (Albany, N.Y.: State Education Department Office for Planning, Research and Support Services, 1993), 9.

72. *Roman Catholic Schools in New York State*, 3, 5–6.

73. Marla K. Kale, "Inner-city Schools: What's in It for Catholics?" *U.S. Catholic* 57 (April 1992): 23; Francis Ryan, "The First to Opt Out: Historical Snapshots of Catholic Schooling in America," *Educational Horizons* 71 (Fall 1992): 63.

74. Elizabeth Kolbert, "School That Battles to Save Small Souls," *New York Times*, 8 November 1991.

75. Chira.

76. "Challenging Tradition: Hayes High Changes with the Bronx," *New York Times*, 10 June 1992.

77. Kale, 24.

78. "Why Are Schools Closing?" *The Pilot*, 22 November 1991.

79. Educational policies and practices in parish schools have been administered by diocesan school departments since the early twentieth century. Centralization of inner-city and low-income school financing, therefore, need not adversely affect local benevolent initiative.

80. *Roman Catholic Schools in New York State*, 18. Using four "multiple risk factors," the authors found no significant difference between Catholic and public schools in the percentage of students at risk. *Roman Catholic Schools in New York State*, 4, fig. 1.

81. *Roman Catholic Schools in New York State*, 10.

82. In rare instances, turn-of-the-century parishioners aimed to endow their schools. For example, a gift of $500 endowed a scholarship *"in perpetuum"* for a student in St. Agnes parochial school in New York City in 1912. And St. Charles parochial school in Philadelphia hoped to build an endowment to cover faculty salaries. However, the vast majority of parishes were barely able to cover operating expenses of their schools at this time. In 1990, nearly 25 percent of elementary schools, few of them in low-income parishes, report having an endowment or development fund. Burns, 1969, 278; *The Pilot*, 24 August 1990.

83. A recent analysis of Catholic high schools concludes that they are genuinely "common schools" since they enroll "a broad cross section of Americans in terms of race, social class, and even religion" and are not "narrow, divisive, or sectarian" in their curricula. See Anthony S. Bryk, Valerie E. Lee, and Peter B. Holland, *Catholic Schools and the Common Good* (Cambridge: Harvard University Press, 1993), 340–41.

84. Ernest Bartell, *Costs and Benefits of Catholic Elementary and Secondary Schools* (Notre Dame, Ind.: University of Notre Dame Press [c. 1964]), 260.

85. Kale, 21.

86. A late-1980s Gallup survey reported very strong support among Catholics of subur-

ban public schools. As commitment to suburban parochial schools declines, appreciation of low-income and inner-city parochial schools as genuine charitable institutions may rise. For a discussion of the Gallup findings, see Gallup and Castelli, 125–26.

87. Peter Gelzinis, "Teaching Nuns: It Hurts," *Boston Sunday Herald*, 26 January 1992; "Archdiocese of Boston to Close Five High Schools," *Boston Herald*, 19 November 1991.

88. "Catholic Population, Number of Schools, and Enrollment," *Catholic School Journal* 40 (January 1940): 27–29.

89. Bartell, 142.

90. Hannefin, 228.

91. "Response of Women Religious to Bishops' Statement on Schools," *Catholic Mind* 66 (April 1968): 54.

92. "A Religious Order's View of Renewal," 8.

93. What two inner-city boys' schools sponsored by Jesuits in New York and Boston are accomplishing could be undertaken on a much broader scale by dioceses. Financial support for the Boston school comes from individuals, the Jesuits, the archdiocese, foundations, and corporations. The most critical element in keeping the institution tuition-free, however, is its volunteer faculty, who contribute one or two years to the work, receiving only a $200 monthly stipend. There has been no problem in finding qualified volunteers. "We're not having any trouble at all," reported an administrator at the school. "They know they're on a kind of spiritual mission here. It gives the school a very positive attitude." "New Jesuit-run School Dedicated in Roxbury," *The Pilot*, 8 March 1991; "History and Mission," *Nativity: The Newsletter of Nativity Preparatory School* (November 1991): 1, 7.

8. Recent Trends in Catholic Giving

1. In 1990, 80 percent of Catholics were listed in parish registers. Joseph C. Harris, *An Estimate of Catholic Household Contributions to the Sunday Offertory Collection during 1991: A Study Conducted for the Life Cycle Center of the Catholic University of America*, December 1992, 41.

2. Robert Wuthnow, *The Restructuring of American Religion: Society and Faith Since World War II* (Princeton, N.J.: Princeton University Press, 1988), 86; Philip Gleason, "Catholicism and Cultural Change in the 1960's," *Review of Politics* 3 (1972): 95–96; Norval D. Glenn and Ruth Hyland, "Religious Preference and Worldly Success: Some Evidence from National Surveys," *American Sociological Review* 32 (February 1967): 73–85; Andrew M. Greeley, *Religion and Career: A Study of College Graduates* (New York: Sheed and Ward, 1963).

3. Marlys Harris, "The Squeeze on Churches and Synagogues," *Money* (April 1982): 98, 106; John L. Ronsvalle and Sylvia Ronsvalle, *A Comparison of the Growth in Church Contributions with United States Per Capita Income* (Champaign, Ill.: empty tomb, 1988), 142, table 2. Unitarian-Universalists tied with Catholics for last place in 1980.

4. J. C. Harris, 51. This may be too strong an assumption. Hoge and Griffin, p. 48, report a per capita annual donation in offertory collections of $80 to $84.

5. The average Catholic contribution for 1990 was $320 versus the $580 Protestant record, according to Andrew M. Greeley, *The Catholic Myth: The Behavior and Beliefs of American Catholics* (New York: Scribner's 1990), 128. See also Andrew Greeley and William McManus, *Catholic Contributions: Sociology and Policy* (Chicago: Thomas More Press, 1987), 2, 10–11. Given the diversity among Protestant denominations, Dean Hoge questions the usefulness of aggregate Protestant-Catholic comparisons. See his "Determinants of Religious Giving by American Denominations: Data from the General Social Survey," paper presented at the annual meeting of the Social Science History Association, Baltimore, November 1993, 9.

6. Greeley, 1990, 129; Greeley and McManus, 27–28. See pp. 11–13 for their data sources.

7. *Boston Globe*, 9 March 1993; 12 March 1993. In 1984, Catholics contributed, on average, $140 to non-church philanthropic causes, Protestants $180. When their income levels are taken into account, the difference is insignificant. Greeley and McManus, 19, 87.

8. U.S. Bishops' Ad hoc Committee on Stewardship, *Stewardship: A Disciple's Response* [first draft] (Washington, D.C.: National Conference of Catholic Bishops, 1992), 4–5. This statement did not appear in the final version of the pastoral letter. (Publication no. 567-4, U.S. Catholic Conference, Washington, D.C., 1993.) According to Greeley, the proportion of born Catholics who in 1991 no longer defined themselves as Catholic was identical with the 1961 proportion, 15 percent. "The Catholic Imagination and the Catholic University," *Current Issues in Catholic Higher Education* 12 (Summer 1991): 37.

9. Greeley and McManus, 64, 78, 135. Because Greeley attributes half the 1963–84 decline to this disaffection, he views the introduction of tithing, stewardship, and sacrificial giving plans as presently ill-advised. Greeley, 1990, 130. There is enthusiasm in other quarters for stewardship programs, however. See, for example, Tim Unsworth, "Parish Finances: Are Catholics Reluctant to Pay Their Own Way?" *U.S. Catholic* (September 1987): 32–38.

10. Hoge and Griffin, 48; "Trends in the '90s" [NCR/Gallup Poll Supplement], *National Catholic Reporter*, 8 October 1993, table 4. Fifty-seven percent of the 1993 respondents also agreed that they could be good Catholics without donating time or money to their parishes.

11. "Why Are Schools Closing?" *The Pilot*, 22 November 1991.

12. Ireland, 1903, 344–45.

13. *Chronicle of Philanthropy*, 15 May 1990, describing an analysis by Virginia Hodgkinson of Independent Sector data.

14. Ibid.

15. Michael J. Scanlan, "Meetings of Diocesan Directors of Charities," *Catholic Charities Review* 4 (October 1920): 238–39. See also O'Grady, "Lay Participation," 384.

16. O'Grady, 1930, 446, 448–49.

17. Jane A. Marra, Lecture [c. 1940], Series W-4, Box 2, DDCW.

18. "Dangers of Too Much Centralization," *Catholic Charities Review* 34 (December 1950): 249.

19. Gerald O'Keefe, Memorandum on Membership in Charities Boards, 31 August 1963, Box: Catholic Charities, Folder: Catholic Charities-Archdiocese of St. Paul, Annual Charities Dinner, AASPM.

20. Lawrence Corcoran, Catholic Charities: Where It Has Been—Where It Is Going [Address at meeting of Minnesota Catholic Conference], 17 April 1974, 2–4, UCUM 33/04 Minnesota-Catholic Charities, Archdiocese of St. Paul-Minneapolis, AUND.

21. Mark A. Peterschmidt to Robert Haas, 26 June 1979, Folder: Coordinated Catholic Charities Appeal 1979, CC-USA.

22. Bernard J. Coughlin, *Church and State in Social Welfare* (New York: Columbia University Press, 1965), 68.

23. Joseph T. McGucken, Archbishop's Report, Catholic Charities, Archdiocese of San Francisco, Report to the Community, 1975–76, Box: NCCC Projects, CC-USA. Government and United Way funds accounted for approximately two-thirds of archdiocesan charity income at this time.

24. Flyer and accompanying letter, Thomas J. Holbrook to Dear Friend of Catholic Charities, 5 May 1975, Box: NCCC Projects, Folder: Catholic Charities Campaign Material, CC-USA.

25. *First Annual Report, Catholic Charities, Diocese of Stockton, CA*, 1 May 1984, Box: NCCC Projects, CC-USA.

26. *The Good News, 1987*, Annual Report, Catholic Charities, Boston Regional Office.

27. *Annual Survey of Diocesan Agencies* (Alexandria, Va.: Catholic Charities USA, 1991). Ninety-five percent of the 163 dioceses that provide social services through Catholic Charities responded to this survey.

28. *New World*, 11 June 1993. Aggregate contributions to the United Way nationally fell 4 percent between 1991–92 and 1992–93, the worst year experienced by the agency since World War II. *Chronicle of Philanthropy*, 10 August 1993.

29. *Today's Catholic*, 31 May 1992; *National Catholic Reporter*, 13 March 1992.

30. "The Grant That Saps Our Life," *Catholic Charities Review* 36 (February 1952): 26.

31. Daniel McLellan, "A History of the Catholic Charitable Bureau of the Archdiocese of Boston" (Ph.D. diss., Notre Dame University, 1984), 307–308.

32. Dorothy Day, *October 1965 Appeal; Spring 1967 Appeal; March 1968 Appeal*, W-l Box 1, Folder: Appeals, 1933–76, DDCW.

33. M. D. Blundall et al., "Planning Study of Selected Social Services of the Archdiocese of Boston" (M.S.W. project, Boston College School of Social Work, 1978), 28.

34. Minutes of the Meeting with Representatives from Select Institutions, New York City, 30 May 1975, Box NCCC Projects, Folder: Institutions . . . 1975 Project-NCCC, CC-USA. The representatives were directors of hospitals, a geriatric center, and children's homes and schools. They included three religious brothers, three sisters, and one layman.

35. Survey of Catholic Institutions: A National Survey of Catholic Institutions Conducted for the National Conference of Catholic Charities Membership Committee, January 1 to June 10, 1972, 16, Box: NCCC Projects, Folder: Institutions . . . 1975 Project-NCCC, CC-USA. Respondents asked national charity leaders to "take a hard, penetrating and realistic look at your organization and set new goals and directions based on today's problems and needs."

36. Raymond Wey, A Survey of Catholic Charities in Minnesota-1974, 9, UCUM 33/04 Minnesota-Catholic Charities-Archdiocese of St. Paul-Minneapolis, AUND. Respondents included Catholics and Lutherans.

37. McLellan, 308; Avery Dulles, Address, 18th Annual Meeting of the Mission-Sending Societies, 18 September 1967, Washington, D.C., RG-10.6, Folder 4: Correspondence (5 July 1967–18 November 1967), Society for the Propagation of the Faith Records, AASPM.

38. Mary L. Gibbons, "Presidential Address," *Catholic Charities Review* 23 (September 1939): 220.

39. Minutes of the Meeting of the Catholic Charities Appeal Committee of the National Conference of Catholic Charities, 24 September 1970, CC-USA.

40. Lynn B. Carroll, "New Volunteer Team Lines Up behind Catholic Charities," *Charities USA* 16 (May–June 1989): 25; Joseph Semancik, "Cadre's Spirit Lives, But Influence Dims," *Charities USA* 19 (Third Quarter 1992): 21.

41. Francis X. Clines, "A World of Serenity Offers a Place to Heal," *New York Times*, 19 March 1993.

42. *The Good Shepherd of Angers*, 74.

43. Ibid., 59.

44. Carol Quigley, An Account of Our Stewardship, IHM Central Administration: Report of the General Superior, 1982–1988, 61, Archives, Sisters, Servants of the Immaculate Heart of Mary, Monroe, Michigan.

45. Catholic Charities Parish/Neighborhood Volunteer Program, typescript, agenda item for National Conference of Catholic Charities Board of Directors Meeting, Kansas City, 24–26 June 1976, CC-USA.

46. John B. Ahern, "Bringing Catholic Charities to the Parish," *Proceedings of Forum on Religious and the Social Welfare Mission of the Church* (Washington, D.C.: National Conference of Catholic Charities, 1971): 83–84.

47. Jim Stackpoole, "Archdiocesan Collection Tops $8 Million," *National Catholic News Service*, 9 June 1982.

48. Vatican Council II Decree on the Bishops' Pastoral Office in the Church [*Christus Dominus*], Chapter 2, nos. 22–24, called for "a fitting revision of diocesan boundaries." Walter Abbott, S. J., ed., *The Documents of Vatican II [1963–1965]* (New York: Guild Press, 1966), 412–14.

Bibliography

Primary Sources

Manuscript and Archival Collections

Archives, Archdiocese of Baltimore, Maryland.
Archives, Archdiocese of Boston, Massachusetts.
Archives, Archdiocese of Chicago, Illinois.
Archives, Archdiocese of Los Angeles, California.
Archives, Archdiocese of New Orleans, Louisiana.
Archives, Archdiocese of Philadelphia, Pennsylvania.
Archives, Archdiocese of San Francisco, California.
Archives, Archdiocese of St. Louis, Missouri.
Archives, Archdiocese of St. Paul and Minneapolis, Minnesota.
Associated Catholic Charities Collection. Archives, Archdiocese of Chicago.
Archives, The Catholic University of America, Washington, D.C.
Archives, Josephite Fathers, Baltimore, Maryland.
Archives, University of Notre Dame, Notre Dame, Indiana.
Bureau of Catholic Indian Missions Collection. Archives, Marquette University, Milwaukee, Wisconsin.
Archives, Catholic Charities USA, Alexandria, Virginia.
Archives, Sisters of St. Joseph, Brighton, Massachusetts.
Archives, Sisters of St. Joseph, Brentwood, New York.
Archives, Sisters of St. Joseph, Chestnut Hill, Pennsylvania.
Archives, Sisters of St. Joseph, St. Louis, Missouri.
Archives, Sisters of St. Joseph, St. Paul, Minnesota.
Archives, Daughters of Charity of St. Vincent de Paul, Albany, New York.
Archives, Daughters of Charity of St. Vincent de Paul, St. Louis, Missouri.
Dorothy Day-Catholic Worker Collection. Archives, Marquette University, Milwaukee, Wisconsin.
Guild of Catholic Women of St. Paul, Minnesota, Collection. Minnesota Historical Society, Minneapolis, Minnesota.
Rev. Peter A. Baart Collection. Archives, University of Notre Dame, Notre Dame, Indiana.
Archives, Sisters of the Blessed Sacrament, Bensalem, Pennsylvania.
Archives, Sisters of Charity of Nazareth, Nazareth, Kentucky.
Archives, Sisters of Mercy, Burlingame, California.
Archives, Sisters of Mercy, Belmont, North Carolina.
Archives, Sisters of Mercy, Windham, New Hampshire.
Archives, Sisters of Mercy, Providence, Rhode Island.

Selected Bibliography

Listed are works cited in more than one chapter and important works on Catholic philanthropy.

Amberg, Mary Agnes. *Madonna Center: Pioneer Catholic Social Settlement.* Chicago: Loyola University Press, 1976.

Baart, Peter A. *Orphans and Orphan Asylums.* Buffalo: Catholic Publication Co., 1885.

Bailey, James H. *A History of the Diocese of Richmond: The Formative Years.* Richmond: Diocese of Richmond, 1956.

Bartell, Ernest. *Costs and Benefits of Catholic Elementary and Secondary Schools.* Notre Dame, Ind.: University of Notre Dame Press, c. 1964.

Baudier, Roger. *Annunciation Parish: A Century of Parish Activities, 1844–1944.* New Orleans, c. 1944.

Beirne, Kilian. *From Sea to Shining Sea.* Valatie, N.Y.: Holy Cross Press, 1966.

Betten, Neil. "The Great Depression and the Activities of the Catholic Worker Movement." *Labor History* 12 (Spring 1971): 243–58.

Boyea, Earl. "The National Catholic Welfare Conference: An Experience in Episcopal Leadership, 1935–1945." Ph.D. diss., Catholic University of America, 1987.

Bryk, Anthony S., Valerie E. Lee, and Peter B. Holland. *Catholic Schools and the Common Good.* Cambridge: Harvard University Press, 1993.

Burns, J. A. *The Catholic School System in the United States: Its Principles, Origin, and Establishment.* New York: Benziger Bros., 1908.

Burns, James A. *The Growth and Development of the Catholic School System in the United States.* 1912. Reprint, New York: Arno Press, 1969.

Campbell, M. Anne Francis. "Bishop England's Sisterhood, 1829–1929." Ph.D. diss., St. Louis University, 1969.

Casterline, Gail Farr. "St. Joseph's and St. Mary's: The Origins of Catholic Hospitals in Philadelphia." *Pennsylvania Magazine of History and Biography* 108 (July 1984): 289–314.

Cathedral Records: From the Beginning of Catholicity in Baltimore to the Present Time. Baltimore: Catholic Mirror Publishing Co., 1906.

Catholic Charities and the Constitutional Convention of 1894 of the State of New York. Report of the Committee on Catholic Interests of the Catholic Club. New York: O'Brien and Son, 1894.

A Century of Service for the Sacred Heart in the United States by the Brothers of the Sacred Heart, 1847–1947. New Orleans: Sacred Heart Brothers, 1946.

Church, Thomas de Cantillon. "Father Drumgoole's Work." 2 parts. *Donahoe's Magazine* 2 (September 1879): 199–206; 2: (November 1879): 427–38.

Clarke, Richard H. "Catholic Protectories and Reformatories." *American Catholic Quarterly Review* 20 (July 1895): 607–40.

Coughlin, Roger L., and Cathryn A. Riplinger. *The Story of Charitable Care in the Archdiocese of Chicago, 1844–1959.* Chicago: Catholic Charities of Chicago, 1981.

Coy, Patrick J. *A Revolution of the Heart: Essays on the Catholic Worker.* Philadelphia: Temple University Press, 1988.

Crimmins, Thomas, comp. *The Diary of John D. Crimmins from 1878 to 1917.* New Rochelle: Knickerbocker Press, 1925.

Cross, Robert D. "Catholic Charities." *Atlantic Monthly* 210 (August 1962): 110–14.

Crumlish, Mary John, and Celestine McCarthy. *Daughters of Charity: 1809–1959.* Emmitsburg: St. Joseph's Central House, 1959.

Cushing, Richard J. "The Survival of Our Private Charities." *Catholic Charities Review* 34 (April 1950): 86–91.

Day, Dorothy. *House of Hospitality.* New York: Sheed and Ward, 1939.

———. *Loaves and Fishes.* New York: Harper & Row, 1963.

Dolan, Jay P. *The Immigrant Church: New York's Irish and German Catholics, 1815–1865.* Baltimore: Johns Hopkins University Press, 1975.

———. *The American Catholic Experience: A History from Colonial Times to the Present.* Garden City, N.Y.: Doubleday, 1985.

Donahoe, James. *The Scope of Charity.* St. Paul: Webb, 1914.

Donohoe, Joan Marie. "The Irish Catholic Benevolent Union." Ph.D. diss., Catholic University of America, 1953.

Donohue, Francis J. "Financial Support for Early Catholic Schools." *Catholic Educational Review* 40 (April 1942): 199–216.

Duffy, Consuela M. *Katharine Drexel: A Biography.* Cornwells Heights, Pa.: Sisters of the Blessed Sacrament, 1966.

Ellis, John Tracy. *The Formative Years of the Catholic University of America.* Washington, D.C.: American Catholic Historical Association, 1946.

A Friend of the House of the Angel Guardian. *The Life of Father Haskins.* Boston: Angel Guardian Press, 1899.

Gallup, George, Jr., and Jim Castelli. *The American Catholic People: Their Beliefs, Practices, and Values.* Garden City, N.Y.: Doubleday, 1987.

Gavin, Donald P. *The National Conference of Catholic Charities, 1910–1960.* Milwaukee: Bruce Press, 1962.

Gerdes, M. Reginald. "To Educate and Evangelize: Black Catholic Schools of the Oblate Sisters of Providence (1820–1880)." *U.S. Catholic Historian* 7 (1988): 183–99.

Gibbons, James. "Wealth and Its Obligations." *North American Quarterly* 152 (April 1891): 385–94.

Gleason, Philip. *The Conservative Reformers: German-American Catholics and the Social Order.* Notre Dame, Ind.: University of Notre Dame Press, 1968.

The Good Shepherd of Angers: Province of St. Louis—U.S.A. St. Louis: Sisters of the Good Shepherd, 1989.

Gorman, M. Adele Francis. "Evolution of Catholic Lay Leadership, 1820–1920." *Historical Records and Studies* 50 (1942): 130–65.

Greeley, Andrew. *The Catholic Myth: The Behavior and Beliefs of American Catholics.* New York: Charles Scribner's Sons, 1990.

Greeley, Andrew, and William McManus. *Catholic Contributions: Sociology and Policy.* Chicago: Thomas More Press, 1987.

Guilday, Peter. *The Life and Times of John England, First Bishop of Charleston (1786–1842),* 2 vols. New York: America Press, 1927.

Hannefin, Daniel. *Daughters of the Church: A Popular History of the Daughters of Charity in the United States, 1809–1987.* New York: New City Press, 1989.

Harris, Joseph C. *An Estimate of Catholic Household Contributions to the Sunday Offertory*

Collection during 1991. A Study Conducted for the Life Cycle Institute of the Catholic University of America, December 1992.

Hassard, John R. G. *Life of the Most Reverend John Hughes, D.D.* New York: Appleton, 1866.

————. "Private Charities and Public Money." *Catholic World* 29 (1879): 255–83.

Hayes, Patrick J. "The Unification of Catholic Charities." *Catholic World* 117 (May 1923): 145–53.

Hecker, Isaac T. "The Charities of New York." *Catholic World* 8 (November 1868): 279–85.

Helmes, J. W. "Thomas M. Mulry: A Volunteer's Contribution to Social Work." Ph.D. diss., Catholic University of America, 1938.

Hennesey, James J. *American Catholics: A History of the Roman Catholic Community in the United States*. New York: Oxford University Press, 1981.

Herron, M. Eulalia. "Work of the Sisters of Mercy in the United States, Diocese of Chicago, 1846 to 1921." *Records of the American Catholic Historical Society of Philadelphia* 32 (1921): 314–43.

Hewit, Augustine. "Duties of the Rich in Christian Society." 6 parts. *Catholic World* 14 (February 1872): 577–81; 14 (March 1872): 753–57; 15 (April 1872): 37–41; 15 (May 1872): 145–49; 15 (June 1872): 289–94; 15 (July 1872): 510–18.

Hogan, Peter E., Robert E. McCall, and Peter J. Kenney. *The Josephites: A Century of Evangelization in the African American Community*. Baltimore: The Josephites, 1993.

Hoge, Dean R., and Douglas L. Griffin. *Research on Factors Influencing Giving to Religious Bodies*. Indianapolis: Ecumenical Center for Stewardship Studies, 1992.

Hynes, Michael J. *History of the Diocese of Cleveland: Origin and Growth (1847–1952)*. Cleveland: World Publishing, 1953.

Ireland, John. *The Church and Modern Society*. New York: McBride, 1903.

————. "The Charity of Christ." *St. Vincent de Paul Quarterly* 12 (August 1907): 225–34.

Jacoby, George Paul. *Catholic Child Care in Nineteenth Century New York*. 1941. Reprint, New York: Arno Press, 1974.

Johnson, Peter L. *Daughters of Charity in Milwaukee, 1846–1946*. Milwaukee: Daughters of Charity, 1946.

Jones, Gene D. L. "The Chicago Catholic Charities, the Great Depression, and Public Monies." *Illinois Historical Journal* 83 (Spring 1990): 13–30.

Kauffman, Christopher J. *Faith and Fraternalism: The History of the Knights of Columbus*. Rev. ed. New York: Simon & Schuster, 1992.

Kavanagh, D. J. *The Holy Family Sisters of San Francisco*. San Francisco: Gilmartin, 1922.

Keegan, Robert F. "Developing Catholic Organization to Meet Present Day Needs." *Catholic Mind* 30 (8 December 1932): 449–59.

Kerby, William J. "Social Work of the Catholic Church in America." *Annals of the American Academy of Political and Social Science* 30 (November 1907): 473–82.

————. "Who Is My Neighbor?" 4 parts. *Catholic World* 87 (June 1908): 347–55; 87 (September 1908): 743–54; 88 (December 1908): 323–29; 88 (February 1909): 607–21.

————. "Problems in Charity." *Catholic World* 91 (September 1910): 790–800.

————. "The Catholic Charities of a City." *Ecclesiastical Review* 48 (June 1913): 677–95.

————. *The Social Mission of Charity: A Study of Points of View in Catholic Charities*. New York, 1921.

Koenig, Harry C., ed. *Caritas Christi Urget Nos. A History of the Offices, Agencies and Institutions of the Archdiocese of Chicago.* 2 vols. Chicago: Archdiocese of Chicago, 1981.

Kremer, Michael N. "Church Support in the United States." D.C.L. diss., Catholic University of America, 1930.

Lavey, Patrick B. "William J. Kerby, John A. Ryan, and the Awakening of the Twentieth Century American Catholic Social Conscience, 1899–1919." Ph.D. diss., University of Illinois, 1986.

Loh, Teresa Teh-Ying. "A Study of the Organization of Catholic Charities." M.S.W. thesis, Catholic University of America, 1947.

Luers, John. "Pastoral Letter, Feast of the Ascension, 1865." *Ave Maria* 1 (3 June 1865): 49–52.

Lynch, Claire. *St. Joseph's Home for Children, 1877–1950.* St. Paul: North Central Publishing, 1982.

McAvoy, T. Thomas. "The Catholic Minority in Early Pittsburgh: The First Bishop: Michael O'Connor." *Records of the American Catholic Historical Society of Philadelphia* 72 (December 1961): 67–83.

McCann, Mary Agnes. "Archbishop Purcell and The Archdiocese of Cincinnati." Ph.D. diss., Catholic University of America, 1918.

McCauley, Bernadette. " 'Who Shall Take Care of Our Sick?' Roman Catholic Sisterhoods and Their Hospitals, New York City, 1850–1930." Ph.D. diss., Columbia University, 1992.

McColgan, Daniel T. *A Century of Charity: The First One Hundred Years of the Society of St. Vincent de Paul in the United States.* 2 vols. Milwaukee: Bruce, 1951.

McCray, M. Gertrude. "Evidences of Catholic Interest in Social Welfare in the United States, 1830–1850." M.A. thesis, Notre Dame University, 1937.

McGann, Agnes Geraldine. *Mother Columba Carroll, Sister of Charity of Nazareth, 1810–1878.* Nazareth, Kentucky: Sisters of Charity of Nazareth, 1973.

McGuinness, Margaret M. "A Puzzle With Missing Pieces: Catholic Women and the Social Settlement Movement, 1897–1915." *Cushwa Center [Notre Dame University] Working Paper*, Series 22, no. 2 (Spring 1990).

McLellan, Daniel. "A History of the Charitable Bureau of the Archdiocese of Boston." Ph.D. diss., Notre Dame University, 1984.

McManus, William E. "Stewardship and Almsgiving in the Roman Catholic Tradition." In Robert Wuthnow and Virginia A. Hodgkinson, eds. *Faith and Philanthropy in America: Exploring the Role of Religion in America's Voluntary Sector.* San Francisco: Jossey-Bass Publishers, 1990, pp. 115–33.

Magri, Joseph. *The Catholic Church in the City and Diocese of Richmond.* Richmond: Whittet & Shepperson, 1906.

Meiring, Bernard J. *Educational Aspects of the Legislation of the Councils of Baltimore, 1829–1884.* 1963. Reprint, New York: Arno Press, 1978.

Miller, Lawrence. "A Study of Angel Guardian Orphanage." M.A. thesis, University of Chicago, 1943.

Mooney, Bernice M. *Salt of the Earth: The History of the Catholic Diocese of Salt Lake City, 1776–1987.* Salt Lake City: Catholic Diocese of Salt Lake City, 1987.

Mulry, Thomas M. "The Society of St. Vincent de Paul." *St.Vincent de Paul Quarterly* 4 (1899): 95–106.

Mundelein, George W. *Two Crowded Years*. Chicago: Extension Press, 1918.

National Conference of Catholic Bishops. *Stewardship: A Disciple's Response*. Washington, D.C.: U.S. Catholic Conference, 1992.

"The National Conference of the Society of St. Vincent de Paul." *St. Vincent de Paul Quarterly* 16 (1911): 193–221.

"The Negroes and the Indians." *Catholic World* 48 (March 1889): 727–40.

Nolan, Hugh J., ed. *Pastoral Letters of the United States Catholic Bishops*. Washington, D.C.: National Conference of Catholic Bishops, 1984.

Noll, John F. "The Practical Way of Supporting Religion." *Ecclesiastical Review* 62 (1920): 273–75.

O'Brien, David J. "Social Teaching, Social Action, Social Gospel." *U.S. Catholic Historian* 5, no. 2 (1986): 195–224.

O'Grady, John. "Lay Participation in Catholic Charity." *Catholic Charities Review* 9 (December 1925): 378–84.

———. *The Catholic Church and the Destitute*. New York: Macmillan, 1929.

———. *Catholic Charities in the United States: History and Problems*. Washington, D.C.: National Conference of Catholic Charities, 1930.

———. "The Catholic Settlement Movement." *Catholic Charities Review* 15 (May 1931): 134–44.

Oates, Mary J. "Organized Voluntarism: The Catholic Sisters in Massachusetts, 1870–1940." In Janet Wilson James, ed. *Women in American Religion*. Philadelphia: University of Pennsylvania Press, 1980, pp. 141–69.

———. "The Role of Laywomen in American Catholic Philanthropy." *U.S. Catholic Historian* 9 (Summer 1990): 249–60.

———. "Economic Change and the Character of Catholic Philanthropy, 1790–1940." In Conrad Cherry and Rowland Sherrill, eds. *Religion, the Independent Sector, and American Culture*. Atlanta: Scholars Press, 1992, pp. 31–49.

Osborne, William Audley. "The Race Problem in the Catholic Church in the United States: Between the Time of the Second Plenary Council (1866) and the Founding of the Catholic Interracial Council of New York (1934)." Ph.D. diss., Columbia University, 1954.

"Our Roman Catholic Brethren." *Atlantic Monthly* 21 (April 1868): 432–51.

Pillar, James J. *The Catholic Church in Mississippi, 1837–65*. New Orleans: Hauser Press, 1964.

"The Pope Creates Mrs. Ryan a Countess." *St. Vincent de Paul Quarterly* 12 (1907): 390–91.

Prindiville, Kathryn. "The Catholic Life of Chicago." *Catholic World* 67 (July 1898): 476–93.

Reardon, James M. *The Catholic Church in the Diocese of St. Paul*. St. Paul: North Central Publishing, 1952.

Reilly, David F. *The School Controversy 1891–1893*. Washington, D.C., 1943.

"A Religious Order's View of Renewal." *Catholic Mind* 66 (January 1968): 8–10.

Remembrance of the Diamond Jubilee, 1850–1925. St. Louis: German St. Vincent's Orphan Society, 21 June 1925.

"Response of Women Religious to Bishops' Statement on Schools." *Catholic Mind* 66 (April 1968): 51–55.

Rezek, A. J. "The Leopoldine Society." *Acta et Dicta* 3 (July 1914): 305–20.

Ring, Thomas F. "Catholic Child-Helping Agencies in the United States." *Proceedings of the National Conference of Charities and Correction* (1896): 289-314.

Roemer, Theodore. "The Leopoldine Foundation and the Church in the United States (1829-1839)." *U.S. Catholic Historical Society, Monograph Series* 13 (1933): 141-211.

———. *Ten Decades of Alms.* St. Louis: B. Herder Book Company, 1942.

Roman Catholic Schools in New York State: A Comprehensive Report. Albany, N.Y.: State Education Department Office for Planning, Research and Support Services, 1993.

Roohan, James E. "American Catholics and the Social Question, 1865-1900." *Historical Records and Studies* 43 (1954): 3-26.

Rouse, Michael F. *A Study of the Development of Negro Education under Catholic Auspices in Maryland and the District of Columbia.* Baltimore: Johns Hopkins University Press, 1935.

Scanlan, Michael J. "Diocesan Charities and Their Organization." *Catholic Charities Review* 2 (1918): 297-301.

Schuller, M. Viatora. "A History of Catholic Orphan Homes in the United States, 1727 to 1884." Ph.D. diss., Loyola University, 1954.

Sharp, John K. *History of the Diocese of Brooklyn, 1853-1953: The Catholic Church on Long Island.* 2 vols. New York: Fordham University Press, 1954.

Sharum, Elizabeth L. "A Strange Fire Burning: A History of the Friendship House Movement." Ph.D. diss., Texas Tech University, 1977.

Sheedy, Morgan M. "The Catholic Parochial Schools of the United States." In *Report of the Commissioner of Education for the Year 1903.* Vol. 1. Washington, D.C.: Government Printing Office, 1905, pp. 1079-1101.

Smith, John Talbot. *The Catholic Church in New York.* 2 vols. New York: Hall and Locke, 1905.

Sorin, Edward. *The Chronicles of Notre Dame du Lac.* Ed. James T. Connelly. Notre Dame, Ind.: University of Notre Dame Press, 1992.

Souvenir of the Silver Jubilee in the Episcopacy of His Grace the Most Rev. Patrick Augustine Feehan, Archbishop of Chicago, November 1st. 1890. Chicago, 1891.

Souvenir Sketch of St. Patrick's Church, Philadelphia, 1842-1892. Philadelphia: Hardy and Mahony, 1892.

Spalding, John Lancaster. *The Life of the Most Rev. Martin J. Spalding, D. D., Archbishop of Baltimore.* New York: Catholic Publication Society, 1873.

St. Francis in Eddington: A History of the Transition of an Institution, 1888-1988. c. 1988.

Sweetser, Thomas P. "The Money Crunch: Why Don't Catholics Give More?" *Chicago Studies* 30 (April 1991): 99-111.

Tentler, Leslie Woodcock. *Seasons of Grace: A History of the Catholic Archdiocese of Detroit.* Detroit: Wayne State University Press, 1990.

Tifft, Thomas W. "Toward A More Humane Social Policy: The Work and Influence of Monsignor John O'Grady." Ph.D. diss., Catholic University of America, 1979.

Toward a Renewed Catholic Charities Movement: A Study of the National Conference of Catholic Charities. Washington, D.C.: National Conference of Catholic Charities, 1972.

Tucker, Frank. "The Finances of Private Charities." *St. Vincent de Paul Quarterly* 5 (1900): 210-16.

U.S. Catholic Elementary Schools and Their Finances, 1989. Washington, D.C.: National Catholic Educational Association, 1989.

Walsh, Marie de Lourdes. *The Sisters of Charity of New York, 1809–1959.* 3 vols. New York: Fordham University Press, 1960.

Weitzman, Louis G. "One Hundred Years of Catholic Charities in the District of Columbia." Ph.D. diss., Catholic University, 1931.

"Who Shall Take Care of Our Sick?" *Catholic World* 8 (October 1868): 42–55.

"Who Shall Take Care of the Poor?" *Catholic World* 8 (February 1869): 703–15; 8 (March 1869): 734–40.

Wood, Thomas O. "The Catholic Attitude toward the Social Settlement Movement, 1886–1914." M.A. thesis, Notre Dame University, 1958.

Zwierlein, Frederick J. *The Life and Letters of Bishop McQuaid.* 3 vols. Rochester, N.Y.: Art Print Shop, 1925.

Index

Maxwell House (New York), 57. *See also* Settlements
Mennonites, 46
Mercy Action Fund, 173
Mill Hill Fathers, 60, 65, 190n69
Mill Hill Sisters, 65
Minnesota Irish Emigration Society, 38
Mission Helpers of the Sacred Heart, 65
Missions: collections for, 58, 61, 116, 190n79
Mitty, John, 198n17
Montavon, William, 95
Montgomery, George, 86
Mormons, 61
Morrell, Louise Drexel, 66, 150
Morse, Samuel F. B., 4
Mount Hope Institution, Mount Hope Retreat (Md.), 40
Mullanphy, Bryan, 183n34, 202–203n17
Mullanphy, John, 10, 30
Mullanphy Hospital (St. Louis), 9, 41
Mullen, John K., 138
Mulry, Thomas, 51, 56, 94, 187n23
Mundelein, George, 80, 89, 100, 101, 106, 123, 131, 195n82, 198n18, 206–207n99
Murray, John, 84
Mutual-aid societies, 9

National Association of Church Personnel Administrators, 140
National Catholic Educational Association, 155
National Catholic War Council, 95
National Catholic Welfare Council, 90, 95, 113, 117
National collections, 3, 62, 115, 116, 117, 137, 140, 201n80, 206n90
National Conference of Catholic Bishops, 139
National Conference of Catholic Charities, 51, 57, 75, 83, 90, 93, 94, 95, 169, 171, 172
National Council of Catholic Men, 95
National Council of Catholic Women, 75, 90, 95
National League of Catholic Women, 82
National School of Social Service, 90
Native Americans. *See* Indians; Missions
Neale, Francis, 142
Newsboys' Night School (New Orleans), 86
New York Catholic Protectory, 24
New York Charity Organization Society, 51, 52, 57
New York Committee on Charities, 53
New York Constitutional Convention (1894), 72

New York Foundling Hospital, 22, 56, 86, 126
New York Foundling Society, 23
New York Roman Catholic Orphan Asylum, 21, 99
New York State Charities' Aid Association, 78, 188n32
Noll, John, 149–50
Notre Dame University, 138, 149–50, 205n81

Oblate Sisters of Providence, 59
O'Brien, Timothy, 205n72
O'Connell, William, 76–77, 80, 83, 87, 88, 129, 131
O'Connor, Ann, 16
O'Connor, James, 66, 68, 128, 191n98
O'Connor, Michael, 14, 20
Odin, John, 60
O'Grady, John, 75, 79–80, 81, 90, 91, 94, 113, 114, 168
Onahan, William, 39
Orphanages: financial support of, 12, 19, 64, 74; location of, 29–30; criticism of, 72. *See also* Diocesan collections; Institutions; Protestants; *specific orphanages, orphan societies, and donors*
O'Shaughnessy, Ignatius A., 138

Paid professionals: in religious philanthropy, 73, 89, 90, 93, 96, 99, 193n25
"Painless Giving," 107, 108
Parishes: trustee system in, 1, 9; support of, 2, 3, 5, 124, 129, 178n5; charity institutions of, 8; and diocesan charity organization, 17, 19, 31, 101, 118; and distribution of charity contributions, 171, 173–74; outreach programs of, 174. *See also* Diocesan collections; Institutions; Parochial schools; Pew rent system; Pledging; Subscriptions; *specific parishes*
Parmentier, Rosine, 191n96
Parochial schools: poverty of early, 22; opposition to, 55; financing of, 98, 155; public funds for, 142, 145, 159, 161, 208n18; as charitable works, 143, 156, 159, 160–61, 163; tuitions in, 143, 144, 155, 158, 159, 162; lay teachers in, 144, 148, 154, 156, 162, 210n61; subsidization of by sisters, 146–47, 150–51; class tensions and, 148; religious test in, 152, 157; urban, 156, 157–58; suburban, 158–59, 210–11n86; as "common schools," 211n83. *See also* Sisterhoods
Partnership for Quality Education, 160
Penny-a-week programs, 4

Mary J. Oates is professor of economics at Regis College. She has written extensively on the American Catholic experience. Her publications include *Higher Education for Catholic Women: An Historical Anthology.*